THE STORY OF
SOUTHAMPTON DOCKS

THE STORY OF
SOUTHAMPTON DOCKS

MIKE ROUSSEL

I would like to dedicate this book to
my wife Kay.

First published in Great Britain in 2009 by The Breedon Books Publishing Company Limited, Breedon House, 3 The Parker Centre, Derby, DE21 4SZ. ISBN 978-1-85983-707-8

This paperback edition published in Great Britain in 2013 by DB Publishing, an imprint of JMD Media Ltd

ISBN 978-1-78091-113-7

Printed and bound by Copytech (UK) Ltd, Peterborough

CONTENTS

ACKNOWLEDGEMENTS

To complete a work such as this would have been impossible without the support of family, friends and colleagues, and the 'dockies', mariners and others who have taken part in the interviews and have given me permission to use some of their own material for my book. They are: Cllr Derek Burke, Terry Adams, Bill O'Brien, Cyril Duro, Don Archbold, Edwin Praine, Ernest Gay, Gordon Brown, Gus Shanahan, Harold Lloyd, Joan Rogers, Kenneth Fielder, Maurice Allen, Norman Sibley, Peter Godwin, Peter Wareham, Ray Strange, Ron Williams and Wally Williams.

My thanks also go to all who gave their time to be interviewed and allowed me to see their work first hand from 2003. They are: Captain Mike Evans, John Hardwick, Gareth Mead, Nigel Allen, William Heaps, Lisette Rimmer, Ron Dawson, Captain Mark Bookham, Gary Toomer, Vernon Nock, Martin Thomas, Richard Thomas, Gary Joyce, Derek Smith, Lynsey Haynes, Chris Wright, John Wright, Tony Giles, Ben Paddington, Lynn Fox, Paul Mitchell and John Tindall.

My thanks go to Keith Hamilton of the *Daily Echo* for arranging an article asking anyone who had worked in the docks to contact me and tell me their stories, and also for his interest in the progress of the book.

I am indebted to Jessica Emery who gave me permission to use material that her father, Colin Hall, had sent me from South Africa. Colin Hall had been a Southampton docker but had moved to work in South Africa. Although Colin and I had never met in person, we kept frequent contact by email until he sadly passed away in June 2007.

I am deeply indebted to author Jim Brown for his sustained interest, advice and support in my project; for spending many hours proof-reading the draft, and especially for his ongoing encouragement to complete the book.

My special thanks go to maritime author Bert Moody for his valuable advice and time, the loan of material from his collection and for proof-reading the draft; and to Sheila Jemima, manager of the Oral History Unit for her advice and valuable support for my project.

I thank Terry Yarwood and Jim Delderfield of the Tug Tender Calshot Trust for the information and photographs that they gave me for my research.

My sincere thanks also go to ABP, especially Doug Morrison, port director, Beth Evans and Lorraine Nottley for their help and permission to use photographs of the port and its history.

I am indebted to all who have given me permission to use photographs and material from their collections. They include: Richard de Jong, Mick Lindsay, Nicki Goff, Poole Flying Boats Celebration and Solent Sky; and my sincere gratitude to the many others who have helped in one way or another but are not mentioned here.

My special thanks go to my friends and colleagues, Alan Passfield, Jeff Graham, Geoffrey Le Marquand and Doreen Russell, who contributed their thoughts and feelings on the last day of the *QE2*, and to Pete Fry for giving me the opportunity to be on the quayside in the evening.

Finally, a huge thank you to my wife Kay, who has patiently put up with the many hours I have spent in my study and has continuously encouraged me to complete the book.

INTRODUCTION

Harbours and Ports

The distinction between a harbour and port is often confused, but the easiest way to think of it is that a harbour (haven) is a place of shelter for ships to anchor or dock without danger from rough waves or high winds; however, a port is a man-made facility where ships can load and unload goods and passengers. It will have quays, berths, piers, jetties, cranes and storage facilities in close proximity and road and rail transportation for distribution of imported goods across the country and for bringing goods for export to load onto ships at the dock.

There are natural harbours and man-made harbours. Natural harbours are protected by natural bays, peninsulas (a piece of land that is almost surrounded by water or projecting out into the sea), headlands (high land jutting out into the sea) and offshore islands. Most natural harbours have to be maintained by regularly dredging deep-water channels to accommodate the increasing draught of the larger ships being built, and examples include New York, Sydney and Southampton.

A man-made harbour is constructed with breakwaters that provide a sheltered bay where there is no natural shelter along a coastline. One such harbour in the United Kingdom that is a very busy commercial port and also a harbour of refuge is Dover. It is a very important harbour because of its close proximity to the Continent, especially for cross-Channel passenger ferries and 'drive-on drive-off' car ferries.

There are two main types of harbours, and these are defined as 'commercial' and 'naval' harbours. A commercial harbour provides facilities for docking, repairs, refuelling, unloading and loading cargo and terminals for ferry and cruise passengers. Naval harbours, however, include all the facilities of a commercial harbour for docking and repairs, but they also have facilities for the storage and handling of munitions.

Some harbours can be both a commercial harbour as well as a naval harbour, and an example of this is in Portsmouth; however, some harbours around the world are known specifically for being a place of refuge where ships may shelter from storms, especially in areas susceptible to unpredictable weather such as tropical storms, hurricanes and typhoons.

Why a Port is Established

Ports are established mainly because of trade. The early Phoenicians, Greeks and Romans traded throughout the Mediterranean Sea, and it was during the Roman invasion that some ports were created in Britain from AD 43. Both Dover and Southampton had ports developed by the Romans that were used to unload and load trading goods from ships, which were to be taken inland or shipped to other trading countries. Ships need enough deep water to sail in and out of the port as many times as possible in 24 hours. Many ports have two high tides a day, but the Port of Southampton is more fortunate in having four high tides each day.

Communications to and from the port are also important. Cargo and passengers start and end their sea journeys at the port, and this makes communication links inland important. That is why many ports were built on or near rivers, as water was the easiest way to move a large amount of goods. In Britain a network of canals was first built to transport goods inland, but when the railways arrived they became more important than the canals. This was because of the increased speed with which they could transport goods from one place to another. With the advent of better road systems, such as motorways, railways began to lose their significance because road transport could collect from or deliver goods directly to the customer. When goods were transported by the railways, most would finish in a railway depot and would then have to be delivered by road transport to the customer. The railways still have an importance for some trades, however, and although many car transporters and container lorries can be seen taking a load of cars and containers to and from the docks, some car manufacturers send trainloads of cars direct to the docks for export. Containers are also taken by rail long distances to different parts of the country for delivery by lorries to the customer.

As a port expands so does the number of industries in the surrounding area that import and export raw materials, because to be situated close to a port reduces their transport costs. For example, flour millers would often build their mills near ports to handle imported grain. Major refineries are also situated near ports to import crude oil and to export refined products. It is the development of these industries that attracts workers, and so the local community benefits and grows. With the growth of jobs, communication links grow to keep the trade moving and so the port itself develops.

One of the advantages of the Port of Southampton is that vessels are protected by the Isle of Wight when sailing up the Solent and into Southampton Water. It has deep-water channels that are regularly dredged, a wide range of industrial development, including the Fawley Esso and Hamble BP oil terminals, and very good rail and road communications to and from the port.

Southampton from Roman Times

Southampton began as an important port for the Romans on the east side of the River Itchen, in an area now known as Bitterne Manor, to transport goods up and down the River Itchen from Winchester, which had been established as a centre of trade in

AD 45. The Romans named it Venta Belgarum after the Belgae tribe who lived there. They called the port Clausentum, and it was used until the Romans left Britain in AD 407.

Although the Romans were suffering from the increasing Anglo-Saxon raids, the main reason the Roman army left Britain in AD 407 was because they needed to help defend Rome against an invasion from northern Europe. The Anglo-Saxons then settled in the area, but Viking invaders became a threat to the Saxons, and by the 10th century the Viking King Canute was crowned in Southampton after defeating the Saxon King Ethelred. It is King Canute who is said to have failed in his attempt to order the tide on Southampton's waterfront to retreat. It is thought that he did this because his courtiers treated him like a god, and he wanted to prove to them that they were wrong. Today there is a sign on the Canute Hotel in Canute Road that states, 'Near this spot AD 1028 CANUTE reproved his courtiers'. The hotel has now been closed and refurbished as residential apartments.

The port became very important to the Normans after 1066. William the Conqueror used the port to transport goods between England and Normandy, and Southampton became prosperous as the main port for trade between Winchester and Normandy. Trade at the time was mainly in wine and wool. Richard the Lionheart sailed from Southampton on the Third Crusade to the Holy Lands in 1187, and in 1415 Henry V left from Southampton on his way to France for the Battle of Agincourt.

The first record of Watergate Quay was in 1411. It was at the bottom of the High Street and was used until the 18th century, when it became disused due to competition for continental trade from London. Trade in wool with Italy and Flanders flourished, and this instigated the building of the Wool House in 1417 as a warehouse at the bottom of Bugle Street, opposite the Watergate Quay, the site of today's Town Quay. The Wool House is now occupied by the Southampton Maritime Museum.

The Pilgrims set sail for America in the *Mayflower* and her sister ship the *Speedwell* from Southampton on 5 August 1620. The *Speedwell* was leaking so badly that they called in at Plymouth to attempt repairs, but these were not successful. Ultimately it was only the *Mayflower* that set sail from Plymouth on 6 September 1620.

The development of Southampton as a port for the next two centuries was very slow, apart from trade with the Channel Islands, France and Spain, and the continued sailings of passenger-carrying ships. The earliest record of the mail and passenger services was in 1781 when a sailing cutter with passengers, mail and parcels left the port once a fortnight for the Channel Islands. During this time however, the town had become more important as a fashionable spa patronized by royalty.

By the end of the 18th century and the start of the 19th century came the Industrial Revolution, the expanding shipbuilding activities of the port and the increasing opportunities of access to the world. Southampton was identified by the business community as an attractive proposition for the building of a major port. Combined with its double tide and easy access to the English Channel, the citizens of Southampton wanted action to capitalise on the wealth that would be created if a port was developed to handle the trade and commerce with the world.

The purpose of this book is to trace the development of the docks from its early beginnings up to the present day, and included are personal recollections based on interviews.

PART 1

CHAPTER 1
INTRODUCTION TO MANAGEMENT OF SOUTHAMPTON DOCKS

The Development of Southampton Docks from 1803

This is a brief introduction to the management of the docks from 1803 to 2008, which highlights the development of the docks from the time of the appointment of the Southampton Harbour Commissioners.

SOUTHAMPTON HARBOUR COMMISSIONERS 1803

The development of Southampton Docks really commenced when an Act of Parliament was passed in 1803 that made the building of quays and warehouses possible, supervised by the Southampton Harbour Commissioners who were appointed and authorised to see it carried out. In the same year a new quay (known as Town Quay) was constructed, replacing the one previously known as Watergate Quay. The old West Quay jetty, where Henry V's army had passed through West Gate to board ships to sail to France in 1415, and from where the Pilgrim Fathers had left in the *Mayflower* in 1620, had over time become dilapidated. It was eventually sold in 1810 and then demolished.

By 1818 regular sailing links with Southampton and Le Harve had been established, and in 1833 the Royal Pier was opened by the Duchess of Kent, accompanied by her 14-year-old daughter, Princess Victoria. It was originally named Royal Victoria Pier but was eventually shortened to Royal Pier. This pier was to enable the berthing of the steam packet boats already servicing the Isle of Wight, the Channel Islands and France.

SOUTHAMPTON DOCK COMPANY 1836

Developing the port was an expensive business, and the commissioners did not have the means of raising the money needed to fund the amount of construction to build the docks; however, a number of influential people saw the financial benefits that could be achieved by building a port in Southampton, and in 1836 they formed the Southampton Dock Company. The first general meeting was convened at the George and Vulture Tavern, London, on 16 August 1836, with up to 50 businessmen from London, Liverpool, Manchester and Southampton present. Parliamentary approval had been given, with an authorised capital of £350,000, to develop a dock. It was considered that the area was the most eligible in the United Kingdom for development of a commercial dock, with its advantages of deep water and double tides. The chairman of the new company announced that an area of 216 acres of mud land adjoining Town Quay had been acquired at a 'fair and full price' of £5,000, and the plans for construction the docks were soon put in place.

In 1877 an Act of Parliament created the Southampton Harbour Board, successors to the Southampton Harbour Commissioners formed in 1803.

The Gas Column, Quay and Victoria Pier in about 1840. (Engraving by Phillip Brannon)

Royal Victoria Pier, with Town Quay to the right. (Engraving by Phillip Brannon)

Although the new board had similar jurisdiction to the previous commissioners, what the Act did was to ensure that the limits were more clearly defined and that the docks came under separate ownership.

The loss in trade in 1880, partly due to the earlier move of P&O to London, put pressure on the Southampton Dock Company to increase the dock facilities to attract more trade, and so they took a loan from the L&SWR (London and South-Western Railway) to build the Empress Dock.

LONDON AND SOUTH WESTERN RAILWAY (L&SWR)

By 1892 the Port of Southampton was the only port at the time able to take the deepest draught vessels at any state of tide, but the Dock Company was not financially secure and on 1 November the same year Southampton Docks was purchased by the London and South Western Railway for £1,360,000. They subsequently took over the management of the port.

The port became more prominent, and shipping lines began to transfer their services from other ports to Southampton. With more of the famous shipping lines now using the port there was a need for further expansion in the old docks for quayside space and dry docks, especially to cater for the needs of the larger liners being built. This was also the time in the early 20th century when the *Titanic* sank on her maiden voyage, bringing worldwide attention to the Port of Southampton.

Southern Railway (SR)

An important development took place in 1923 when the L&SWR amalgamated with other railways in the South and Southampton Docks was taken over by the new Southern Railway. The 1920s and 1930s were the heyday of transatlantic travel when Cunard's slogan 'Getting there is half the fun!' became a household phrase and the 'Queens', the famous *Queen Mary* and *Queen Elizabeth* ocean liners, were launched. It was also the time Britain was facing increased competition from the United States and the Continent, however, and the docks began to have difficulties. This was not helped by the German air strikes of World War Two, which caused so much damage to the major ports, including Southampton. A six-week docks strike over pay in 1945 led to the post-war Labour government sending in troops to keep the docks open. Although the strike was not officially recognised by the Transport and General Workers Union, it only ended when the leaders of the TGWU agreed to negotiate with the government for a change in the dockers' working conditions. This led to the NDLS (National Docks Labour Scheme), introduced in 1947 by the Labour government for the registration of labour and the provision of fall-back pay when no work was available. As John Hovey said: 'This was the scheme for registration of labour and the provision of fall-back pay when no work was available throughout the country, by the Labour government in June 1947. Registration books were stamped for each half-day's work. Those men who did not obtain work on the "call stand" had their registration books stamped or "bomper". For some men the Dock Labour Scheme was a blessing.'

At the end of the war there was a need to repair and reconstruct the damage done by the German bombing. The Port of Southampton alone had 69 air raids that destroyed or seriously damaged 23 sheds and warehouses. The Labour government voted to nationalise the country's transport-related industries under the British Transport Act of 1947. This legislation created the new British Transport Commission (BTC), which operated through six executive branches: the Docks and Inland Waterways Executive; the London Transport Executive; the Railway Executive; the Road Hauler Executive; the Road Passenger Executive and the Hotels Executive.

British Transport Commission (BTC)

From 1948, when British transport was nationalised, the port was managed by the British Transport Commission, through the Docks and Inland Waterways Executive, and the nationalisation of the railway network changed Southern Railway to British Railways. It became clear by the late-1950s, however, that having the six executive branches under one umbrella was a mistake, and so the government looked at possible ways of restructuring the BTC. By 1960 the government had come to a final decision and published a white paper calling for the abolition of the BTC, which was finally completed in 1962. Five new authority bodies took the place of the BTC. These were the British Railways Board, the British Transport Docks Board, the British Waterways Board, the London Transport Board, and the Transport Holding Company.

British Transport Docks Board (BTDB)

When the British Transport Commission was finally abolished in January 1963 the British Transport Docks Board took over management of the ports. They quickly ran into difficulties because the labour relations had remained bad throughout the 1950s and 1960s with strikes over wage, and the casual dock employment situation was breeding resentment among the dock workers. Eventually the frustration and resentment of the dock workers boiled over, leading to a six-week strike, crippling the industry in the 1960s. The dock workers felt humiliated by the number of traditional practices that gave them no guarantee of employment. This was highlighted by way the port owners would choose their workforce from the dockers who attended the 'pool' daily with the hope of getting work. Those that were chosen were lucky and got a day's work, but the unlucky ones went home. These and other practices finally led to the dock workers' strike in 1967.

The result of the strike was a victory for the dock workers, and in 1967 the British government passed a new British Dock Labour Scheme replacing the one that had been initiated in 1947. This became known as decasualisation. The casual labour system was now abolished with the port owners employing only registered dock workers. Those that did not obtain work from the pool were still paid, although at a lower scale. The most important feature of the BDLS was the lifetime guarantee of employment, known to the dock workers as 'Jobs for Life.' Dock workers were registered under the Docks Labour Scheme and could not be sacked, except for misconduct! It was at this time that mechanical technology, especially containerisation, started in the docks, and the speed at which this occurred meant that there was a drop in the number of dockers required for work each day. This meant that a number of the total men registered would not be required on some days but would still have to be paid. Another problem for the employers was the restrictive practices, outdated systems of work and the high manning levels. With the move towards containerisation the employers wanted to gain the full benefit of the 24-hour working that the container ports could offer, and they also wanted the dockers to work more flexible hours. The dockers saw this as the employer's way to reduce jobs and impose new conditions of work, and this led to poor working relationships between the management and the dockers, leading to strikes throughout the late 1960s and early 1970s.

Furthermore, the dock workers' victory placed the dock owners under even greater pressure. As well as having to meet the full wage cost, they were confronted in the 1970s with the competition from the more modern, government-subsidised ports in Europe. The larger ports on the Continent, such as Rotterdam, Hamburg and Antwerp, who were better equipped and able to take the newly built, larger ships which required deep-water berths, began to take business away from the British ports and forced the shipping companies to use these ports. This put pressure on the Labour government in the late 1970s to consider privatisation of some industries, and the docks were among the first to be considered; however, the Conservative government, led by Margaret Thatcher, came to power and in 1982 the British Transport Docks Board was abolished. A new body, Associated British Ports (ABP), was prepared for privatisation and given control of 19 of the country's ports, including some of the largest ports such as Southampton, Hull and Cardiff.

Associated British Ports (ABP)

When Associated British Ports (ABP) took over the running of the port in 1982 they came under increasing financial pressure. They had to meet the demands and payroll guarantees of the National Dock Labour Scheme and the competition from the more efficient, less labour intensive operations of the European ports through their installation and operation of new machinery, vehicles and equipment.

In 1989 the Conservative government, led by Margaret Thatcher, abolished the Dock Labour Scheme and, with the reduction in costs through not having to meet the payroll requirements of the Dock Labour Scheme, ABP was able to divert these savings into modernisation of equipment and compete with the European ports on a more level playing field. The dockers came out on strike in July, but by then it was all too late.

In 2000 Associated British Ports (ABP) submitted an application to develop Dibden Terminal on port-owned land. ABP saw the need for the new Dibden Bay Container Terminal in terms of competing for the container trade with other ports, both in the UK and on the continent, that were already upgrading their facilities to meet the future developments in the container trade. With larger and larger container ships being built, the shipping companies using Southampton would not hesitate to transfer their business to the ports that could best meet their needs in speed and efficiency if Southampton were not ready. After public consultation and a final decision by the government, however, the application was not granted.

One of the developing areas in Southampton after 2000 was the cruise industry, with an increasing number of cruise liners visiting the port. In 2003 more than 214 cruise ships called at the port, which was quite an increase on 1997 when just 91 cruise ships called at Southampton. Also during 2003 ABP invested more than £10 million in the reconstruction and refurbishment of the two existing cruise terminals. This included rebuilding the Mayflower Cruise Terminal in the Western Docks, used mainly by P&O cruise ships as their home port, and the modernising of the Queen Elizabeth II Passenger Terminal, Cunard's traditional home berth in the Eastern Docks. Also in that year the third cruise passenger terminal, the City Cruise Terminal, was officially opened by the Lord Lieutenant of Hampshire, Mary Fagan. A fourth terminal is being built in the Ocean Dock and will open in April 2009.

Admiral Acquisitions Consortium

Admiral Acquisitions Consortium, an American consortium, became the new owners of the Port of Southampton in August 2006. The takeover bid was led by US bank Goldman Sachs, who own 23 per cent of the company, with the Prudential Group investments owning 10 per cent and a Canadian pension fund and Singapore government investments owning one third each. This is the first time in its long history that the port has been owned by a foreign consortium of investors.

START OF THE DEVELOPMENT 1803–2009

Southampton Harbour Commissioners 1803–36

Following the Act of Parliament of 1803 making it possible for the building of quays and warehouses, the Southampton Harbour Commissioners were appointed to supervise the development of the waterside work. They first went about to demolish Watergate Quay and a section of the town wall to create better access to the Town Quay from the High Street. Part of the town wall can be clearly seen at the end of the High Street today.

The Harbour Commissioners then sought the advice from John Rennie, who was a celebrated engineer, well known for his work on canals, bridges and dockyards. John Rennie attended a meeting with the Harbour Commissioners on 5 June 1805, (a memorable year because of the Battle of Trafalgar on 21 October 1805). Rennie, with the assistance of John Doswell Doswell, a Southampton surveyor, prepared a detailed report for the Harbour Commissioners to consider. One year later John D. Doswell was appointed as surveyor to the Harbour Commissioners and, following the suggestions of John Rennie, prepared plans for a quay wall from the Town Quay westwards. This was to be the initial stage in the building of the Southampton Docks.

Until the introduction of paddle steamers the cross-channel packet services to Le Harve were undertaken by sailing ships. The first steamship seen in the Solent was the yacht *Thames* when it sailed into Portsmouth in June 1815. The first Isle of Wight and Southampton service was undertaken by the wooden paddle steamer *Prince of Coburg*, which made its first crossing on 24 June 1820. This service was to be for three crossings a day, and it proved more reliable service than the old sailing packets because it could sail at any state of the wind and tide. In 1821 the *Prince of Coburg* was joined by two further steamships. By 1822 the wooden paddle steamer *Medina* had been launched and became the first steamship to provide services to the Channel Islands, and its duties also extended to a number of crossings to Le Harve in 1824. At the same time a weekly service to Le Harve was undertaken by the French steamship the *Triton*. It was the success of these services that influenced the building of the steam packet *Camilla* for the Le Harve service and the steamer *Adriadne*, which was to be used for the Channel Islands service.

By the 1830s the number of passengers using the steamers had increased considerably and was estimated at over 100,000 a year. During the summer months, and especially when the Cowes Regatta was on, there would be an increase in the weekly traffic, but it was found that, despite the work of the Harbour Commissioners to increase the size and access to the Town Quay, it was still too small to handle the both the cargo and passenger traffic.

With such a busy quayside the result was that passengers were left 'having to clamber over barrows, ropes, piles of merchandise and drunken sailors to get on and off the steamers.' The captain of a steamer was left with the only option: to disembark passengers into lighters that could land them on one of the hards or on the mud of the foreshore.

John D. Doswell was commissioned to prepare plans for the building of a new pier in 1831. He presented a plan for a stone pier and a wooden pier at approximately half the cost of the stone pier. It was the wooden pier that was chosen, and it was built by William Betts, a local builder. The building of the pier only took six months, and it was opened by Princess Victoria, who named it the Royal Victoria Pier. This was later to be shortened to the Royal Pier. Within five years, however, the wooden pier was infested by a marine insect called the gribble. To combat the damage caused by the gribble the timber piles were covered with thousands of iron nails, which were expected to rust and so create a protective layer over the wood.

The Development of Southampton Docks from 1836 Southampton Dock Company

Once the Southampton Dock Company was formed in 1836 the business began of drawing up the initial plans for developing the 216 acres of mud land to the east of Town Quay. Also in 1836 the Itchen floating bridge opened. It was a steam-driven chain ferry invented by J.M. Rendel, a pupil of Thomas Telford, and was similar to two other floating bridges that had been installed in Dartmouth and Saltash.

On 12 October 1838, the year of Queen Victoria's coronation, the foundation stone of the new docks was laid by Rear-Admiral Sir Lucius Curtis in the presence of approximately 20,000 people. A newspaper reported at the time that, 'The interest was immense. At an early hour of the morning the bells of the parish churches rang their merry peals and announced to the town that the preparations had commenced, vessels in the harbour were dressed in colours, streamers manned their yards and the town and neighbourhood put on that appearance of gaiety which the occasion deserved. The number of strangers that flocked into the town from all quarters was immense, and as the hour for the appearance of the procession approached all the shops were closed.'

The Development of the Southampton Docks Begins

Once the Southampton Dock Company had been formed in 1836, and the foundation stone laid in 1838, work began on the planning and construction of the docks area. From 1838 the first plan was initially for the building of a tidal or open dock which became known as the Outer Dock, with three graving docks and a closed dock. The closed dock (Inner Dock) was the only non-tidal dock ever constructed in Southampton Docks.

Laying the foundation stone of Southampton Docks, 1838. (Courtesy of ABP)

The Outer Dock

The Outer Dock, the first tidal dock, was opened on 29 August 1842 and measured 16 acres with 2,600ft (792.48m) of quays and would accommodate two ships of the Peninsular & Oriental Steam Navigation Company, the 780-ton *Tagus* and the 500-ton *Liverpool*. The Outer Dock was opened to general trade on 1 July 1843 and the P&O *Pacha* was the first ship to use it. The largest ocean-going ships berthed there as it was the biggest dock in England. The introduction of the railway to Southampton in 1840 gave the opportunity to link the services directly into the docks, and so railway lines were laid along the Outer Dock quayside. This allowed the ships to discharge their cargo directly into rail wagons, thus speeding up the distribution of goods to all parts of the country, as well as bringing goods to the port for loading directly on to the ships.

Dry Docks

Another important development in the Outer Dock was the introduction of three dry docks for the maintenance, overhaul and repairs to ships. No. 1 Dry Dock, which was 401ft (122.2m) in length, 378ft (115.2m) at floor level and had gates that were 66ft (20.1m) width, was opened on 27 July 1846. The first ship to use it was the Royal Mail Steam Packet Company's 1,939-ton *Forth*. The other two dry docks opened in 1847 and 1857. The dimensions of these docks were as follows: No. 2 Dry Dock, opened in 1847, was 281ft (85.6m) in length, 240ft (73.1m) at floor level with a gate width of 51ft (15.5m) and No. 3 Dry Dock, opened in 1854, was 523ft (159.4m) in length, 501ft (152.7m) at floor level and had a gate width of 80ft (24.3m).

The Inner Dock

The Inner Dock, the only non-tidal basin built in the port, was opened to shipping in 1851. It consisted of 10 acres with 2575ft (784.8m) of quays and had an entrance that was 46ft (14m) in width. There were two single lock gates, and with the advantage of the Southampton phenomenon of a double high tide it was possible to keep the lock gates open for six hours per day. The opening of the Inner Dock coincided with the Great Exhibition of 1851, and a wrought-iron crane exhibited there was bought by the Docks Company and subsequently used on the dockside. Due to the increasing size of ships being built and using the port it was necessary in 1859 to extend, deepen and widen the entrance to the Inner Dock. The first vessel to enter the dock after completion of the work was the P&O Company's *Pera* on 20 May.

Quay Extensions

A decision was made to build quays along the west bank of the River Itchen to the south of the Outer Dock. The construction of the Itchen Quays, known originally as the Old Extension Quay, commenced in 1873 but was not completed until 1895. Despite Berths 30–33 being opened in 1876, this was too late to stop P&O leaving Southampton in 1875 due to pressure from London merchants and the need for more berths and deeper water.

The No. 4 Dry Dock was completed in 1879, and its measurements were: 479ft (146m) in length, 453ft (138m) floor length and a gate width of 56ft (17m). The Union Line started using the Itchen Quays.

The Empress Dock

The loss in trade in 1880, partly due to the earlier move of P&O to London, put pressure on the Southampton Dock Company to increase the dock facilities to attract more trade, and a decision was made to build a new deep-water dock, and the

The Inner and Outer Docks in the late 1800s. (Courtesy of Mick Lindsay Collection)

Southampton Dock Company took a loan of £250,000 from LSWR to construct it. This was to be the last extension undertaken by the Southampton Dock Company before being taken over by the London and South Western Railway Company.

Work started in 1886 and was completed in 1890, and on 26 July that year the new Empress Dock was opened by Queen Victoria. It had an area of 18½ acres with 3,880ft (1182.6m) of quays and an entrance width of 165ft (50.9m). A memorable sight for those who had been invited to attend the opening was the royal yacht *Alberta* sailing into the dock and breaking the ribbon at the entrance.

In his *Reminiscences of Public Life in Southampton 1866-1900* Sir James Lemon gives an interesting first-hand account of the opening of the Empress Dock. He starts by commenting on the skills of seamanship on the royal yacht *Alberta*: 'The new deep water dock was opened by Her Majesty Queen Victoria on July 26th, 1890. The royal yacht steamed into the new dock and subsequently was moored alongside the quay. I well remember the long time it took to get alongside the quay; it certainly showed the most miserable want of seamanship I remember. The captain of one of the Isle of Wight steamers would have accomplished it in about one-fourth of the time.'

Sir James Lemon comments on the members of the town council, borough magistrates and town officials assembling at the municipal offices earlier in the day where they robed up and boarded a special train at the railway terminus to be taken into the docks. Sir James Lemon: 'At about 1.30 luncheon was served in an elaborately decorated and spacious shed on the quay opposite to which the royal yacht was to stop a few hours later.'

Mr Steuart Macnaughton, chairman of the Dock Company, presided and was supported by the Archbishop of Canterbury, the Earl of Northbrook, Mr James Bishop, Mayor of Southampton and the Bishop of Guildford.

At the Empress Dock seats were provided for a number of people, and the space reserved for the public was quickly filled. Sir James Lemon: 'and people swarmed into the dock from noon until 4 o'clock. Across the entrance to the basin a ribbon was extended, and in the centre of it was a bouquet of flowers. The *Alberta* was steered straight for the centre knot, and when the ribbon parted there was a loud and prolonged cheering and the Union Jack

P&O's *Arcadia* leaving the Outer Dock in 1888. The Dry Docks No. 1, 2 and 3 can be seen from the left in the foreground.

The Thames twin-screw steam yacht *Sapphire* in No. 4 Dry Dock. (Courtesy of Bert Moody Collection)

Berth 34 looking up the River Itchen. The entrance to Empress Dock can be seen before the ships moored at Berths 32 and 33. (Courtesy of Mrs Maureen Webber)

exchanged for the Royal Standard at the entrance. The yacht broke the ribbon at two minutes to five, having made the journey from Cowes in about 40 minutes, and it was nearly 20 minutes before she was brought alongside the West Quay.'

Once the royal yacht was alongside, a guard of honour of the Royal Marines Light Infantry presented arms and the band played the National Anthem, 'and people present cheering with great enthusiasm. The Archbishop of Canterbury specially dedicated the new basin and then requested everyone present to join in the Lord's Prayer, and his request was generally complied with'.

The chairman of the dock and officials boarded the yacht and were presented to Queen Victoria. Sir James Lemon: 'The chairman then handed in an address, which was beautifully got up. Her Majesty graciously replied and handed the chairman the following written reply, viz.:

"I received with pleasure your loyal and dutiful address. It gives me great pleasure to inaugurate this important addition to the docks of the Port of Southampton, and to see so striking an illustration of the energy of commercial enterprise in my kingdom. I trust that the Port of Southampton will feel the benefit of the great work you have completed and in the future increasing developments of trade and prosperity."'

At that point a large white ensign was unfurled, 'disclosing to the interested spectators the arms of the Southampton Dock Company and beneath, in large letters, the words Empress Dock.'

After the presentation of a bouquet, and the presentation of arms with the playing of the National Anthem, 'the ropes were then unfastened and the royal yacht slowly steamed away amid renewed cheering, and duly arrived at Trinity Pier, East Cowes, at about 7 o'clock.'

The Dock Company showed their thanks to all who had worked on the construction of the Empress Docks by giving them a supper in the 'luncheon shed'.

(The extract from Sir James Lemon's account of the opening of the Empress Docks is courtesy of Genevieve Bailey.)

Coal Barge Dock

Also in the late 1880s the coal barge dock on Berth 28 was opened for storing coal in lighters for the bunkering of outward-bound vessels. It had two jetties and the length of the quayside was 360ft (110m). The coal dock was finally closed in 1979. An account of this work is given here:

The entrance to Empress Dock in the late 1920s. (Courtesy of ABP)

A coal porter's postcard. (Courtesy of Bert Moody Collection)

'And the men worked in the barges digging coal into baskets which was transported on what we call a small derrick, to be transferred into the ship's coal-ports and that carried on all day long. Seven in the gang, that would be two trimmers and five; the five that'd be three diggers, the man on the stage is four and the man on the spinners heavin' it up. That's the five. As the coal was put in the ship, into the coal-ports, these people were in the bunkers trimming the coal, stowing the coal back.

'The Union Castle boats used to take approximately about 3.000 tons each, which used to take three or four days, sometimes quicker than others.

'To me they were the finest crowd of men you wished to work for, or work with; t' say they were rough, but they were decent and they could work.' (*Oral History Unit, Southampton.*)

London & South Western Railway 1892-1923
By 1892 the management of the Port of Southampton was taken over by the L&SWR (London and South Western Railway). Due to the port being able to berth the largest ships of the day, at any state of the tide, more shipping lines were attracted to the port. The American Line transferred its New York mail service from Liverpool to Southampton, with the liner *New York* commencing the service on 4 March 1893.

Development of the Old Docks
In 1895 the No. 5 Dry Dock in the Empress Dock was opened by His Royal Highness the Prince of Wales and from then on was known as the Prince of Wales Dry Dock. It was 745ft (227m) long, had a 729ft (222m) floor length and a gate width of 91ft (27.7m). At the time it was the largest dry dock in the world. With the increase in traffic more berth space was needed, and so work was started on the South Quay and Test Quays. In 1902 South Quay (37 Berth) and Test Quays (Berths 38–41) were opened. The South Quay, Berth No. 37, is 425ft (129.5m) in length and was

Prince of Wales (No. 5) Dry Dock. (Courtesy of ABP)

Trafalgar (No. 6) Dry Dock. (Courtesy of ABP)

first used by the Rotterdam Lloyd Steamship Company and the Nederland Royal Mail Line for their outward bound steamers to the Dutch East Indies. This berth was later taken over by the Union Castle Mail Steamship Company's continental steamers. The Test Quay is 2,227ft (678.7m) in length and takes Berths 38 to 41.

Trafalgar Dry Dock
A new dry dock was required to take the increasing size of ships being built. This was to be known as the No. 6 Dry Dock, and prior to its opening the first 50-ton electric crane was installed.

No. 6 Dry Dock was 912.3ft (284.1m) long, had a 852ft (259.6m) floor level and was 100ft (30.4m) wide at the entrance. It was opened on the 100th anniversary of the death of Nelson by the Marquis of Winchester, Lord Lieutenant of the County, and thereafter was called the Trafalgar Dock. *Dunluce Castle* was the first ship to enter the Dry Dock, on 17 November 1905.

Dock Enlarged for SS *Berengaria*
The Trafalgar Dry Dock, although at the time the largest in the world, was not large enough to take the SS *Olympic* and had to be enlarged. In 1922 it was necessary to enlarge the dock yet again to accommodate the SS *Berengaria*. This was accomplished by cutting a V-shaped section into the head of the dry dock for the liner's bows. This only left 10in (0.25m) between the sides of the ship and the dock wall.

White Star Dock – Ocean Dock
This dock was originally called the White Star Dock because it was built to accommodate the White Star North Atlantic express service. Construction commenced in 1906. At that time the Old Dock only extended to 40 Berth, where the International Cold Store had been built in 1902. Although the Trafalgar Dock had been built and opened in 1905, the area between 40 Berth and the dry dock was mudland with a chalk bank at the southern end. The chalk bank was useful to the construction of Berths 43–46, and part of berth 47 in the White Star Dock, because it could act as a barrier or dam,

The White Star Dry Dock in 1910–11, with Union Castle liner *Carisbrook Castle* at Berth 46. (Courtesy of ABP)

White Star liner *Olympic*. (Courtesy of Nikki Goff collection)

meaning that the work could be undertaken while dry without the problem of the tides. Once the dock had been completed the chalk bank was opened up to let the water in. It was not possible to do this for Berths 48, 49, jetty 42 or Berth 41. Other forms of construction were needed due to the River Test washing up to the banks.

The White Star Dock was opened on 14 June 1911 and was built specifically to accommodate the new White Star Olympic Class liners, *Olympic, Titanic* and *Britannic*.

The 46,439-ton *Olympic*, the first of the three vessels built, was launched on 20 October 1910 and was the first passenger liner to use the White Star Dock in 1911. The *Olympic* departed from 43–44 Berths on her maiden voyage from Southampton to New York on 14 June after first stopping at Cherbourg and Queenstown, both times to pick up passengers and mail. She left New York on 28 June 1911 for her eastbound maiden voyage across the Atlantic to Southampton. After calling in at Plymouth to discharge passengers and mail she continued on to Cherbourg to discharge more passengers and mail and then continued back to her home port of Southampton. As well as the *Olympic*, the other White Star liners using the dock regularly were the *Majestic, Oceanic* and *Teutonic*.

The name of the White Star Dock was changed to Ocean Dock in 1922 due to other famous companies using the dock, especially the Cunard Line.

DOCK LABOUR IN THE EARLY 20TH CENTURY

For a young lad wanting to get a job in the docks after leaving school at the age of 14 there was only the opportunity to become messengers or shed boys. It was while working with and taking the advice of the experienced dockers that they learned the job. This account highlights the experiences of one lad who started work in 1914: 'Before you became a docker you had to be 21 years of age, because the physical side of the job was pretty hard going. You couldn't expect a boy of 14 to pull a bale of wool weighing about 5 cwt! They were all good, good old fellows in them days. You know, they'd say, "Come on nipper, this is the way to do it. Do what I do, follow me and you won't go wrong", and they used to help you a lot. Well that's how you learned. My father always

White Star liner *Majestic*. (Courtesy of Nikki Goff collection)

A postcard showing dockers at work.

used to say: "Look, do what he tells you, it'll come in handy later." The first job I had was as a shed boy, and that was like a general factotum that was, at everyone's beck and call: "Just get the shed boy, call him up!" My wages were five shillings a week. The "Canute" opened at five in the morning then, and I used to take one of these jars with the cane all round them, filled up with beer for the day for my three bosses in the office. A gallon for eight pence! The Channel Islands cattle had to stay in the docks for a few days, and us boys used to creep in when the cattle-man wasn't looking, dip our own mugs into the buckets of creamy milk and run off with it. But most of the milk was distributed around the bosses. There was some men stood up there and I stood by them and watched them. Not that I wanted a job because I'd signed on the West Indie boat. The fellow that was taking on the men then, he pointed to me and said: "Would you like a job?" I said I'd just signed on the *Aruba*. "Well," he said, "It doesn't go out before Friday." He said to go aboard the *Magdalena*. Go down the hold and sew up all the coffee bags that was all broken. I got four pence an hour.' (*Oral History Unit, Southampton.*)

Working on the Cranes

It was the same 'learning on the job' for lads leaving school who wanted to become crane drivers. As all the crane drivers were employed in the docks by the railway company, most boys would start work as a messenger boy before moving on to become scaler lads or crane lads. Then they moved on to maintenance and finally became a crane driver. This account explains the experience of one lad who wished to become a crane driver: 'I worked for Mr Dewey on his milk round and when I went for a job in the docks 'course I jumped off his cart and went to Maritime Chambers and met my father there, we went up to the top of the chambers and we had to sign a big form and then he patted me on the back and said: "Go on, you young devil!" And shortly afterwards I started in the docks as a scaler lad.

Ocean Dock in the early 20th century. (Courtesy of Mick Lindsay Collection)

Electric cranes. (Courtesy of ABP)

'I went in a tinsmith's shop. We used to do the cooks' dishes and things on the Royal Mail boats. When they used to come in the docks we used to go to the ship with a pair of trucks, pick up the old dishes and pans, take them back to Conroy's to re-tin them, make them nice and bright again, and the next time the ship come in we took them back again and got another lot.

'They blowed the boiler down first and then took the manhole covers off. Two of us scaler lads used to go in underneath the boiler and clean the flues out all the way round and used to get as black as anything.

'We used to have eight of us inside the boilers cleaning the scale off the plates and round the furnaces and all that. And you'd get smothered in candle fat and dust; chalk dust off the sides goes like powder in there, see. Your hair used to be smothered in candle grease. Candlelight was all we had; we used to make our own candlesticks on a bit of string and flat iron and a nut on the other end.

'As a crane lad I used to clean the cranes. I had to do what the driver told me, they were very strict. For those seven steam cranes there was only two crane lads. I was on the 12-ton steam crane, my friend was on the 15 ton. The other drivers worked on their own.' (*Oral History Unit, Southampton.*)

From being scaler lads the boys moved on to different jobs and gained more experience: 'The scaler lads all went on to other jobs. One chap, he went on to the 30-ton steam crane and there was three of us went into this stoke-hole here. Some went on to the engines, shunting. They were brake boys and they all sort of disappeared into different jobs. They electrified everything and didn't want no scaler lads then.

'I was asked whether I would rather go on the engines or go on the cranes. I preferred at that time to go on the cranes because I was in the Boy Scouts and the other job meant shift work and I shouldn't be able to attend them.

'They wouldn't train you to be a driver, not the steam drivers. No, they never trained us at all, but when we went to the electric cranes we were just on as greasers, and they trained you to become a crane driver then an electric crane driver.

'As I was learning, I lowered down too heavy on a 2-ton crane. Oh they were fast, and I came down and didn't stop them before they touched the quay. I hit the quay and busted three barrels of wine. They went all over the quay. I got me billy can out then and went down and filled it up.' (*Oral History Unit, Southampton.*)

The skills involved in shipbuilding or boilermaking included plating, rivetting and welding, and as they were employed by the London and South Western Railway the company would employ men to work in their workshops. The lads had the opportunity to either work on the cranes or on the engines and would 'often move between working on ships to locomotives and cranes'.

'It was such a variety you might get two or three different jobs in a day and some you'd never see again. Today you might be working on a loco', tomorrow'd be working on a ship, another day on the cranes. In fact, you may work on all three in a day as small jobs came off of them, old steam cranes an' all.

'The job meant crawling about in all parts of the ship, in the bilge tanks, underneath the boiler seatings, repairing all parts of ships, you see. Repairing the boats, all the lifting gear in the docks we used to do. We had locos to repair. All the cranes to repair, all the dry-dock work, all the moorings over in the Channel Islands, all the gangway work, all that sort of thing. If you were in a shop, a railway shop or something like that, you'd get thousands of things to make. Well, we never, for us half a dozen was quite a number to make. Made work interesting too!

'In the early days I would help the plater mark out the various sizes because there wasn't the electric welding and there wasn't the acetylene burning as there is today. Everything had to be developed out on the flat and then bent up and flanged and drilled and all had to fit together – not "cut and fit" as it is today.

'The lengths of jobs varied. You'd have a job for two or three days on one ship and then leave. Another ship, if it was in for a fortnight, you might work on it for 10 days or so.

'The boilermakers were a little superior because their money was higher than other trades, but we all thought that our particular trade was the best – I naturally thought plumbing was good.' (*Oral History Unit, Southampton.*)

Responsibilities of the Crane Driver

The crane driver was not only responsible for the operation of the crane, but also for the safety of dockers working onboard and on the quayside. His working conditions were not always very comfortable, especially in cold weather, as the following account explains:

'The first cranes they had in the Ocean Dock were different altogether. You had to watch when you were derricking out with the jib because you could only go so far. You'd hit the stop blocks and you could soon get the counter weight off the back. You had about eight ton swinging up and down. They were awkward at night, you couldn't hear nothing. All you could do was watch your wire at the side of you, the light shining on it. That's the only way you could see whether it was faster or slower. So you had to keep one eye on the wire and one on the hatchway, one and one.'

'Then you had the gear cranes, they was all in gear. Well you had an emergency footbrake, but you didn't use it because everything was in gear. Once you left neutral everything stopped so it was fast, but we didn't like it much because it was too dull. We always wanted something with a bit of life in it.'

Working in the first electric cranes was not very comfortable, as described by one crane driver: 'The conditions in the first electric cranes was very poor. We had a paraffin oil stove for our heat, and it used to smoke and your feet was absolutely freezing. There was no partition in the cranes. From the driving cab into the machines was all one. Later on, some of the drivers used to make their own partitions, so that kept the cabs bit warmer and with less row from the barrels and gears.'

'If you were driving a five-ton and they asked you to pick up six-ton, you refused to do that. You couldn't actually tell the weight, you'd have an idea from the power you were using and the strain of the crane when you pushed the lever. But the thought was in your mind that it was overweight. You'd say: "Here, this is heavy".

'The hatchwaymen would give the signals to the driver. The crane driver could see his own way to get into the hatch, but when he was down below the hatch he couldn't see. It was very awkward. Sometimes the driver could see down the hold but if the tide rose, he couldn't see.

'If you had a light load, like "Quaker oats" or something like that, and the wind blew, you'd get a swing and that's where the art of crane driving came in. If it wasn't put on the board right it could blow it off or it could slip through the net or the sling and come down.' (*Oral History Unit, Southampton.*)

Unloading Channel Island tomatoes at C Warehouse, No. 1 Berth in 1931. (Courtesy of ABP)

SOUTHERN RAILWAY 1923-1948

An important development took place in 1923 when the L&SWR amalgamated with other railways in the South and the management of Southampton Docks was taken over by the new Southern Railway. At the same time parliamentary agreement was obtained to plan for a new docks extension. This was to be for 7,000ft (2133.6m) of deep-water quays, including a graving dock 1,200ft (365.7m) in length, 1141.6ft (347.9m) floor length and 135ft (41.1m) width at the entrance. The early planning was for two graving docks, but only one was built.

The Old Docks from the 1920s

The warehouses in the Outer Dock were equipped with electric hoists and housed coffee, cocoa, dried fruits, tobacco and cigars and also had vaults for the cool storage of wines. This was where the Southern Railway steamers berthed for passengers, mails and cargo to and from the Channel Islands and France. The Inner Dock was used for grain, timber and fruit imports and was partly bordered by grain warehouses on the North and East Quays. These warehouses also had dry vaults for storing wines and spirits.

Many ships up until the 1930s were fuelled by coal. Berth 13 was a coal depot, and bunkering of the vessels with coal was

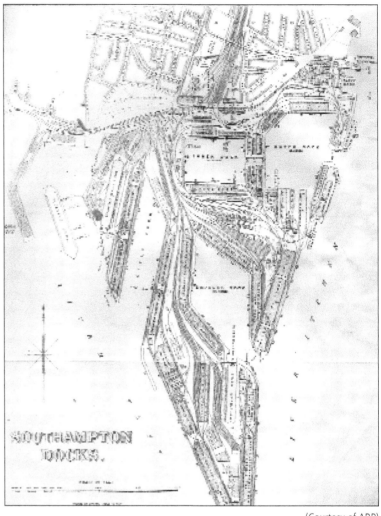

(Courtesy of ABP)

undertaken by coal barges that could carry up to 2,000 tons of bunker coal at a time. This was done by hand by the coal porters directly from a barge into the ships' coal bunkers.

Berths 14, 15 and 16 were used by the fruit traffic, and Simons (Southampton) fruit brokers' auction sales room was at Berth 14 and could accommodate up to 300 buyers. This enabled a faster movement of fruit, as it would only take a few hours to unload the fruit, sort it, sell it in the sale room and then transport it by rail to various parts of the country.

The shallow-draught facilities in the old Inner Dock restricted the type of vessel using this particular dock considerably, with

mainly 'coaster' or 'feeder' vessels being the only ones able to use this basin in the latter days of its history.

As in most ports around the country, these old docking areas were surrounded by large 'multi-storey' brick-built warehouses, with (jibbed) rope-tackles on their outer platforms to lift packages onto the various storage levels. The inner floor surfaces were thick wooden planks which had been worn rickety over the years, making the use of hand-trucks comparable to 'working in a ploughed field!'

The Inner Dock. (Courtesy of Bert Moody Collection)

Goliath Crane. (Courtesy of ABP)

The old warehouses in the original dock areas were identified by code letters, 'L', 'M', 'N', 'O', 'P' and 'Q' being those at the Inner Dock. They were later specifically used to accommodate 'special' cargoes, usually those held under Customs' bond. For example, 'O' warehouse was mostly used for the storage of cased tobacco, where the dockers laboriously trundled the old wooden-framed, iron-wheeled hand trucks laden with 2cwt cases of leaf tobacco over the wooden furrows of those original floors, which were built in the early Victorian era.

The Empress Dock in 1929 had eight berths, 20–27, mainly used by Royal Mail Steam Packet Company's 'A' Class steamer to transport mail, passengers and cargo to Brazil. Cargo such as meat, butter, grain and fruit was sent from the docks by rail to London, the Midlands and the South Coast. Berth 20 in the Empress Dock was used for trooping operations from Southampton.

Berths 30–33, previously known as the old Extension Quay, along the River Itchen, were used by the Canadian Pacific Steamships, Rotterdam Lloyd and Nederland Royal Mail Line steamers to the Dutch East Indies, and Peninsular and Oriental Steamship Company to the Far East. Following on from Berths 30–33 are Berths 34–36, originally known as the Prince of Wales Quays, and they were one of the first projects by the London & South Western Railway after taking over the docks. They were known by the 1920s as the Itchen Quays. By 1929 a new double-storey shed was built on the site of an old transit shed at Berth 34. Both Berths 35 and 36 have double-storey sheds and were all used in 1929 by the Union Castle Steamship Company's ships from South Africa. The majority of imports at the time were wool, skins, hides, grain and fruit. To assist in the handling of the cargo the 'Goliath' electric cranes at the rear of the sheds were used.

The South Quay was Berth 37 and was first used by Rotterdam Lloyd Steamship Company and Nederland Royal Mail Lines, but by 1929 it was used by the Union Castle Mail Steamship Company's steamships to the Continent.

The Ocean Dock, looking from 42 Berth. (Courtesy of ABP)

The *Leviathan*.
(Courtesy of Mick Lindsay Collection)

The Test Quays were Berths 38–41, with Berth 40 having the International Cold Storage Company premises on the quayside, storing cargoes of meat and other perishable foods. Berths 38 and 39 were used for weekly sailings passengers, mail and cargo to South Africa by a fleet of 10 Union Castle Mail Steamship Company vessels.

In the Ocean Dock, Berths 43–47, along with sheds, passenger gantries and cranes, were used mainly at the time by the White Star Line, Cunard and United States Line, however, Berth 45 was used exclusively for a large timber trade, with a timber shed to store large quantities of goods.

Following on from Ocean Dock are Berths 48–51. By 1929 there were some 42 miles of railway track within the docks area linked with the Southern Railway system. This increased by the middle of the 20th century to 78 miles of track.

Boat Trains in 1926

Boat trains were timetabled to meet deadlines for the arrival and departure of the liners. A boat train could leave within 90 minutes of the arrival of the ocean liner, and within a further 90 minutes passengers would arrive in London. Many passengers for the ocean liners would travel by the special boat trains from Waterloo Station, which was laid on to connect with the liners at Southampton Docks. In just one month, November 1926, the liners the boat trains met included the *Leviathan*, *Olympic*, *Minnadosa*, *Mataroa*, *Saxon*, *Ascania*, *Avon*, *Majestic*, *George Washington*, *Athenic*, *Arundel Castle*, *Empress of France*, *Berengaria*, *Rotorua*, *Homeric*, *Melita*, *Ausonia*, *Almanzora*, *Walmer Castle*, *Mauretania*, *Edinburgh Castle*, *Antonia* and *Arcadian*.

The *Arundel Castle*. (Courtesy of Mick Lindsay Collection)

Coal and Oil Bunkering

Coal and oil bunkering was undertaken by R & J.H. Rea Ltd and the British Mexican Petroleum Company, which had a fuel oil bunkering station on the east side of the River Itchen from 1923. These facilities supplied the large Atlantic liners such as *Majestic, Olympic, Mauretania* and *Homeric.* Kenneth Fielder remembers the liners taking on fuel oil: 'It is nice to remember how the liners were refuelled. They were basically refuelled originally by Brit Mex. From Woolston there was a jetty, and on the end of the jetty was what they called the jetty barge, where the crews of the refuelling barges would leave to go aboard. The refuelling barges would normally anchor off, and on occasions they would have to come in to take oil on board, which was pumped to them from the depot oil storage tanks, possible coming originally from the Esso refinery. Some were known as dumb barges because they had to be towed to the liners. There were two self-propelled ones. One was called the *Inveritchen* and the other was the *Francunion.* They would be responsible for definitely refuelling the railway boats just after the Second World War. They would have been most certainly refuelling all the Cunard vessels by that time. When the barges used to go in to Fawley refinery to be loaded to take the oil to the liners there was just one pontoon at the end of the jetty. There is an area inside of the refinery that is still known as the old refinery.'

The following account describes working on an oil barge: 'I was on an oil barge. We used to be towed by the Red Star tugs to down off of Fawley, where the oil-tankers used to come in. They were much smaller them days than they are now, carrying round about 10–12,000 tons of fuel. The barge I was in used to carry approximately 800 tons. We used to be towed back, either to the depot or to one of the liners. It could be the *Majestic* or the *Aquitania,* the *Mauretania,* any of those that were bunkered, and we could pump on 800 tons. We could pump that in two hours. We pumped 400 tons an hour.

'There was three men on a barge them days, and whoever was on watch had to keep steam up during the night, especially in winter-time. Our money was £4 a week, but we was doing three weeks in one. We were working night and day, up and down. It sounded like a lot, but it was in fact one of the hardest jobs I've ever had in my life. Four pounds a week. I reckon we was earning about £24 a week!' (*Oral History Unit, Southampton.*)

The Floating Dry Dock

The new ships being built in 1924 were larger, and that put pressure on what vessels the Trafalgar Dock could accommodate; however, a decision was made in 1924 to employ a 60,000-ton floating dock that would quite easily take the larger ships. The

The *Berengaria* in the floating dry dock at Berth 50. (*Courtesy of ABP*)

A postcard of the floating dry dock.
(Courtesy of F Stuart)

floating dock was officially opened by H.R.H. the Prince of Wales on 27 June 1924 and was placed alongside 50 Berth. The dimensions of the dry dock were 960ft (292.6m) in length with a 170ft (51.8m) outside width. The floor area covered 3½ acres, and it had 14 electrically driven centrifugal pumps which ensured that lifting could be completed in four hours. The floating dock could accommodate the larger liners such as the *Olympic*, *Majestic* and *Berengaria* (formally the German Liner, the *Imperator*).

From the Town Quay you could easily look across at the floating dry dock. Bert Moody describes what he saw as a boy: 'If you moved along to the Town Quay you got a good view of the big floating dry dock there. The joy of watching as a boy was to see a boat entering and the dry dock coming up, lifting the boat out of the water. I saw the *Mauretania* and the *Olympic* come into that floating dry dock, and the *Aquitania*, because all the big ones went in there. The *Bremen* came in there about 1930, but I have no recollection of seeing the ship go in. I was about nine or 10 then, but I know she did go in there twice. The only dry dock in Germany that could take her was occupied by the *Europa*, her sister ship. The *Europa* had been damaged by fire before she entered service. Before the *Bremen* entered service she came in just to have her bottom cleaned up, that was all. I don't remember *Bremen* at all, although she definitely was there, but according to me she was the only foreign ship to use the dry dock while the dock was in Southampton. The dry dock was only there from 1924 and by 1934 it was out of use because of the No. 7 King George V Graving Dock being ready. In 1940 the floating dock was taken to Portsmouth and then ended up in Rotterdam.'

One young lad describes the terrifying moment he had while greasing the wires on one of the cranes: 'There used to be two cranes on the floating dry dock, and they were high up when you went up to the top of one of those. I remember once, I had to grease the wires on the floating dock-cranes, and, of course, the dry dock was high up out of the water and these cranes were on top of that again, so they were probably 200 or 300ft up in the air. We wanted the crane driver to lower a bit, and instead he "slewed", and oh! The heart went out of your mouth. Instead of lowering the ball, as we intended him to, he swung the jib with us on the end. That was one of the dangerous moments.'

Ken Fielder also clearly remembers the floating dry dock: 'Obviously we became conversant with the docks, and prior to the King George V Graving Dock the larger liners were put into the floating dry dock, which was at Berth 50. It used to submerge and the liner would go in, and then the water was pumped out and it would rise above water level, and literally by going to the old Town Quay you could see a huge liner a few yards away. I can clearly remember seeing the *Olympic* out of the water.'

'There was also a very large floating crane which could be taken around the dock where its facilities were necessary for the dock's purpose. In later years Berth 50 became the base for the BOAC flying boats.'

For the heavy lifts the floating crane had three separate hoisting gears. The main hoist was able to lift 150 tons on two hooks with a speed of 8ft (2.43m) per minute, 75 tons at 16ft (4.87m) per minute and had a maximum radius of 106ft (32.3m).

A 150-ton floating crane.
(Courtesy of ABP)

The Itchen floating bridge. (Courtesy of Mrs Maureen Webber)

The Itchen Floating Bridge

The floating bridge was used frequently by dock workers who crossed the River Itchen to work in the docks. It was especially useful for those who worked on the railway steamers leaving the Outer Dock for the Channel Islands and France, as the Marine berths were close to the nearest dock gate to the bridge. The floating bridge also had a royal passenger when the Prince of Wales crossed the river to Woolston to visit the Supermarine factory in 1924. In 1956, while visiting friends, the artist L.S. Lowry painted the floating bridge. The Itchen floating bridge was replaced by the new Itchen toll bridge in 1977 (after 141 years of service).

Moving Cargoes by Hand

The conditions that the dockers worked in during the 1920s and 1930s were often harsh, especially with some of the cargoes they would have to move by hand. Weather and unsociable working hours had to be endured by the dockers because of their need to work to feed their families. This is an account of how one docker viewed the work at the time: 'It was pretty fast working. Where fruit was concerned you had 50 cases of oranges on a board, and the speed was terrific. You had three sets of men lifting them off a board, as it came. It landed on a scooter top, went into the shed and you had to break them down and four men had to sort them onto the floor and truckers took them away to the stacks. They had straight barrows, we called them hand trucks. They were used for carrying anything: baggage, fruit, wool and skins, anything you like. Fork trucks are used now.

'Sometimes we used to come in at six in the morning for the Havre boat and as soon as the passengers was finished we used to go on either the tomato boat or the potato boat if it was in and we used to work 'til one o'clock at night, Sundays as well.

'A Dundee boat came in with all seed potatoes in the winter just about February. I know we worked one day and it was that cold and the rain was coming down and it was freezing up against the sheds. We had to work out in it, trucking in and trucking in. We couldn't stop the whole time.

'Then you had the wet hides. They was hides that had been salted down, tied up with rope, with a metal tab on. And you used to look at the tab and sort them all out for all these different firms that used to handle these hides. Stinking job it was, even the cat ran away from you when you come home. He wouldn't have nothing to do with you.

'You had to put something back, especially in the summertime when it was real hot out there, 'cos that sun used to bake down on you and you couldn't get out of it. The hatches were all open and we used to have what they called 'plain board', like for what they used to make floorboards and that. When the sun shined on that, it used to hit you; it would sort of reflect back on you and you wanted about four pints of beer, I can tell you, to put the sweat back in you again after you'd been out there for four hours.

'We used to have this other cargo that's given a lot of people asbestosis. We used to work that and take no notice of it. It used to go up out of the hatch in sacks, perhaps the sacks would be torn on the way up and it used to come out just like snow and

we used to think it was funny, but it's not so funny now they've found out about it.

'One job we used to hate doing was being transferred to the Royal Mail meat boats. They used to land the meat on the platform trucks which used to bring it in to the shed. Four men used to lift up these lumps of meat and if you were one of the carriers, they used to place this on your back. Then you had to carry it up a steep plank into a lorry and that was hard work. I remember the heaviest I had on my shoulder weighed 300lbs and it's all iced, you

Various cargo imports, including hides. (Courtesy of ABP)

Jersey potatoes. (Courtesy of ABP)

see and you had no protection for your shoulders. Carrying this frozen meat all day long must have set up rheumatism in lots of people, but we were young and strong and it didn't bother us that much. You had two men to take it off your back. Well sometimes you'd get two weaklings up there and they used to drag it off your back. Well, of course, if you drag a piece of beef off your back all the time you know you got it, you only had a bit of canvas on your shoulder and they used to knock seven bells out of you sometimes.

'We was doing a Cape Boat and this old bloke, a passenger, nobody would do his baggage. In them days, a tip was a tip. This bloke had some damn old bags and stuff. I happened to be going up and I saw him trying to struggle with this, so I took it up to the train for him and he was a proper Dutch Boer and hardly understood a word. When he gave me a tip I said: "What the hell's that?" I didn't know what it was. Put it in me pocket. I gets home and I shows it to me father. "You want to keep that", he says, "It's a Kruger". So I put it on me watch chain. Cor, a gold sovereign for a tip! Somebody had a lucky find later for I lost my watch, chain and all in a crate of apples I was loading.

'I went as a Customs cooper in the cage; all the cargo that came ashore, I used to have to open. Cases of silks, cotton, books, all different kinds of everything you could mention. You used to put it out and show them and examine it and then pack it all back again and do up the cases. Sometimes, three or four thousand cases of whisky would come over, different kinds of whisky, rum and brandy used to pass through the Customs and barrels of wine as well. I've had about a hundred barrels of wine in the shed and I had to knock the bungs out and they used to dip them for measurements and everything like that, and afterwards I used to scribe them with the numbers and date.' (*Oral History Unit, Southampton.*)

The Western Shore in the 19th and early 20th Century
As young lads in the 1920s and 1930s Kenneth Fielder and Bert Moody could remember what it looked like before the New Docks were built. The railway line ran along from the Redbridge Station to Millbrook Station, opened in 1861, and on to the Blechynden/Southampton West Station. This area along the railway line from the Redbridge causeway to Millbrook and Southampton West Stations and around to the Western Esplanade was along the water's edge. It was called West Bay.

Ken Fielder could remember the path from Millbrook Station into Southampton. Only part of the path is still there today, fenced and listed as a cycle track: 'Millbrook in the 1930s, my school days, my very early days. We used to go down the old Millbrook Station, and there you would have a path that would take you all the way into Southampton. At high water the Test used to come up to a small shingle beach. It wasn't very safe, and we wouldn't paddle in the water in case you cut your feet, but there was an old landing stage there, an old decrepit one, and that preceded the creation of the new dock.' Bert Moody was not so bothered about cutting his feet: 'The water used to come up to Millbrook Station, and I used to paddle in it.'

CONSTRUCTION OF THE NEW DOCKS

By 1927 the trade in the port was increasing considerably, and there was a need to extend the quays even further. An ambitious scheme, the brainchild of Sir Herbert Walker, the chairman of Southern Railway, had been planned for an extension of the docks, and the New Docks scheme officially commenced on 3 January 1927 with the reclamation of land between the Royal Pier and Millbrook Point. This was to be called the Extension Quays and an area of 400 acres of mud land within a marshy bay would be pumped dry. One hundred and forty-six massive concrete and steel piles would provide 1½ miles (2.41km) of deep-water berths.

Ken Fielder talks about the process they used to reclaim the land for the New Dock: 'The New Dock was created when they built what was the new quayside and pumped the water into the River Test. They then dredged the Test, and the material from the dredging became what we know as the New Dock area.'

In 1929 the work had progressed with dredging the soft mud and the start of the construction of the quay walls. At the time the plans were for a quay wall 7,400ft (2225.5m) long with six cargo sheds 900ft (274.3m) long by 150ft (45.7m) wide, with rail tracks and adjoining roads. There was also a plan to construct a jetty running parallel with the quay wall. The jetty was to be 5,000ft (1,524m) long and 400ft (121.9m) wide so that vessels would be able to berth on both sides. This would have allowed the berthing of up to 20 of the largest vessels of the day, but in the end the jetty was not built. Although the plans also allowed for two graving docks at Millbrook Point, only the King George V Graving Dock was built. Planning also included two connections to the main railway line, one at Millbrook Station where a siding would leave the main railway line and the other would link with the Harbour Board's railway at the Royal Pier. A recreation area of 10 acres was planned and is known today as the Mayflower Park.

Bert Moody remembers the docks in the 1920s and 1930s and the building of the New Docks: 'I was born in Totton in 1921, and my father worked for Southern Railway. He died in 1924 and my mother, who was his second wife, said she was going to leave Totton, and so we moved to Southampton. She was a qualified pianoforte teacher and decided to take a shop. It was on the corner of Simnel Street and Bugle Street. It's not there today because it has been demolished and there is a block of flats on the site. It was about 50 yards away from Tudor house. In between the shop and Tudor house was St Michael's lodging house, where a lot of dock workers and construction workers stayed, particularly when building the New Docks in the 1930s. You could get a bed for 9d a night, but they had no food arrangements at all. They used to come into our shop for a pennyworth of cheese and a pennyworth of corned beef and half penny's worth of milk. The shop sold all sorts of little things, and you had to sell a lot to make a living.'

The continuous noise of the building of the New Docks is still very clear in Bert Moody's memory: 'I saw all of the new docks being built. Horrible noises, pile drivers all the time and the dredgers grinding away, because they did a lot of dredging. A massive area was filled in by the dredging.'

Millbrook shore looking towards Southampton. (Engraving by Phillip Brannon)

Looking from Forest View towards Weymouth Terrace in the Western Shore Road, now all demolished. Today you would see the West Quay shopping centre where water is in this picture. (Courtesy of Mrs Maureen Webber)

The first ship to use New Docks quays was the Cunard Lines' four-funnel *Mauretania* (the 'Grand Old Lady' of the Atlantic) who docked at 102 Berth on 19 October 1932. Bert Moody: 'The first ship to go up into the new docks was the *Mauretania* in 1932, and she went up there to lay up for the winter, just to get her out of the way. She went into 102 Berth. While she was there she went into dry dock and was painted all white. She became a cruise ship in 1933 and 1934.'

Kenneth Fielder also remembers the old *Mauretania*: 'The old *Mauretania* had four funnels and was known as the "white lady" because her hull was white. Before she was taken away to be broken up she berthed in what became the New Dock, and I always remember seeing her funnels and the white hull before she went to be broken up.'

The first day of July 1935 was a very sad day for many in Southampton. It was the day that the *Mauretania* left on her way to the Metal Industries Ltd scrapyard at Rosyth. Bert Moody mentions being in what later became the Mayflower Park when the *Mauretania* sailed out. Her masts had been cut down to go under the Forth Bridge. 'The *Mauretania* was laid up at the end of 1934, and I was in the park the night she sailed for scrap. I saw men crying that night. It didn't mean much to me at the time, but it did to them. The whole of the park and the whole of the dock were full of people when she sailed that night. Of course she had the tops of her masts cut off because she was going to Rosyth.' She was followed three months later by the *Olympic*, sister ship of the *Titanic*, and a year later by the *Majestic*. The *Majestic* was built in Hamburg and originally launched as the *Bismark*, but she later passed to the White Star Line as part of the war reparations and was renamed. She was 915.5ft (279m) in length, 100.1 ft (30.5m) in beam and had a four screw, steam turbine steamer burning fuel oil.

The New Docks was fully completed by 1934, and one of the features of the Docks Extension Scheme was to provide an industrial estate close to the new berths. Approximately 131 acres were set aside for this and the Solent Flour Mill of Joseph Rank Ltd was the first to be built on the site in 1934. Kenneth Fielder: 'Industries soon built up on the New Dock. Industries such as Martini, Rank's Flour Mill and Standard Telephone and Cables were there and extended up to what is now the container berth.'

An original plan of the New Dock showing two graving docks and a site for a future jetty. The site of the isolation hospital can be seen to the left of the plan.

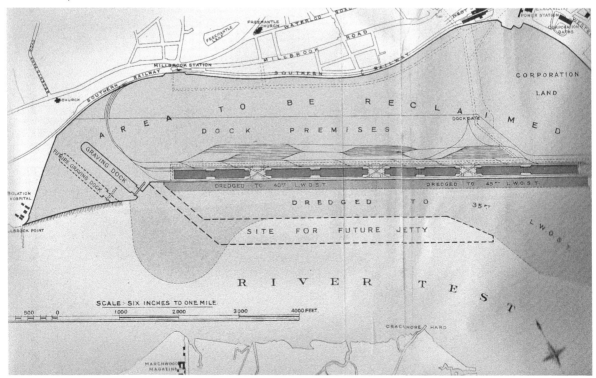

The *Mauretania*, the first ship to berth at the New Docks in October 1932. (Courtesy of ABP)

The *Mauretania* leaving Southampton New Docks for Rosyth to be used for scrap. (Courtesy of Bert Moody Collection)

King George V (No. 7) Graving Dock under construction, which was started in 1931. (Courtesy of ABP)

Gradually other factories were built before the war, including Montague L. Mayer Ltd, Timber Merchants and General Motors (built 1938–39) and later Cadbury and Fry Chocolate Manufacturers; however, after the war, due to the bombing of the docks, new buildings were erected including a new cold store as a replacement for the International Cold Storage and Ice Company bombed in 1940.

Kenneth Fielder also remembers that there was an isolation hospital in the locality: 'Something, unfortunately that has faded in the memory, is the fact that in that locality there was an isolation hospital built but was never used.' The isolation hospital in question was close to Millbrook Point, just at the edge of the reclaimed land for the New Docks and near to the King George V Dry Dock. It did not appear to be used because a large proportion of the beds would always be empty, except in times of epidemics. The 30 beds were reserved for smallpox cases and were deemed by the authorities 'to be necessary in the public interest,' but it was considered a rare occurrence for any of the beds to be occupied.

The King George V Dry Dock (No. 7 Dry Dock)

The need for a larger dry dock was included in the plans for the New Docks at the Millbrook Point end of the development. The construction of the dry dock had started in January 1931. It was named the King George V Graving Dock and opened on 26 July 1933. At the time it was the largest dry dock in the world. The area the dock was built on was tidal mudland, and this area had to be dredged and became reclaimed land. There was also a second dry dock on the initial plans, although this was never built.

The opening of King George V Graving Dock, with the royal yacht *Victoria and Albert*. (Courtesy of ABP)

The completed New Docks and the RMS *Queen Elizabeth* in the George V Graving Dock. (Edmund Nuttall Ltd)

Kenneth Fielder talks of the completion of the new docks, including the new dry dock, and his knowledge of its opening gained from the first-hand account of his brother who attended the event. Kenneth Fielder: 'The King George V Graving Dock was named after King George and Queen Mary who opened the dock when the original royal yacht *Victoria and Albert* initially sailed into it. I can remember that quite concisely because my elder brother, who was a schoolboy himself, was invited to be part of the audience on the staging put in for them to sit on.' The royal yacht *Victoria and Albert* sailed into the dock, breaking the red, white and blue ribbon at the entrance.

At the opening ceremony the king said, 'I have much pleasure in declaring the dock open for use and in naming it The King George V Dry Dock, and I pray that, by God's blessing, it may serve to foster and increase the commerce of Southampton.'

Southern Railway Steamer Services

In 1926 the Southern Railway Company Marine Services had sailings to the Channel Islands, Le Harve, St Malo, Caen, Cherbourg and Honfluer. A boat train was laid on for passengers to travel by train to and from London and Southampton. In the 1920s Maurice Allen's father spent a number of years on the Southern Railway ships which went to the Channel Islands and France. His father was also a first-aid man, and at that time there were quite a lot of injuries in the docks so it was necessary for every shed to have a first-aider. There was a bonus to that because the first-aider got extra pay.

The cross-channel services brought in cargo including vegetable and fruit produce from France and the Channel Islands for the UK markets. Some of this cargo was transhipped onto the Ocean Liners docked in the port. The dockers who worked for the Southern Railway Marine Department, apart from the 'perms' who had permanent jobs for the company, would attend the SR 'call-stand' on a daily basis in an attempt to get work. This was always very competitive, and some advantage was gained by those dockers who were known as the 'preference' men. These were dockers who had particular experience in handling certain cargoes.

An example is given of what it was like trying to get work on the SR Marine Department ships in the 1920s and 1930s: 'A weekly worker had a fair living, a permanent man had a good living and a shed-man had a poor living. That's how it went.

'On the Marine side you had different gangs for the various docking times; the "Jersey gang", "St Malo gang" and the "Havre gang". The gangs you had on the docks side were timber, grain and meat gangs. If a meat ship came in all the meat men got called up. You had a number and the meat man's number came in the first lot, but if you hadn't been to work and a meat boat came in, and it was your turn to go on, well the meat men would jump over you because they were the proper gang for the job.

'We used to go round to the call-stands all over the place in the docks. There was quite a number and you used to pick up the odd half-day when there was one going. If all the registered dockers were in then us outsiders were allowed to take a job afterwards. If we didn't get in anywhere we used to make our way back to what we called "the cattle shed", which was the Southern Railway call-stand. It was just a large shed with pens in where different sections of men used to stand, and the labour-master used to walk about and pick where he liked.

'You wouldn't believe it, men fighting to get a brass tally for four hours' work, literally grabbing for work. He used to come out with a great long brass box along his arm and he'd stand on the platform, and there'd be hundreds of the poor devils all wanting a job. He'd hand out tickets and they'd grab, grab, grab for half a day's work, knocking each other's hats off like a lot of animals.' (*Oral History Unit, Southampton.*)

By 1929 the two newest Southern Railway steamships, the *Dinard* and *St Briac*, both sister ships, represented the most modern design of the time for passenger services. They could carry 1,300 passengers and both were oil driven. Vessels in the Southern Railway fleet based in Southampton included the passenger vessels *Hantonia, Normannia, Lorina, Alberta, Vera, St Briac, Dinard, Princess Ena* and *Ardena*. These docked at Berth 7, 8 and 9 in the Outer Dock where a Marine passenger station had been built. The cargo vessels were the *Haslemere, Fratton, Ringwood, Ada, Bertha, Brittany* and *Cherbourg*.

Prior to World War Two approximately 300,000 passengers were carried by the Southern Railway's cross-channel steamers between Le Havre, St Malo and the Channel Islands.

Banana Trade

In 1931 the banana ships of Elders & Fyffes started running from the West Indies and discharged their cargo of bananas in the Empress Dock. Bert Moody talks about how the bananas came in on the stem, before they were boxed: 'Bananas started running in 1931, and they mainly came in on the stem then. When I got involved in railways they had the banana ships and the banana trains. Each railway box van had straw on the floor to lay the banana stalks on. You couldn't stack the bananas into the box van otherwise the lower ones would have been squashed in. None of the box vans were full, which tended to waste space. Carrying bananas in boxes didn't start until about 1960. Until then they were on the stems.'

It was well known that with the bananas various creatures, such as spiders and snakes, could be found lurking in among the stems. To protect themselves the stevedores would tie up their sleeve ends and the bottom of their trousers to stop any creature crawling up their arms and legs. Sometimes another stevedore would play a trick on an already nervous colleague by tickling them on the back of their neck with a straw, making them think that there was a spider on their collar! The bananas would be unloaded onto a continuous conveyor belt, which would transport the bananas to the train where they would be loaded into the railway box van.

In the June 1953 *Southampton Docks Shipping List & Shipping Guide*, published by the Docks and Inland Waterways Executive, under 'Topical Items' included details of the first cargo of bananas since the war arriving in Southampton on 1 February 1953. It also states that with two shipments a month during the year the port expected the total of 2,550,000 stems, equalling 33,900 tons, to be brought into the port. To transport the first cargo by the *Viator*, 480 railway vans were required to take the bananas to London, the South Coast, the Midlands and South Wales.

In 1959 the new banana accommodation on Berth 25 in the Empress Dock was completed, and British Railways provided a special distribution service from the docks around the UK. One of the banana trains seen in Southampton Docks was the GWR 6999 *Capel Dewi Hall*, Hall Class 4–6–0 and built in 1949. The locomotive was withdrawn from service in 1965 and finally scrapped.

Kenneth Fielder talks about the Southern Railways Dock (Outer Dock): 'We were very much conversant with the old docks as well. The area we now know as Ocean Village was where the old cross-channel steamers left for the Channel Islands, and I do know they went across to St Malo and Le Havre. It was also known as the Princess Alexandra Dock.'

Joan Rogers's father, William Richard Taylor, also sailed on the Southern Railway ships. William Taylor came from a maritime background. His father was Commodore Captain Richard William Taylor, sailing out of Liverpool, and his brother Frederick Taylor worked for the Union Castle Line. Joan Rogers: 'Dad was a happy, hard-working man, and he ran away to sea when he was supposed to be at

A banana boat, Fyffes *Changuinola*, unloading bananas for the first time with the new gantries. (Courtesy of ABP)

Bananas being loaded into a railway box van. (Courtesy of ABP)

college, and for that reason he was not very popular with his father. Dad did not come from a poor family, like mum, but after years in the merchant navy, travelling the world, he became second officer and was able to take other jobs that was offered him on board ships. He was a bosun, AB and quartermaster but never achieved the position of captain.'

After years of sailing the world, William Taylor eventually joined the Southern Railways steamer, *St Briac*. At the time he joined the *St Briac* the family was living in Jersey. Although they loved living in Jersey, they moved back to Southampton because that was where Mrs Taylor wanted to give birth to her new baby, Joan.

It was while sailing aboard the *St Briac* that William Taylor became involved in a rescue at sea. They were sailing in rough seas and an SOS was received from a sinking yacht. The captain asked for volunteers to go to the aid of those on board. Joan Rogers: 'My dad, with some of the other seaman, launched a lifeboat and set sail in very high seas and rescued the people from the yacht just before it sank.' William Taylor was awarded the Board of Trade medal and a purse of money for taking part in the rescue of sailors from the sinking yacht. His medal, seaman's book and references are now with the Southampton Maritime Museum.

The banana train GWR 6999 *Capel Dewi* leaving Southampton. (Courtesy of Richard de Jong Collection)

The Southern Railway steamship *St Briac*. (Courtesy of ABP)

The Royal Pier. The PS *Bournemouth Queen* can be seen berthed at the pier, with the naval fleet in the background. The damage to the railway line is thought to have been done in 1919–20 when a ship struck the pier. (Courtesy of Terry Cooper Collection)

The Royal Pier and Town Quay

Bert Moody remembers the Royal Pier from when he was boy in the 1930s: 'When I got older I would walk down Bugle Street to the Royal Pier to see the paddle ships. The *Balmoral* and *Lorna Doone* were the summer boats, but in the winter you could see them down at Northam on the mud. You had also the *Solent Queen*, *Her Majesty*, *Princess Helena* and, of course, *Princess Elizabeth*.' They were the ones that kept the service going through the winter. He would also enjoy walking along to the Town Quay to observe the ships: 'Of course, on the Town Quay you saw the coasters. Coast lines came in there, Clyde Shipping Company and also right on the top end you had the British and Irish Steam Packet Company *Lady Cloe*. There was always a policeman on the Town Quay, so you waited until he was otherwise engaged and then you would nip in. That's how you got on to the top of the Town Quay. Right at the top end there was always a stack of Guinness barrels, the empties going back to Dublin for refilling. The ships docking would bring in the new lot of filled Guinness barrels. You had the *Lord Elgin*, the paddler that used to go across to Cowes, taking general freight and cars.'

Ken Fielder also remembers the Royal Pier: 'The Royal Pier was significant in our lifetime because the Isle of Wight boats used to leave from there. They had lovely names. There was the *Lorna Doone*, *Balmoral* and *Princess Elizabeth*, as I remember.

They used to go to Ryde, Southsea and sometimes round the island going into Ventnor and Sandown. One used to go to Bournemouth, either the *Balmoral* or *Lorna Doone,* and from Bournemouth to Cherbourg in the same day. You had the Royal Pier Pavilion then when you had dances and concerts. It was a very popular venue. People used to fish off the pier.'

A Red Funnel Daily Steam Packet Service timetable from 1939. (Courtesy of Cyril Duro)

A postcard showing the PS *Princess Elizabeth*. (Courtesy of Terry Cooper Collection)

Red Funnel Day Excursions

It was in 1900 that the Isle of Wight Company began day-return excursions to Cherbourg via Bournemouth with the Paddle Steamer *Balmoral* from June to September. The PS *Balmoral* was 473 tons, 236ft (72m) in length and 27ft 1in (8.2m) wide. In 1935 the Isle of Wight Company changed to Red Funnel. The *Balmoral* was licensed to carry 1,033 passengers and was the only Red Funnel vessel to cross the channel twice weekly to Cherbourg, either from Southampton to Bournemouth and on to Cherbourg, or via Southsea to Sandown, Shanklin and then on to Cherbourg.

Working on the Paddlers

Cyril Duro comes from a family of mariners. His grandfather was a captain and great uncles were either captains or mates. 'When I left school in 1937 I started my sea career with the Isle of Wight Company, Red Funnel. My grandfather was the shore captain. His brother was Captain Harry Dennis, captain of the *Lorna Doone*. Another brother, Jack Dennis, was the mate on the *Gracie Fields*. Her captain was Captain Larkin. I joined the *Gracie Fields* and worked for 32 shillings and sixpence a week (£1.65) as a deck boy. I remember the captain telling me, "whatever you do, the men you're going to work with are going to be old enough to be your father, just respect them." I stopped on the *Gracie Fields* for a year or so and then joined the *Balmoral* as an ordinary seaman.

A postcard showing the PS *Lorna Doone*. (Courtesy of Terry Cooper Collection)

'The money went up, and that gave me two pounds nine shillings a week (£2.45). I thought that was a fortune at the time. The *Balmoral* was built in 1899 and could make 20 knots. She used to sail across to Cherbourg, and that was where I met my wife. We used to go from Southampton to Bournemouth and then on to Cherbourg. We also went from Southampton to Ryde to Shanklin, Sandown and across to Cherbourg that way.'

The *Balmoral*'s average time was four hours for the channel crossing, but Cyril Duro remembers the fastest time they completed the trip: 'She was quite a fast boat, and the fastest we did it was within three hours and eight minutes, which was quite quick for a paddle boat. We were allowed to have 392 passengers on board, which was the limit when we went to Cherbourg. If we were not going to Cherbourg and were going down to Brighton or Torquay then we could take 1,200 people.'

A postcard showing the PS *Gracie Fields*. (Courtesy of Terry Cooper Collection)

Working hours were long and left little time for leisure for the crew when off duty. Cyril Duro: 'Our hours of work on the paddle steamers were very long. We used to start very early in the morning and not get home till 11 at night.' The crew would be paid for working overtime, but that was only between 48hrs and 70hrs. Cyril Duro: 'We got paid for 48hrs work, so many shillings for 54 hours, 60 hrs and 70 hrs, but

A postcard showing the PS *Balmoral*. (Courtesy of Red Funnel)

The Ocean Dock in 1929. (Courtesy of ABP)

no more after 70hrs. We worked well over 100 hours a week. Not many in today's world would be happy working those hours.'

Due to the long hours of work Cyril Duro found great difficulty in getting home at the end of the day and would have to sleep on board. 'By that time I couldn't go home at night. I could when I was on the *Gracie Fields* because I got back in time to get the last tram from the Royal Pier to Shirley where I lived. On the *Balmoral* sometimes she was later, but even if she was early I couldn't get the last tram back. I couldn't get a tram early enough in the morning to get in by 5am when we started work. We were called at 5am and left at 7am for Bournemouth and then on to Cherbourg. If we left at 7.15 we were on the Ryde, Shanklin to Cherbourg route.'

Despite the long hours the crew still enjoyed going to work. Cyril Duro: 'We enjoyed it. If you had good weather we would be over Cherbourg by about 1 o'clock and left about 4pm. Our captain, Capt Goldsmith – "Old Goldy" we called him – got the Freedom of Cherbourg.' Apparently Captain Goldsmith would often celebrate the honour bestowed upon him when visiting Cherbourg!

Cyril Duro left the *Balmoral* to join the newly built *Vecta* in 1938, but by this time it was leading up to the start of World War Two.

Ocean Dock in the 1930s

Ken Fielder remembers the pre-war era and seeing the large liners in the Ocean Dock: 'Then you had the Ocean Dock, and they were originally berthed by the Cunard and White Star liners. The White Star liners were the *Majestic*, *Olympic* and *Homeric*, and the Cunarders were the *Aquitania*, *Mauretania*, *Berengaria*, and in 1936 the *Queen Mary*.' By 1938 the Ocean Dock was very busy with the large liners, such as the RMS *Queen Mary* and *Aquitania* who docked for their North Atlantic services. The dockside equipment to handle the cargoes of these liners included 16 electric cranes, whose lifting capacity ranged from 35 cwts to 5 tons with a lifting height of 100ft (30.4m), and four single-storey transit sheds.

A late 1930s postcard showing the Old Docks. (Courtesy of Bert Moody Collection)

CHAPTER 2

MILITARY EMBARKATION PORT AND WARTIME PRE-WORLD WAR TWO

Henry V set sail on 15 August 1415 from Southampton with approximately 300 ships carrying his army to France for the Battle of Agincourt. It was not till the middle of the 19th century, however, that Southampton really began to develop as an important military embarkation and trooping port. By the time of the Crimean War there was an urgent need to care for the returning casualties of war back in Britain. It was for that reason that the Royal Victoria Hospital, Netley, on Southampton Water, was built for troops who were sick or wounded in the war.

The Royal Victoria Military Hospital

During the 1854–56 Crimean War Southampton was used as the principal military embarkation port, and as many as 54,000 British soldiers were sent to the Crimea to fight against Russia. Of these, 18,000 soldiers died and a further 9,000 returned as invalids. Only 10 per cent of the number that died was from battle wounds, with the majority dying from diseases such as typhoid, typhus, cholera and dysentery.

Florence Nightingale came to prominence in the Crimean War. She had become concerned about the reports about the terrible conditions for wounded soldiers and left for the Crimea on the 21 October 1854, taking 38 members of staff, whom she had trained herself. They arrived at Selimiye Barracks in Scutari, Istanbul, Turkey, in November and found that a lack of hygiene was causing mass infections to the soldiers' battle wounds. Florence Nightingale and her staff set about bringing cleanliness and order to the hospital.

The British government came under immense pressure over the condition of the wounded soldiers and planned for a hospital to be built to care for the sick and wounded returning from the Crimea. It purchased land at Netley, which looked out on to Southampton Water. Queen Victoria, who took a personal interest in the welfare of her troops, was impressed by the work of Florence Nightingale and her volunteer nurses and laid the foundation stone for the hospital in May 1856.

The building was 468 yards (427.9m) long and was built to house 1,000 beds. At the time it was one of the longest buildings in the world and the largest British Military Hospital. The location of the hospital was ideal to receive wounded soldiers landed

A postcard showing the Peninsular and Oriental Steam Navigation Co. steamship *Ripon* leaving Southampton Docks for the Crimea carrying the Grenadier Guards in 1854. (Courtesy of Bert Moody Collection)

The *Clive*, built in 1882, saw service as a troopship on the Indian service. (Courtesy of Mrs Maureen Webber)

from hospital ships; however, the Royal Victoria Hospital, Netley, was finally completed in 1863, after the Crimean War. A cast-iron pier approximately 560ft (170.6m) in length was built in 1869 and sited opposite the central block of the hospital. Wounded soldiers were transferred from the ships onto 'tenders' (one of which was named *Florence Nightingale*) and landed on the pier where they were then taken to the hospital. The Royal Victoria Hospital was used to tender the wounded from other wars, including the Boer War, World War One and World War Two. Florence Nightingale died on 13 August 1910 and is buried in the graveyard at St. Margaret's Church in East Wellow, Hampshire.

Trooping and Principal Embarkation Port

In 1894 the British government chose Southampton as the principal base for Indian and Colonial transport services. This was for the seasonal trooping that took place between autumn and spring. One of the ships chartered for six months during 1894–95 for trooping by the British government was the P&O *Britannia*.

The British government also chose Southampton in 1899 as its principal embarkation port to take troops to Africa for the Boer War. One of the advantages was the connection by rail from the barracks in Aldershot right on to the berth alongside the troopship. The men were thus able to embark onto the ships directly from the train. Many ships were used as troopships at the time, one of which was the Union Castle Line *Dunottar Castle*.

The total number of troops passing through the port to and from South Africa amounted to 25,384 officers, 502,616 men and 27,922 horses. In addition to these numbers were the families who travelled and the large quantities of luggage and stores required.

World War One

In World War One, between the years of 1914 and 1918, the docks were placed under government control and it became the number one military embarkation port. The British Expeditionary Force embarked from the port in 1914, and outside Dock Gate 4 there is a plaque to the memory of the Old Contemptibles who sailed from the docks for France. From 1914, apart from the reduced cross-channel services run by the London and South Western Railway from the Outer Dock, most of the normal seagoing services had ceased. Over 7,000,000 troops embarked and disembarked from the port during this time, and approximately 3,800,000 tons of stores were moved. At times between 20 and 30 ships would leave the port in one night.

During World War One a number of the Red Funnel fleet were requisitioned for service. These included the *Duchess of York*, *Lorna Doone*, *Solent Queen* and *Balmoral*. The *Bournemouth Queen* was renamed HMS *Bourne* and was used as a patrol vessel and for minesweeping.

There was a story printed in the *Daily Echo* in November 1988, where it appeared that Cary Grant had spent the summer of 1914 working in the docks. The story originated from the writing of his biographers, Chuck Ashman and Pamela Trescott. His name was then Archie Leach, he lived in Bristol and volunteered as a 13-year-old to work as a messenger during the summer months. It is thought by his biographers that witnessing 'the cream of British youth leaving for France to die in the trenches had a profound effect on him.' After returning to his secondary school in Bristol his experiences in the docks must have made him think carefully about his future. He became involved in the theatre after a visit to the Bristol Hippodrome and then later moved on to greater things as a film star and assumed the stage name of Cary Grant. It is quite possible that when he travelled on the transatlantic liners and landed at Southampton he would remember his experiences in the docks as a messenger.

After World War One the German ships that had survived were taken by the allies as war reparations and renamed. The *Imperator* became the Cunard *Berengaria*, the *Vaterland* was renamed *Leviathan* and sailed as the flagship of the United States Lines and the *Bismark* was renamed as the *Majestic* and sailed for the White Star Line. All were seen regularly sailing in and out of Southampton.

A number of the liners were sunk while in service for the British government during World War One and Two. The

The PS *Bournemouth Queen* with a picture of Captain Prewett. (Courtesy of Terry Cooper Collection)

The hospital ship *Asturias* in 1917. (Courtesy of Mick Lindsay Collection)

Lusitania was approaching the coast of Ireland when she was sunk by torpedoes from the German submarine *U20* on 7 May 1915. She sank in 18 minutes, and of the 1,257 passengers and 650 crewmen that sailed from New York on 1 May 1915 1,198 were lost, including 128 American citizens. The sinking of the passenger liner brought about world condemnation and it is thought that it was one of the factors that eventually brought the US into World War One. Another liner lost was the White Star's *Britannic*, third of the Olympic Class trio, which was sunk by a mine in the Aegean Sea while supporting the Dardanelles offensive.

Kenneth Fielder has a family maritime history, and his father also served in the Dardenelles: 'My dad served 24 years in the Royal Navy and in the First World War saw service in the Atlantic. He was in the Dardenelles, and then he was seconded to the Japanese Navy in the Far East, and he had a scroll commending him for his service to the Japanese Navy. He would receive messages on the warship, and someone would then translate the order into Japanese. His last time away was two years, and we went down to meet him when he came back. He had been made up to a PO and was measured up for his uniform in Portsmouth, and then he served with the Fort Blockhouse signal station during the later years of his 24 years in the navy. At the outbreak of the Second World War he volunteered to go back into the Royal Navy. Sadly he had developed kidney trouble and was sent up to the east coast, in the Norfolk area, but the cold wind was too severe for him and he was discharged, he had a relapse and died in 1944.'

Other family members were mariners and served in World War One. Kenneth Fielder: 'I had an uncle that was bedroom steward on the *Majestic* and an uncle who was killed when the battleship HMS *Queen Mary* blew up in the Battle of Jutland. There was another uncle on my mother's side that was in the Royal Navy as a stoker and ultimately then when he came out of the navy was employed in Southampton Docks as one of the fitters/attendants of the graving dock.' Perhaps the family maritime history is why Kenneth Fielder says: 'I can never live away from the sea. I always saw the sea as a challenge, and I always remember Alec Rose who sailed around the world. He wrote a book, and in there I remember one paragraph, "Man will never conquer the sea, he can only come to terms with it and survive it."'

White Star Line's *Majestic* in the floating dry dock. (Courtesy of Mick Lindsay Collection)

CHAPTER 3
DEVELOPMENT OF CANALS AND RAILWAYS

The development of canals and railways became important to the development of the transport links with Southampton, especially with the expansion of the Port of Southampton for the carriage of freight and passengers.

It was during the mid-18th century that the Industrial Revolution began in Great Britain. With it came a move away from an agricultural economy to an industrial economy and a consequent change in the lives and work of many people. Manual work on the land became scarcer with the introduction of machinery, and people began to move to the towns where they could get work in factories. Coal mines required a reliable means of transport to move bulk quantities of coal to the factories to fuel the steam engines, and factories also needed transport to convey their finished goods.

The road system at the time was poorly maintained, and the transportation of goods tended to be very slow due to the muddy conditions on many of the tracks and roads. Although new roads were beginning to be built, it was the canal system, most of which had been completed by 1815, that was used to transport heavy loads such as coal and other bulk materials. The labour needed to complete the building of the canals and railways came from the rural labourer, and many of these men did not return to the country but remained in the larger towns and cities, working in factories instead.

With the development of steam locomotion the canals began to face competition from the railways by the mid-19th century. In the beginning both canals and the railways worked in conjunction, with the railways mainly carrying passengers and lighter goods, and the canals concentrating on the bulk goods; however, gradually more and more of the bulk goods, especially coal, began to be carried by the railways, mainly because of the quantities that could be carried at one time and also the speed of delivery.

The Andover to Redbridge Canal

The Andover Canal, built in 1794 from Andover to Redbridge, was 22 miles long, and along its course were 24 locks. The canal was mainly used to transport slate, coal and agricultural products, but after 63 years of use it was not very profitable, and the name of the company was changed in 1857 to the Andover Canal & Railway Company. The canal was closed, and from 1859 it was filled in and a railway line built along its route, enabling goods to be transported in a faster time than could be completed by canal boats. The Andover and Redbridge Railway was taken over by the L&SWR in 1863, and the line opened in March 1865. The line is well known as the Sprat & Winkle Railway Line, possibly because it carried seafood from Southampton to Andover. The route of the Sprat and Winkle line from Redbridge was via Romsey to Andover.

This line was very useful in World War One and Two to transport troops and equipment from the Salisbury Plain army camps to Southampton for embarkation on ships to fight in France; however, with Lord Beeching's closure of many local railway lines in the mid-1960s the services only continued between Andover Junction and Andover Town until it was finally closed in 1967.

The Southampton to Salisbury Canal

The Southampton to Salisbury Canal was authorised by an Act of Parliament in 1795 and was to be built from the Itchen River at Northam, but this section was never built. The line ran along the shoreline at Millbrook to link with the Andover Canal. It was opened in 1802–03, but it too was never fully completed and was discarded from 1808. The canal was filled in, and parts of it later became the route of the railway line from Southampton to Dorchester, which opened in 1847. The railway line passed through Blechynden station, Millbrook station and Redbridge station, where the line branched left over the River Test to Totton and continued via Ringwood to Dorchester.

Blechynden Station

The Blechynden station was opened in 1847, and a link with Southampton Terminus followed shortly after. In 1858 the name was changed to Southampton West station. The railway line ran along the water's edge at the western shore, and the station was sometimes flooded by high tides before the New Docks were built. By 1935 the number of platforms had been increased from two to four and the station renamed Southampton Central. After the Southampton Terminus Station was closed in 1966, the Southampton Central went through a period of rebuilding in 1967, losing its clock tower in the process. Although the station was renamed Southampton, it eventually became Southampton Central again. Redbridge Station opened in 1847 and became more prominent when the L&SWR purchased the Redbridge Wharf and built a railway depot there from 1879.

The Railway Link Between London and Southampton

The need for a railway link between London and Southampton was considered important, and in 1831 the London & Southampton Railway Company was formed, with Francis Giles appointed as engineer. Francis Giles was also the engineer for

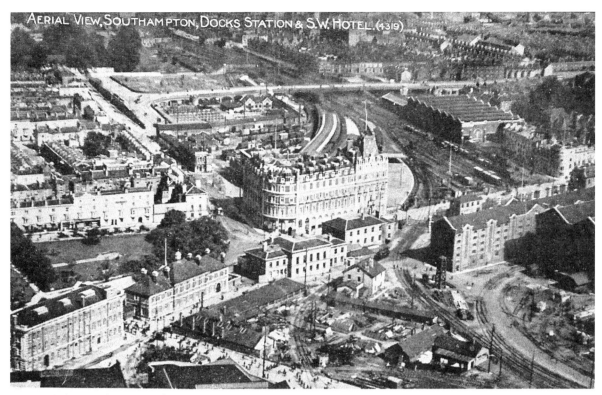

A postcard of the Southampton Docks Station.

the building of the Southampton Docks. It was not until 1834, however, that Parliament gave permission for the line to be built and Joseph Locke replaced Francis Giles as the chief engineer. The line was completed in 1840. Southampton Terminus was the original terminus of the London and Southampton Railway and also opened in 1840 to serve the docks and the city centre. This was an important development because it would speed up the transportation of goods and passengers to and from the port, and consequently it led to famous passenger shipping lines becoming attracted to using the Port of Southampton.

Development of the Docks Railway: Southampton Terminus Station

Southampton Terminus Station was designed by Sir William Tite and built for the London & South Western Railway. The station opened as Southampton Station, with the rail link between London and Southampton completed in 1840. At that time the London end of the railway link terminated at Nine Elms, but when the final link of the London terminus was completed to Waterloo the station was called Waterloo Bridge Station. This was later shortened to Waterloo Station.

The Southampton end of the railway line had its name changed a number of times before finally being called Southampton Terminus. From 1840 it was known as Southampton Station, then it was renamed Southampton Docks Station in 1858, Southampton Town and Docks in 1896, Southampton Town for Docks in 1912 and finally, when Southern Railway took over the management of the docks in 1923, it became Southampton Terminus. The lines were extended to the Ocean Terminal in the docks for the boat trains, allowing passengers to alight on platforms within the terminal.

Southampton Terminus Station was closed on 5 September 1966 by British Railways and remained empty for some time; however, because the main building was listed it was protected from demolition. It remains today and now houses a casino.

Southampton Terminus Station. (Courtesy of Richard de Jong Collection)

Southampton Terminus Station today.

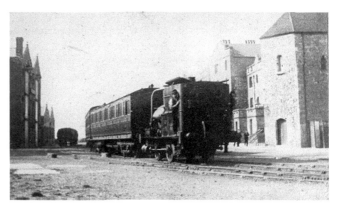

A Royal Pier train. A steam train service ran from Southampton Docks station and the Royal Pier between 1876 and 1914. (Courtesy of Mrs Maureen Webber)

Rail links to the Town Quay and Royal Pier

The London & South Western Railway Company had already laid a rail line to the Town Quay in 1847 for horse-drawn wagons, but they continued expansion into the docks, and by 1871 railway lines had been laid to the Royal Pier. It was not until 1876 that the first steam engine was introduced.

The Adams B4 0-4-0 Dock Shunters

When the L&SWR took over the management of the Southampton Docks in 1892 they gradually introduced the Adams B4 0-4-0T shunters into the docks. All these locomotives were painted in a dark green livery.

When Southern Railway took over the docks in 1923 the dock locomotives' livery was changed over time to black with yellow lettering. By the late 1930s the B4s, which had

A postcard of the Town Quay. (F. Stuart)

The L&SWR B4 0-4-0T shunter *Honfluer* in 1910. (Pamlin Prints postcard)

been built in the 1890s, were becoming worn out, and maintaining them was becoming more difficult. This problem was solved during World War Two by the arrival of the US Army Transportation Corps to Great Britain and the S100 Class steam locomotives they brought with them.

An example of a B4 dock shunter can be seen today at the Bluebell Railway in Sussex. This is the L&SWR B4 Class No. 96 *Normandy*, which was owned by the B4 loco group, part of the Bulleid Society who also worked in conjunction with the Bluebell Railway.

The US Army Transportation Corps

In World War Two the Port of Southampton was chosen as the 14th port of the US Transportation Corps, and in July 1943 US Army Transportation Corps started to prepare for the shipping and supply of equipment for the D-Day landings. It was in 1943 that the first US 0-6-0T steam locomotives, designed by Colonel Howard G. Hill and specifically built for use in Europe, began to arrive in Great Britain. The livery of the USATC 0-6-0T during the war was black with white numbering. At the end of the war Southern Railway purchased 15 of the standard gauge 0-6-0 tank locomotives from the US Army Transportation Corps for service within Southampton Docks in 1946. One of the 15 locomotives purchased was to be used for spare parts. These tank engines were ideal for use in the docks because of the tight curves in the rail track, and they would also be a suitable replacement for the B4s. They were to be used in a shunting role, moving rail wagons and passenger carriages around the docks.

British Transport Commission

Under the post-war Labour government's nationalisation programme, the British Transport Commission came into existence on 1 January 1948. Part of the Transport Act 1947 provided for five executives, one of which was the Docks & Inland Waterways, which took over the running of the docks, and the Railway Executive, which was British Railways. From then on they were all regional; Western, London Midland, Eastern, North Eastern, Southern and Scottish.

British Rail Numbering System for the 0-6-0 Tank Locomotives

Up until the nationalisation of the railways in 1948 the livery of the USA Class Tank engines was black with yellow lettering, which spelt SR, for Southern Railways, on the sides of the locomotives. The tank engines were given the British Rail numbers 30061 to 30074 and were in service in the Southampton Docks from 1946 until the diesel shunters took over in 1963.

Nine of the engines continued in BR departmental service from 1963, and some continued until the end of steam in 1967. Two USA Class Tank engines USATC numbered WD 1968, SR 65, BR 30065 *Maunsell* and WD 1960, SR 70, BR 30070 *Wainwright* were still in service in the Ashford Wagon Works until 1967. They were renumbered as departmental stock, DS237 (30065) and DS238 (30070), and painted in the Southern Railway green livery. Both these engines have been preserved by the Kent and East Sussex Railway.

Other USA Class Tank engines can be traced to railway preservation groups. For example, the USATC tank engine carrying the War Department number WD 1959, SR 64 and BR 30064 was transferred to the Eastleigh Railway Works as a shunter. In 1967 it was sold to the Southern Loco Preservation Co. Ltd and is now on display at the Bluebell Railway in Sussex. It has been painted in its War Department livery with the WD number 1959. The USA Class Tank engine BR number 30067 was also still working at Eastleigh Railway Works in the late 1950s.

A number of the other USA Class engines from Southern Railway remained for a time working as shunters but were eventually scrapped during the 1960s. BR Department Stock DS234 (30062) was a shunter at Meldon Quarry, now part of the Dartmoor Railway, running on the old Southern Railway line from Crediton to Okehampton and Meldon Quarry. DS235 (30066) and DS236 (30074) both acted as shunters at the Lancing Carriage Works, and DS 233 (30061) worked as a shunter at the Redbridge Sleeper Works, alongside the Redbridge Wharf, from 1962 to 1967 when the locomotive was scrapped.

0-6-0 USA tank engine BR 30064. (Courtesy of Richard de Jong Collection)

0-6-0 USA tank engine BR 30064. (Courtesy of Richard de Jong Collection)

Another Southampton Docks shunter, the SR Class USA Tank engine WD 1973 (30072), is being preserved by the Keighley and Worth Valley Railway in West Yorkshire.

London and South Western Railway first opened the Redbridge site as a depot in 1879, and it was used by Southern Rail and British Railways until its closure in 1989. The site has been used by ABP for the storage of cars, and they have donated some of this land for the Redbridge Wharf public park. The access to the six-acre park is across the footbridge at Redbridge Railway Station.

The Eastleigh Railway Works

The London & South Western Railway decided in the mid-1880s to build a wagon and carriage works at Eastleigh, Hampshire. They began building in 1889, and by 1891 the company had relocated its carriage and wagon works from Nine Elms in London to the new works in Eastleigh. In 1909 the locomotive building was also transferred from Nine Elms to the Eastleigh works. Southern Railway took over the works in 1923, and over time a large number of locomotives were built there, making it one of the main Southern Railway locomotive building works. When steam trains were phased out in the 1960s the work began to reduce until 2006 when the works finally closed.

Boat Trains

Boat trains would meet the liners and transport passengers to and from Waterloo Station to Southampton Docks. On the day the *Titanic* sailed there were two boat trains. The first train arrived at the docks at 9.30am with the second and third class passengers, and the first class passengers arrived later at 11.30am.

When Southern Railway introduced the Bulleid *Merchant Navy* 4-6-2 class many were named after famous shipping lines, hence the name Merchant Navy Class. Up to 11 of these engines have survived and have been preserved, including BR 35005 *Canadian Pacific* and 35009 *Shaw Savill*, both by the Mid-Hants Railway (Watercress Line). It was Southern Railway that was the last main line to operate the steam express services between Waterloo and Weymouth, and it was the Bulleid Merchant Navy Class 35030 *Elder Dempster Lines* that left Weymouth for Waterloo on 9 July 1967 and signalled the end of steam.

As well as the engines named after shipping lines, Southern Railway also ran their Ocean Liner Specials to carry the passengers from the liners that docked at Southampton Docks to London's Waterloo Station. In the early 1950s there was the *Cunarder*, which was a Pullman Boat Train that met both the RMS *Queen Mary* and RMS *Queen Elizabeth* on the transatlantic service to and from Southampton and New York. This train was in operation until both liners ceased service in the late 1960s. The SR Bulleid Pacific No. 34007 *Wadebridge* was also known to have hauled the Ocean Liner Specials, but it was taken out of service in 1965 and rescued by the Plym Valley Railway from a scrapyard in 1981 for preservation. The locomotive was sold to a group of railway enthusiasts who formed the company Wadebridge (34007) Locomotive Ltd, with the aim to restore the 34007. This was finally achieved in October 2006 when the *Wadebridge* (34007) was again hauling passenger coaches.

There is still the opportunity to travel on special boat trains through the occasional VSOE (Venice Simplon Orient Express) that has been restored to 1920–1950s-style coaches. A special boat train composed of the VSOE British Pullman cars was run for the maiden transatlantic voyage of the RMS *Queen Mary 2* to New York in 2004. The train also met the *Queen Mary 2* and *Queen Elizabeth 2* when they returned from New York to Southampton in tandem the same year.

'Boats and Boat Trains'

Bert Moody had joined the railway in 1938 prior to his war service in the Royal Air Force, and when he returned after the war he was working in the Terminus parcels department and would often refer to a ship as a boat. He recalls getting told off once by a Union Castle man for doing just that. Bert Moody: 'I said to the Union Castle man, "When is the next boat to South Africa?" The Union Castle man told me, "We have no boats sailing to South Africa, and the only boats we have are the little ones that are on the ships!" So I quickly replied, "Why then do the passengers that get off the Union Castle ships travel on boat trains?" He told me that was railway terminology!'

CHAPTER 4

FLYING BOATS

Imperial Airways Service to the Channel Islands

In 1923 the British Marine Air Navigation Company was formed by a joint venture with Supermarine and Southern Railway, the owners of Southampton Docks. The new company began running the first British flying boat passenger service in operation from Southampton to Cherbourg, Le Harve and the Channel Islands. The aircraft used was the Supermarine Sea Eagle, designed by Reginald Mitchell who was later to design the famous Spitfire. The aircraft carried six passengers and two crew members. It was a short venture because on 31 March 1924 Imperial Airways was formed as the choice of the government for the future of the British air services. The British Marine Air Navigation Co Ltd was then taken over by Imperial Airways, who began operating a passenger and cargo flying boat service from the Marine Airport, based on the River Itchen at Woolston, to St Peter Port in Guernsey. During the summer months this was a twice-weekly service, taking 1hr 40min. During the winter months it was a once-weekly service. There were arrangements in place for special flights to either the Channel Islands or to France if requested. In 1929 it cost £3 single fare and £5 10s 0d, (£5.50) return, compared with today's single fare of approximately £77 and taking 45 minutes flying time from Southampton Airport.

The Introduction of the 'C' Class Flying Boat into Southampton

It was in 1936 that the first 'C' class flying boats appeared in Southampton. An order had been placed by Imperial Airways with Short Brothers Ltd, Rochester, Kent, for 28 large flying boats in 1934, and on 2 July 1936 G-ADHL *Canopus*, the first of Imperial Airways' fleet of Short S23 'C' class Empire flying boats, was launched on the Medway at Rochester. G-ADHL *Canopus* was delivered for service at the end of October 1936, and at the time it was the largest British-built passenger-carrying monoplane.

On 5 March 1937 Imperial Airways opened its Hythe flying boat base on Southampton Water for the servicing and maintenance of aircraft on its Empire services. Imperial Airways inaugurated the Empire flying boat services from Southampton Docks in 1937. The first flying boat service to South Africa was undertaken by G-ADHL *Canopus*, leaving Southampton on 2 June 1937. The route included stops at Marseilles, Rome, Athens, Alexandria, Cairo, Khartoum, Mombasa, Mozambique and on to Durban.

Refuelling trials with Imperial Airways G-ADUV *Cambria* flying boat and an Armstrong Whitworth AW23 acting as the tanker began in January 1938. This was under the direction of Sir Alan Cobham, who had become interested in airborne

The Supermarine Sea Eagle. (Courtesy of Solent Sky)

G-ADHL *Canopus*. (Courtesy of Geoff Reichelt)

refuelling in 1931, when he was considering flying non-stop from England to Australia using a means of in-air refuelling. The aim this time was to find ways of using flying boats for a transatlantic air crossing; however, at the same time tests were being conducted with what was known as the Short Mayo Composite, which was long-range seaplane carried piggy back on top of a flying boat for flying longer distances, such as transatlantic flight to the US.

Kenneth Fielder: 'The flying boat was the original introducer of air mail across the Atlantic. It was undertaken by what became known as the 'Piggy Back'. The ship named *Maia* was the mother ship and carried the *Mercury*. The *Maia* was a flying boat, in other words she had a hull in the water and wings with floats. The *Mercury* was a float plane, she was upon two floats and you got aboard the hull up a fixed ladder. To get to the cockpit, once you had got inside, you had to go on your hands and knees and crawl through. They would take the mail first of all and load the *Mercury* with mail and a lot of fuel and then hoist her by crane on to the back of the *Maia*. The *Maia* would be responsible for take-off and flying over the coast of Ireland and would then release the *Mercury*, who would complete the journey to the US. In actual fact the *Mercury* was bombed in a Norwegian Fjord, and the *Maia* was bombed in Poole harbour. The Norwegian campaign preceded the invasion of France, and the *Maia* was bombed after the second move by the flying boats to Poole.'

It was in July 1938 that the first crossing of the North Atlantic took place using the Imperial Airways Short S21 flying boat G-ADHK *Maia* and the Short S20 floatplane G-ADHJ *Mercury*. The *Mercury*, carrying mail and newspapers and piloted by Captain D. Bennett, separated from the *Maia* near Foynes, Ireland, before flying non-stop to Montreal, Canada, and from Montreal to Port Washington in New York. On the return flight the *Mercury* flew to Botwood, then on to the Azores and Lisbon. Also in 1938 the flying boat services transferred to Berth 108, where a new wooden Imperial Airways terminal had been built. The routes were soon extended to Cairo, Mombassa, Bahrain, Calcutta, Singapore and Sydney.

The age of the flying boats had now come to Southampton, with flying boat factories built at Hythe and Woolston. Ken Fielder had worked with flying boats and remembers clearly the development in Southampton: 'Flying boats were originally introduced in Southampton by Imperial Airways, and they were serviced at Hythe. It had a slipway where they would berth.' (This was on the site of the American naval base that was closed in 2006). Kenneth Fielder: 'Originally that was the Imperial

Airways flying boat base where they had big hangers and a slipway. The flying boats would be towed to a slipway, and wheeled legs were put on the main frame and one on the tail, and the boat would be hauled clear and left up on the tarmac. They would be serviced and run up prior to be taken out to the trotter mooring buoy. We used to call them a trot. Originally, pre-war when they were first introduced, there was a raft attached to Berth 108 in the New Dock where they would be hauled in for the mail, the freight, baggage and passengers, prior to their departure. They never flew overnight, only in daylight, and would fly to places like Marseilles, Naples, Alexandria, Mombasa, Victoria Falls or down to somewhere like Cape Town. Some would fly to Rangoon and on to Hong Kong. At Hong Kong they would join up with Quantas Airways, who also operated flying boats.'

Bert Moody worked for the railway and remembers the special trains from Victoria to Southampton for the Imperial Airways flying boats. 'I remember the Imperial Airways, and they had a special train which brought passengers down from Victoria. You usually had about two coaches, no more. I think two coaches and a van for the luggage. It took about six days to get to Australia, because they stopped every night for refuelling.'

The launches were very important because they were responsible for servicing the flying boats when they were anchored off on the buoys and also acted as standby for take-off and departure, which was administered by the Air Ministry launches. Kenneth Fielder: 'The Imperial Airways, as they then were, had launches and launch seaman who sometimes had to tow the flying boats, service them or stand by them, take the crew on board and a test crew if they were a test flight or engineer or fitters if there was work to be done.'

In 1939 Imperial Airways merged to form British Overseas Airways Corporation (BOAC), and in the same year trials were undertaken for the first commercial transatlantic flights with flying boats that had been modified for in-flight refuelling. These flying boats were the 'C' Class G-AFCU *Cabot* and G-AFCV *Caribou* flying the route from Southampton to New York, calling at Botwood, Newfoundland and Montreal, Canada.

When Imperial Airways was officially taken over by BOAC they moved from Berth 108 in the New Docks and took a raft down to anchor off Hythe, where the servicing took place. From then on that was where the departures and arrivals were taken.

Kenneth Fielder was a launch seaman for a time after being injured while serving as a crew member on the *Empress of Britain*. When Ken arrived home after his arm injury on the *Empress of Britain* he stayed ashore to recuperate. His father knew the person in charge of the marine section of BOAC and got him a job working as a launch seaman on the flying boats.

Ken describes what happens next: 'The man in charge of the marine section of BOAC was Mr Perry, and my dad and Mr Perry served on the same ship when they were both in the Royal Navy as signalmen. As the launch crews needed to

A Short Mayo Composite – This consisted of a the S.21 *Maia*, a modified S.23 'C'-class Empire flying boat, and the S.20 *Mercury* seaplane mounted on its back (piggy back). (Courtesy of Poole Flying Boats Celebration: Percy Douglas Collection)

Imperial Airways Empire flying boat G-ADVD *Challenger* at Berth 108 embarking passengers. (Courtesy of Solent Sky)

Imperial House Berth 108 – notice the number of bicycles used to get to work! (Courtesy of Solent Sky)

Imperial Airways landing stage at Berth 108 in the 1930s. Empire flying boat G-AEUB *Camilla* can be seen moored. It was later registered to Qantas Empire Airways as VH-ADU, but it crashed and was destroyed off Port Moresby in 1943. (Courtesy of Bert Moody Collection)

Imperial Airways G-AFCW *Connemara* after the fire, starboard side. (Courtesy of Solent Sky)

communicate with each other, my dad was to train the launch crews in the use of Morse code. So he took me to see Mr Perry, and he said he would employ me as a launch seaman.'

Ken Fielder talks about some of the incidents that happened in Hythe and further afield: 'The original flying boats were known as the 'C' Class and were all named with a 'C', and one, the *Connemara*, caught fire when she was anchored off of Hythe. The man who was refuelling her jumped off her with the hose still in his hand and she perished.'

The fire happened on the evening of 19 June 1939 while the *Connemara* was being refuelled from a barge. The fire had started in the engine room of the barge, but it quickly spread to the flying boat. There were three men on the flying boat and four on the barge. They all dived overboard, but although six were rescued one man was missing and was thought to have drowned.

Kenneth Fielder: 'Another [flying boat] had to make a forced landing in the Belgian Congo, in a swamp. The name of Kelly Rogers is always synonymous with aviation because I think he was one of the first men to fly the Atlantic. His nephew was also known as Kelly Rogers, and it was Captain J.C. Kelly Rogers and another captain went out to the Belgian Congo and stripped everything out of the aircraft, and they were able to put what we call the tail release. They put a very strong rope or wire on to two trees, through the tail to hold her so that what they could actually do was to give maximum power on the four engines and then release the tail so she could take-off. She just about got off! We saw her when she came back, and you never saw such a mess inside. They got her back though!'

This was the G-ADVB *Corsair*, piloted by Captain Alcock, which was flying to Durban on 14 March 1939 when it made a forced landing on the River Dangu in the Belgian Congo. Although an attempt was made in July 1939 by Captain Alcock to fly the *Corsair* off the River Dangu, it was Captain J.C. Kelly Rogers, with First Officer Garner and Radio Officer Dangerfield, on 6 January 1940 that eventually flew the *Corsair* from the Dangu back to Southampton.

Imperial Airways G-AFCW *Connemara* after the fire, port side. (Courtesy of Poole Flying Boats Celebration: Percy Douglas Collection)

The G-ADVB *Corsair*. (Courtesy of Solent Sky)

Captain J.C. Kelly Rogers

On 5 August 1939 Captain J.C. Kelly Rogers was the pilot of the G-AFCV *Caribou* for the first flight of British airmail service across the Atlantic to North America. One year later, and almost to the day, Captain Kelly Rogers, commander, with Capt E. Rotherham (2nd Capt), Capt E. White (navigator), Mr J. Burgess and Mr C. Wilkinson (radio officers) were the crew on the flying boat G-AFCZ *Clare* for the first direct transatlantic crossing from Southampton to New York. The G-AFCZ *Clare* (previously named *Australia*) left Southampton on 3 August 1940, landing at Foynes, Ireland, then on to Botwood, Newfoundland, Montreal and finally landing in New York.

It was also Captain Kelly Rogers who was the pilot of the BOAC Boeing flying boat G-AGVA *Berwick* when the Prime Minister Mr Winston Churchill made the first transatlantic flight by a British prime minister in January 1942. The flight was from Bermuda to Plymouth.

BOAC transferred from Southampton to Poole

BOAC were concerned about the war in Europe and began what was called the 'Horseshoe Route' from Durban to Sydney, calling at Cairo and Athens. A link from England was later created to Durban with 'C' Class flying boat services leaving from Poole.

After the sinking of the *Empress of Britain*, Ken Fielder was discharged and went back to work as a loader on the flying boats for BOAC, but this time at Poole. He had worked on the flying boats before in Southampton. The flying boat services had been interrupted because of the war and were transferred to Poole harbour. 'During the war years, on two occasions they went to Poole because of the danger of being bombed in Southampton, and on the build up to D-Day they went to South Wales, in the Swansea area.'

When the BOAC Flying Boat operation first transferred to Poole the control centre was from a vessel, but the Poole Harbour Yacht Club at Salterns Pier had been requisitioned in 1939 for the war effort, and so it became the base for the flying boat operations in 1940. Passengers would arrive and be transferred to the flying boats by motor launches. Passengers arriving by flying boat would be transferred to a train at Bournemouth West Station and travelled from there to Victoria Station.

There was a Royal Navy Air Station at Sandbanks (HMS *Daedalus II*) where the Fleet Air Arm seaplane training took place. In 1942 the Sunderland flying boats were based at RAF Hamworthy and were part of No. 19 Coastal Command, patrolling from Poole.

A 1943 plan of the Poole flying boat operations. (Courtesy of Poole Flying Boats Celebration)

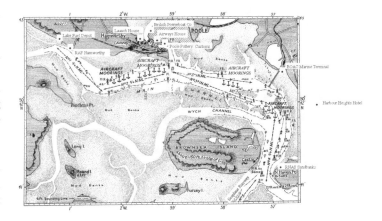

Poole Flying Boats Celebration (PFBC) has been established as a charity (112327) to celebrate the era of the flying boats, both civilian and military, and they are collecting and collating photographs and material to develop an archive that can be accessed by the public. It was in 1948 that the BOAC flying boat service returned to Southampton, and it is fitting that the links between the history of the flying boats in Southampton and Poole are documented. Solent Sky and PFBC are forefront in this venture.

Flying Boat Services after the War

BOAC resumed flying boat services in Southampton from their new terminal, opened on 14 April 1948 on Berth 50. Kenneth Fielder had worked for BOAC after an accident on board the *Empress of Britain* and talks about his memories of that time: 'BOAC came back to Southampton and latterly to Berth 50, which is where the pontoons stretched out and you had the north and south pontoons, as they were called, which went up and down with the tide.'

The 'C' Class boats were superseded by what became known as the 'Hythe Class', which were converted Sunderlands. The Sunderlands were responsible for Coastal Command in the war, and some were based at Calshot. They were modified to take passengers and preceded the 'Solent Class'. The Solent Class of flying boats was more like the 'C' Class but larger in order to carry more passengers, but they had one disadvantage when they were first introduced. Kenneth Fielder describes what must have been a very frightening moment for both crew and passengers when one Solent Class flying boat took off from Southampton: 'When they took off the displacement of water hit the float and damaged it to the extent that one of the passengers, pointing to the float hanging off, asked the steward "Should it be like that?" When the flying boat landed, members of the crew had to get out onto the opposite wing to counterbalance the weight to avoid the damaged wing going down into the water. They were then able to get her up to Berth 50 to unload the passengers. The problem of the floats being damaged by displacement of water was overcome by moving them further out on the wings.'

Ken Fielder remembers some of the passengers who used the flying boats: 'I remember now that the passengers used to fly early in the morning, and those I saw included Seretse Kahn and also King Abdullah of TransJordon and many film stars. One was Robert Newton (originally Long John Silver in *Treasure Island*). When they planned to make a remake of *King Solomon's Mines* the stars of the film were Stewart Granger, Deborah Kerr and the American Richard Carlson. All had to join the flying boat to fly to the location in Africa. Stewart Granger stayed in the Polygon Hotel, Richard Carlson went to the Grand Hotel, I think in Lyndhurst. At the Grand Hotel, Lyndhurst, Deborah Kerr arrived in her own saloon car with her husband, Tony Bartley.

RAF S.25 Sunderland. (Courtesy of Geoff Reichelt)

BOAC Terminal at Berth 50. (Courtesy of ABP)

Deborah Kerr and Tony Bartley arrived later than the other passengers for the flight, but by that time there was no further food available in the hotel. One of the return loaders from BOAC would have been waiting at the Grand Hotel for the coach to arrive from Victoria in London, to off-load the luggage for the passengers. He was aware that in Ashurst, near Lyndhurst, there was a small restaurant called the Angry Cheese, and so the enterprising loader phoned them and they agreed to provide Deborah Kerr with a meal, so they drove down and had a meal there. Kenneth Fielder remembers seeing Deborah Kerr at the Grand Hotel for a few moments before they went off to catch the flying boat and comments, 'I remember her quite well. She was a very petite, very attractive lady; she wore moccasins.'

At the time the Grand Hotel had the BOAC passengers that were going out on an early flight. The passengers who were on the later flight, if there were two flights in the morning, were taken from Victoria to a hotel on the Hogs Back, Guildford. They would complete their journey the following day and be flown off to their ultimate destinations. It was BOAC's own coaches that brought them down for the two or three flights that went out each week.

Ken Fielder remembers seeing Jean Simmons and Stewart Granger, her first husband whom she married in 1950: 'Stewart Granger was at that time very friendly with Jean Simmons, and she stayed at the same hotel the night before he flew off to make *King Solomon's Mines*. The next day when he came to the departure lounge, she sat in the departure lounge waiting for him to finally go.'

In 1949 the Aquila Airways flying boat services was formed by Barry Aikman and provided services to Maderia, Lisbon, Las Palmas and Genoa. Ken Fielder: 'Before BOAC was phased out another airline was started, called Aquila, who were privately owned. They flew mainly to Maderia on weekends. Fly Friday and come back Tuesday. If you had night take-offs or landings, as you occasionally had with Aquila airways, you had to put down a flare path. They were small floats with a light on them. You put them down in one direction and the wind might change and go down in another direction. That was always the danger and was a recognised danger.'

Wally Williams well remembers the near miss that he had with an Aquila Airways flying boat when he worked for Williams Shipping: 'Me and Ernie was going down the river at night in the old Exchange when I pointed out to Ernie, "What's all them green lights there in Lane's Lake?" Ernie says, "I don't know, let's go over and have a look." We were running up this long line of floats with green lights on when suddenly one of the Aquila Airways flying boats just missed the top of our mast. They were practising night landings. There were no port notices in those days about what was happening. You only found out when you came across something like that and you realised that they were going to start night flying!'

This was not the first time a flying boat had been dangerously close to a vessel when landing. In July 1939 an RAF flying boat was coming in to land on Southampton Water, near the RAF base at Calshot, when it clipped the mast of the paddle steamer *Gracie Fields*. The damage to the wings caused the flying boat to crash into the water. Fortunately, no passengers or crew were injured on the PS *Gracie Fields* and the flying crew was rescued unharmed.

The flying boat pioneered the airline routes to Africa, India, Hong Kong and beyond. However, the SR45 'Princess' flying boats came too late to be of any use and also at a time when BOAC were losing interest in flying boats and looking more to the land plane. Only three Princess flying boats were built, but they never went into service. They were eventually scrapped and moored on the banks of the River Itchen, just a short distance from the original Supermarine works. Kenneth Fielder: 'The Princess flying boats were eventually just cocooned at RAF Calshot. One of the pilots was known as Bennett. He was a wing commander, first with BOAC and then in the Royal Air Force, where he was in charge of the path finders who used to mark out target areas over enemy territory. After the war he tried to launch what was known as South American Airways, and they were going to fly the three Princess Flying boats to South America. Unfortunately it did not get off the ground, and the Princess flying boats only flew about 500 hours in test flights.'

The Princess flying boat only flew about 90 hours between 1952 and 1954, when she was finally grounded along with her two sister ships.

The BOAC G-AHIN Short S.45 Solent 3 Southampton. (Courtesy of ABP)

The G-ALUN S.45 Princess flying boat – the only one of three constructed to fly. (Courtesy of Solent Sky)

This is the Catalina that was involved in an unfortunate accident on Southampton Water while publicising the Seawings 2000 event in late July 1998. (Courtesy of Plane Sailing Air Displays Ltd)

Other Flying Boat Accidents

Flying boats were quite a popular way to travel to destinations, but they were not without accidents. Kenneth Fielder remembers some that occurred, and it was the crash of the Aquila Airways flying boat on the Isle of Wight, and the move towards the land-based aircraft, that led to the phasing out of regular flying boat services.

In 1957 there was a serious flying boat crash on the Isle of Wight when an Aquila Airways flying boat came down in a chalk pit on 15 November 1957. Although 15 passengers walked away from the crashed aircraft, the crew and 35 passengers were killed. The reason for the crash was that two of the four engines had failed, and with the aircraft carrying so much aviation fuel on impact it burst into flames. This was the beginning of the end for Aquila Airways, and it was in September 1958 that the last flying boat left Berth 50 in Southampton bound for Maderia. Kenneth Fielder remembers the crash at the time: 'I know that one flying boat had to make a forced landing on the IOW. I can remember their operations, and the importance is that everyone was sorry when they were phased out. Of course the introduction of the Comet and the aircraft that fly today you can understand the reason why.'

Ken Fielder also recalls: 'I do remember one particular incident. They had two American Catalina craft [American long-distance flying boats] which were in Hythe for coastal command. There were two types. They only had two engines, port and starboard, and on one type the Catalina's propellers were positioned closer to the cockpit than the other. Capt Harris was responsible for training the pilots. This was happening in Poole Harbour before they moved back to Southampton. He changed from one type of Catalina to the other and had forgotten that he was in the one where the propeller was closer to the cockpit. He pulled back the shutter, put his arm out to wave that everything was alright, and lost his arm.'

There was a tragic accident on 27 July 1998 when a Catalina sank on Southampton Water after a component in the bow undercarriage bay failed during take-off. The Catalina amphibian was on a trip organised by Southampton City Council to promote the Seawings 2000 air show, to be held in June 2000 to celebrate the city's aviation and maritime history. Two people drowned, including the Mayor of Southampton, but the two pilots and remaining 14 passengers and crew escaped unharmed from the sinking aircraft. The Catalina was recovered and is now stored at an airfield near Dublin awaiting restoration.

Derek Burke was one of the passengers on the Catalina when it sank in Southampton Water: 'On 27 July 1998 we were offered a place on a 1944 Catalina to celebrate our 2000 Seawings celebration. I was deputy mayor at the time, and with the mayor, Mike Andrews, and other passengers we took off from Eastleigh Airport to fly over Southampton. The beauty of it was to land on the water because it was a seaplane. We actually went around and did what they called 'touch and go' and on the second time around the Catalina was taking-off when there was a problem in the undercarriage bay and the aircraft filled with water. I escaped through the emergency exit and swam around until being rescued, but two people downed, including my friend Mike Andrews, the Mayor of Southampton.'

BOAC Flying Boat Timetable
MARINE AIR TERMINAL, BERTH 50.
Arrivals and Departures.
Monday.
11.45am BOAC Hythe Class to Australia
3.00pm BOAC Plymouth Class from Hong Kong
Tuesday.
11.45am BOAC Solent to Johannesburg
12.30pm BOAC Plymouth Class to Hong Kong
Wednesday.
11.45am BOAC Hythe Class to Australia
1.00pm BOAC Hythe Class from Karachi
3.30pm BOAC Hythe Class from Australia

Thursday.
11.45am BOAC Hythe Class to Karachi
3.00pm BOAC Plymouth Class from Tokyo
3.30pm BOAC Solent from Johannesburg
Friday.
11.45am BOAC Solent to Johannesburg
12.30pm BOAC Plymouth Class to Tokyo
3.30pm BOAC Hythe Class to Australia
Saturday.
11.45am BOAC Hythe Class to Australia
3.30pm BOAC Solent from Johannesburg
Sunday.
11.45am BOAC Solent to Johannesburg
3.30pm BOAC Hythe class from Australia
3.30pm BOAC Solent from Johannesburg

A postcard of the Hythe ferry passing the BOAC Terminal at Berth 50. (Tuck Postcard)

The Flying Boat Era Comes to an End

The design and development of the flying boat really came about because there were very few land-based runways that could take the large airliner, but ample space for landing on water was available world-wide; however, at the end of World War Two there were many airfields with long concrete runways which had been laid out during the war, and there was also a surplus of aircraft that could be purchased very cheaply from the United States Airforce after the war, and so land-based airlines were able to get started. This was to be the demise of the flying boats.

We talk today about flying out of Heathrow airport, Gatwick airport or any other regional airport, but it must be remembered that the word 'airport' originated from the flying boat service landing and taking-off in the Port of Southampton.

CHAPTER 5

SHIPPING LINES AND SHIPS

Mail Packet Boats

In the 17th century the British Post Office hired sailing ships to transport the mail. It was in 1688 that a mail packet station was opened in Falmouth, Cornwall, and this service continued until 1850 when the packet station was closed. Most of the routes for sea mail were transferred to Southampton after 1840 once the railway had been built from London, due to the speed at which the mail could be transported to the capital by train.

The sailing ships were known as 'packet boats', and letters carried on them were called packet letters. The vessels were also able to carry bullion, some cargo and passengers, but it was found that the transportation of sea mail with sailing ships was very unreliable. Although the packets boats tended to rely on speed for their security, the weather at sea could drastically affect how long the voyage would take. In a drive for a more reliable service and the need for greater security the government transferred the responsibility of sea mail to the Admiralty in 1823. The efficiency of the service was to be welcomed by the trading companies.

Famous Shipping Lines in the 19th Century

Famous 19th-century passenger shipping lines included the P&O (Peninsular and Oriental Steam Navigation Company) Line, Cunard and White Star Line.

The Peninsular Steam Navigation Company

The Peninsular Steam Navigation Company had started sailing from Britain to Spain and Portugal in 1822, and by 1836 the company had a fortnightly service of steamships in operation. The company tendered for a contract to convey the Royal Mail to the Peninsular, but this was at first rejected. However, the Admiralty did accept their tender in 1837, and the day the contract was signed, 22 August 1837, is accepted as the date that P&O was founded. The first vessel to sail with the mail from Falmouth to the Peninsular ports of Vigo, Oporto, Lisbon, Cadiz and Gibraltar was the 800-ton paddle-wheel steamship *Don Juan*. However, the vessel was wrecked on the return journey.

In 1840 the company was awarded a new contract to extend the service for a monthly run to Alexandria. The 1,787-ton paddle-wheel steamship *Oriental* opened the service, and there was a stipulation in the contract that the voyage from England to Alexandra had to be completed in 15 days. It was at that time the name changed to the Peninsular and Oriental Steam Navigation Company (P&O).

Further contracts were won, including conveying mail from Egypt to the Far East from 1844. The first ship to run the service was the 2,018-ton paddle-wheel steamship *Hindostan*. The service was later extended to Japan. By 1851 the Admiralty awarded P&O the contract for an Australian mail service, operating twice monthly from Singapore to Sydney. This service was inaugurated by the 699-ton iron screw steamer *Chusan*, leaving from Southampton and arriving in Sydney on 3 August 1852 and leaving again for Singapore on 31 August 1852.

Cunard

In 1839 Samuel Cunard established the British and North American Steam Packet Company, known as the Cunard Line, to carry the Royal Mail to Canada and the US. The *Britannia* was the first ship to come under the Cunard name on 4 July 1840.

Famous liners in the Cunard fleet followed, with names such as *Caronia, Carpathia, Aquitania, Mauretania,* and *Lusitania*. It was the *Carpathia* on April 15 1912 that rescued all the survivors from the sinking of the White Star's *Titanic*.

The White Star Line

The White Star Line was the company that owned the *Titanic* who sailed on her fateful journey in 1912. Founded in 1869 as the Oceanic Steam Navigation Company Limited, its house flag was a white star on red

Cunard *Britannia* in 1840.

pennant, taken from the White Star fleet of sailing clippers of the earlier days of sail. By the end of the 19th century the White Star Line ships were sailing to America, Australia and South Africa. However, the early 20th century, the time of the Great Depression, was a difficult time for the steamship lines. It was at this time that Cunard and White Star Lines amalgamated to become the Cunard-White Star Line Limited.

Royal Mail Steam Packet Company (RMSP)

The opening of the Southampton Docks made it more attractive as a port to other shipping companies and the Royal Mail Steam Packet Company's ships began to use the dock on a regular basis with services to South America.

The Royal Mail Steam Packet Company's 232-ton screw schooner *Esk* started a mail and passenger service to South America in 1850. She left Southampton on 10 November 1850 on her maiden voyage, calling at Lisbon, Madeira, Cape Verde Islands, Pernambuco, Bahia and Rio de Janeiro. The *Esk* was 112ft (34.1m) in length, with a beam of 21.5ft (6.5m). She had one funnel, two masts and a wooden hull with a single screw. Her speed was 8.5 knots, and she could accommodate 29 passengers. The ship was built in 1849 by Robert Menzies, Leith. After a short time in the South America service she was transferred to the West Indies inter-island sailings.

The Union Line *Briton*, which was built in 1897 in Southampton Dry Dock. (Courtesy of Mrs Maureen Webber)

The Union Steamship Company

The Union Steamship Company, founded in 1853, also began using Southampton Docks. The company was originally named the Southampton Steam Shipping Company and was used to bring coal to Southampton from South Wales for the P&O and Royal Mail Lines. Later it was renamed Union Steam Collier Company. Five ships were built for this service, the *Union*, *Briton*, *Saxon*, *Norman* and the *Dane*; however, in 1854, with the start of the Crimean War, the ships were requisitioned by the Admiralty for military use. After the war there was a surplus of coal in Southampton, and the ships were laid idle, but in 1857 the Union Steamship Company won the contract for a monthly mail service to South African ports. This service commenced on 15 September 1857 with the sailing of the Union Line's RMS *Dane*, a screw steamer of 530 tons, with a length of 195ft (59.4m), a beam of 25ft 1in (7.6m) and a speed of 9 knots. The *Dane* was built in 1854 by Charles Lungley & Co.

The Union Line *Norman*, built 1894. (Courtesy of Mrs Maureen Webber)

Other Shipping Companies

Also in 1857, the Hamburg-America Line commenced to call at Southampton en route from Hamburg to New York. By 1858 Norddeutscher Lloyd vessels also called on their North American mail service, sailing from Bremen to Southampton, Cherbourg and New York.

In 1858 there was a visit by the newly built *Great Eastern* before her maiden voyage from Southampton to New York on 17 June 1860. The *Great Eastern* was designed by Isambard Kingdom Brunel, built at the London yard of John Scott Russell and Company in Millwall and launched in 1858. She was 692ft (211m) long, 83ft (25.2m) wide, with a draught of 20ft (6.1m) and 22,500 gross tonnage.

Kaiser Wilhelm Der Grosse, which was built for Norddeutscher Lloyd in 1897. (Courtesy of Mrs Maureen Webber)

The Orient Line

The Orient Steam Navigation Company (Orient Line), started the first direct steamship service from England to Australia in 1877. The first ship in this service was the 3,877-ton iron screw steamer *Lusitania,* which arrived in Sydney in August 1877 via the Cape of Good Hope.

The Orient Line was founded in 1878 with the aim to run services to Australia because of the huge trade opportunities this offered. Their first steamship was the 5,386-ton *Orient,* built in 1879. The early attempts of using steamships on the long haul run to Australia, however, with the difficulties of breakdowns and maintenance while at sea, were up against the successes of the famous clipper sailing ships. This problem was gradually overcome, and powered steamships began to make successful return voyages to Australia without the aid of sails.

Shipping Lines' Development Moving into the 20th Century.

From 1892 more shipping lines were attracted to the port and at the same time the management of the Port of Southampton was taken over by the L&SWR (London and South Western Railway).

The American Line

In 1893 the American Line transferred its New York mail service from Liverpool to Southampton. The liner *New York* started the service on 4 March 1893. The reasons for the move were the links the liners would have with the Continent by calling at Cherbourg, better boat rail links to and from Southampton and that the journey from London by rail was 100 miles less than from Liverpool. The *New York* was 517ft (157.5m) in length, had a 64.6ft (19.6m) beam and weighed 10,499 tons. She was built by James and George Thompson, Glasgow, and was launched on 15 March 1888 as the *City of New York,* sailing for the Inman Line, Liverpool to New York. At the time she was the largest ship in the world and the first twin-screw liner on the North Atlantic. On 22 February 1893 she was acquired by the American Line and renamed *New York,* and on 25 February 1893 she sailed to New York on her first voyage for the American Line. It was the *New York* that was pulled away from her moorings alongside the *Oceanic* at Berth 38 by the suction and wave action caused by the propellers of the *Titanic* as it left Southampton on 10 April 1912. The speedy action of the master of the tug *Vulcan* in getting a line on the *New York,* and the assistance of the tug *Hercules,* kept her away from the *Titanic* until she had passed. In 1893 the American Line also purchased the *City of Chester* (4,791 tons), *City of Paris* (10,499 tons) and *City of Berlin* (5,526 tons) from the Inman Line. They were renamed *Chester, Paris* and *Berlin* and from May to December 1893 were sailing from New York to Southampton.

Union Line and Castle Shipping Line Merge

In 1890 the Castle Mail Packet Line's *Dunottar Castle* sailed from Southampton on her maiden voyage, and a year later the service was transferred from Dartmouth to Southampton. Also in 1891 the Union Line's *Scott* left Southampton on her maiden voyage.

In 1899, at the start of the Boer War, both the Union Line and Castle Packet ships were used to transport troops and supplies to South Africa. With the amalgamation of both companies into the Union Castle Line in 1900 this continued with the government requisitioning many intermediate ships for this purpose; however, in 1902 at the end of the Boer War a number of ships were laid up at Netley, Southampton Water, due to the lack of trade at the time.

A new mail contract was put out to tender in 1899, but this time only one shipping company could win the contract. In the past there had been much rivalry between the two companies for trade. That was until the transfer of the Castle Mail Packet line from Dartmouth to Southampton, when both the companies began to work more closely with each other. It was for that

reason that neither company bid for the contract. Finally a joint contract was awarded, and with it the decision to merge both companies was made.

On 8 March 1900 the Union Line and Castle Shipping Line merged to form the Union-Castle Mail Steamship Shipping Line. It was decided that the new fleet would adopt the Castle Line livery. The first sailing of a Union Castle Line ship from Southampton was the *Dunottar Castle,* 5,625 tons, which left the port

The Union Line *Scott,* built in 1891. (Courtesy of Mrs Maureen Webber)

outward bound on 17 March 1900. Prior to the ship leaving Southampton, a reception was held on board commemorating the hoisting of the new Union-Castle flag.

By 1900 other shipping lines started making regular calls to the port, including the Nederland Line and Rotterdam Lloyd. It is said that P&O invented cruising, and although there were cruising holidays as early as the 1840s, in 1904 P&O started offering their first cruising programme – for first class only. The company had the *Rome*, which had been built in 1881, and after conversion for her new role as a 'cruising yacht' she was renamed *Vectis*.

Shipping Lines' Development in the 20th Century: White Star Line and Cunard Line

In 1907 White Star Line's North Atlantic express service was transferred from Liverpool to Southampton and was inaugurated by the 25,000-ton *Adriatic*. The *Adriatic* had been launched in 1906, and her maiden voyage was from Liverpool to New York, leaving on 8 May 1907, but her return journey was to Southampton. She arrived at Southampton on 29 May 1907 with 996 passengers on board. Other White Star Liners at the time were the *Baltic*, *Cedric* and *Celtic*. Also in 1907, Cunard's *Lusitania* and *Mauretania* were launched, and at over 30,000 gross tons they became the world's largest liners.

The White Star Line Olympic Class liners, the *Olympic*, *Titanic* and *Britannic*, were originally planned and built to compete with Cunard's *Lusitania* and *Mauretania* in size and luxury but not necessarily speed. The *Olympic* was the first vessel to be launched on 20 October 1910, then the *Titanic* on 31 May 1911 and finally the *Britannic* on 26 February 1914. The *Britannic* was originally going to be named the *Gigantic*, but after the sinking of the *Titanic* the name was changed to the *Britannic*. The Cunard Line also inaugurated its Canadian service from Southampton in 1911 with the sailing of the *Albania* on 1 May while en route from London.

There were a number of collisions with Royal Navy vessels in the early years of the 20th century, including the *St Paul* who collided with and sank HMS *Gladiator* off Yarmouth on 25 August 1908. Also the *Olympic*, under the command of Captain Edward Smith, sailed out of the newly opened White Star Dock on 20 September 1911 and collided with 7,350-ton cruiser HMS *Hawke* off Cowes Harbour. The *Olympic* was coming around the Bramble Bank, and HMS *Hawke* appeared to be pulled towards her, and, unable to avoid a collision, she struck the starboard side of the *Olympic*. It was thought at the time that the suction created by the *Olympic* pulled the cruiser into its side causing two serious gashes, one below the water line. After the collision the *Olympic* had temporary repairs in Southampton Docks before sailing to Belfast on 3 October for more permanent repairs.

Ships were getting larger, and in 1911 Hapag built the first of their 'Big Three' ocean liners (which were to be the largest ships in the world). The *Imperator* was followed by her sister ships *Vaterland* and *Bismark*. They were the first liners to exceed 50,000 gross tons and were 900ft (274.3m) in length.

By April 1912 the Royal Mail Line had taken control of the Union Castle Line, but it was not till after the collapse of the Royal Mail Line in 1931 that the Union Castle Line became an independent company again. It was also in April 1912 that a great tragedy occurred after the *Titanic* had left Southampton for New York.

The *Titanic*

The year 1912 is synonymous in many minds with the sinking of the *Titanic* (sister ship of the *Olympic*), after sailing from Southampton on 10 April on her fateful maiden voyage. Of the 2,206 on board, 1,503 were lost.

Roy Diaper, who had retired after being harbour master in Littlehampton and was living at the NALGO lodge in Felpham, Bognor Regis, was in his early 90s when he talked to some schoolchildren about his memories of the *Titanic*. He told them that his father was a master mariner who knew Captain Smith (the master of the *Titanic*) well, and he had taken Roy onboard to meet the captain just before the vessel sailed from Southampton. He could remember his father meeting Captain Smith and described the grand staircase that they climbed to meet the captain. He said that as a young boy the staircase must have seemed so much larger than perhaps it would have done to an adult.

The appearance of the *Titanic* with four funnels was misleading as not all of the four funnels were used. The rear funnel was false and mainly used as ventilation for the engine room. It was also thought that the fourth funnel was used to store cleaning

The *Titanic* leaving Southampton on her fateful maiden voyage, April 1912. (Courtesy of Mick Lindsay Collection)

Samuel Williams, who signed on the *Titanic* in his brother Edward's name. (Courtesy of Ron Williams)

gear and sometimes as a radio room. At the time the fourth funnel was designed primarily to attract passengers to what they thought was a more powerful and stable ship in which to sail.

A number of the *Titanic*'s crew had left the ship before she sailed. One of them, Bill Tongs, was a scooter driver in the docks. Norman Sibley got to know a lot of the dockers through playing darts and said, 'Bill was a very quiet, private man who never married. He would always listen to others' points of view before making a decision, but once he had he was never wrong. His nickname in the docks was "Mouldy Tongs". He was engaged as a member of the crew at the age of 14 to sail on the *Titanic*, but just before sailing he had premonition of a disaster and walked off the ship and did not sail on the maiden voyage that ended so disastrously.'

Another of the crew did sail, but under a different name. Ex-stevedore Ron Williams's uncle Samuel was a fireman on the *Titanic* when it went down, but he sailed under his brother's name, Edward Williams. Ron Williams: 'What happened was the day before the ship sailed all the firemen went over to the Oriental pub across the park opposite Gate 4. They were skylarking about and going on about the 'old sinkable'. Anyway, an argument broke out and my uncle apparently hit a policeman. His mates told him to do a bunk so he went and saw his brother Edward Williams. His brother told him that he couldn't sign on the *Titanic* because he had seven children and told him to go down and sign on again as Edward Williams. When the ship went down my gran went down to the White Star offices in Canute Road to claim for it and said his name was Sam Williams. They said that they were sorry Sam Williams didn't go and his place was taken by Edward Williams. She said Edward Williams was sat indoors with his children, it couldn't have been him!'

Samuel Williams had been living with a woman and they had a child, so when the *Titanic* sank she went to claim from the White Star offices in Canute Road. All the men that knew he had sailed on the *Titanic* signed to say it was him and she was paid. The problem for Ron Williams was that all the time his father talked about his brother he would not listen. 'All my adult life I wouldn't listen to my dad. He would always talk about his brother being on the *Titanic* when he was having a pint, but my Uncle Sam went down with the ship. I didn't know the name of the lady he was living with or the name of his child because I wouldn't listen to my dad. I've been trying to find out all my adult life. I had a letter from a woman in Surrey saying that when her dad died he was an illegitimate child of someone off the *Titanic* and she gave me her mum's name. We found out where she lived in Southampton and it was only three streets away from where my uncle lived in 2 Canal Walk, St Mary's. I can't put the two together because it was "child of father unknown" on the birth certificate.'

The news of the sinking of the *Titanic* was a huge shock to Southampton, and one man describes his memory of the mood of the town when the news spread across Southampton:

'My first memories, I think the first memory that stands out, was the sinking of the *Titanic*. Things weren't as noisy as they are now, but the town went absolutely quiet. A great hush descended on the town because I don't think that there was hardly a single street in Southampton who had not lost someone. The ship, as you know, was supposed to be unsinkable. In those days there weren't much assistance for widows and orphans, and I can quite clearly remember going to a concert in aid of the widows and orphans. The admission was 6d.' (*Oral History Unit, Southampton.*)

Another man describes seeing the panic that spread, especially from those who had a family member sailing as a crewman:

'My next recollection in College Street was the sinking of the *Titanic*. People were running up the street shouting, "The *Titanic*'s sunk". There were panic stations everywhere. Women running out and down to the shipping office, you know near the dock gate. Everybody talked about the *Titanic*. It was the unsinkable ship. She had a double bottom tank and all this sort of things, and watertight doors.' (*Oral History Unit, Southampton.*)

The North Atlantic Services Start from Southampton

In 1914 P&O merged with British India Co. and in 1917 had purchased a majority share in the Orient Line. Both P&O and the Orient Line alternated weekly departures from London to Australia.

By 1919 Cunard Line's North Atlantic express service from Liverpool to New York was transferred to Southampton. The service from Southampton to New York was inaugurated by the *Aquitania* when she sailed outward bound on 14 June 1919 with 5,000 Canadian troops on board. One year later the Canadian Pacific Steamship Company based their white 'Empress' ships at Southampton to serve their principal Canadian service to Quebec and Montreal.

The *Aquitania*. (Courtesy of Nikki Goff Collection)

The Class System on the Passenger Liners

For almost a century there was a class system of travel with the first class (luxury), second class (although not luxury, it was decent), third class (basic) and steerage. The steerage passengers were mostly emigrants, and it was the cheapest accommodation, often deep down in the ship at the stern where the steering gear was situated, hence the term 'steerage'. In the early days the steerage passengers would have to find their own food and sleep wherever they could in a hold. Improvements were made, and although the first class was still luxurious the lower classes were improved and these passengers could travel in a reasonably comfortable way – although still basic.

When the *Titanic* sailed she had first, second and third (steerage) class. The third class on the *Titanic* was the steerage passengers and it was one of the first vessels to offer decent yet cheap accommodation for their passengers. The accommodation for many was better than they had at home, and the food was generally better than the third class on other ships. Over time the third class service improved until eventually only a two-class system, first class and cabin class, existed on most liners.

By the 1920s there was a move towards changing class profiles in the P&O and Orient Line. P&O changed second class to tourist class with the Orient Line combining their second and third class to create tourist class.

The Port Becomes Busier

Just after Southern Railway took over the management of the port in 1923 plans were proposed to extend the docks area by building west from the Royal Pier. Southampton was getting busier with more and more traffic in and out of the port. It was at about the same time, in 1925, that P&O decided to transfer its vessels back to the docks to carry cargo to the Far East.

The Union Castle four-funnelled *Arundel Castle* entered service in 1921 and was followed a year later by her sister ship the *Windsor Castle*. The first Union Castle motor-driven ship, the *Carnarvon Castle*, left Southampton on 16 July 1926 for her maiden voyage to South Africa. The Union Castle ships were distinctive to all in Southampton, with their lavender-grey hulls and black-topped red funnels.

Bert Moody recalls his memories of the Union Castle ships: 'I saw the Union Castle ships regularly. We saw them more when they decided to move up to Berths 102 and 104. It was 102 for the inward cargo and then after they had discharged they would move up to 104 to load the outward cargo. Before that they were in Dock Head. They used to come in on Berth 35 on the Itchen side and move around to sail from Berth 38. That was all Union Castle ships because on the Dock Head there were always feeder ships. They had two feeder ships at one time, *Hansa* and *Eider*. They were quite old ships, but they used to do trips to Hamburg and tranship to take cargo from Germany

The *Arundel Castle*. (Courtesy of Mike Edwards Collection)

The *Carnarvon Castle*. (Courtesy of Mick Lindsay Collection)

and South Africa. The ships got a bit old, and it was in about 1936 or 1937 that the new ship, a little ship called *Walmer Castle*, arrived. She was brand new but was lost during the war. She used to do the transhipment of cargo from Southampton every week to Hamburg. Of course after the war it had the same arrangement, but then you had General Steam, little cargo vessels coming in and doing the transhipment. Often they used to take wool because this was brought in from South Africa in bales. Some was definitely transhipped, sometimes over the side onto the quay and then loaded from the quay. Some of the wool went up to the Midlands to Bradford.'

The old four-funnel *Mauretania* held the Blue Riband for over 20 years until 1929 when it was taken away by the *Bremen* on her maiden voyage. The *Bremen* was the first ship to take both westbound and eastbound records on her first two voyages.

The Great Age of the Ocean Liner: The *Empress of Britain*

Kenneth Fielder well remembers the Canadian Pacific Empress ships, and a few years later became a member of the crew on the *Empress of Britain*. He also describes the sailing of the *Bremen* and *Europa*: 'Please bear in mind there were other shipping lines in Southampton, including Canadian Pacific, who in 1931 introduced their flagship the *Empress of Britain*, and they also had the *Empress of Australia*. The *Empress of Britain* would normally berth at 101 Berth. The *Bremen* and *Europa* were the two German ships that used to come into the docks before the war, and they used to berth in the New Docks. They would precede the sailing of the *Empress of Britain* by about one hour. I remember seeing them sail because I was on the *Empress of Britain* as a crew member for a while. The *Empress of Britain* would leave at about 1pm on Saturday and arrive in Quebec the following Thursday. She would sail again on the Saturday and arrive back at Southampton late on the Thursday evening.'

Edwin Praine had joined the *Empress of Britain* as a member of the crew in 1932 and was disappointed because he missed the maiden voyage by one year, on 27 May 1931. Five years later, however, on the 27 May 1936, Edwin Praine was more successful in being a member of the crew aboard the RMS *Queen Mary* when she left on her maiden voyage.

Bert Moody always remembers the *Empress of Britain* as his favourite ship: 'The *Empress of Britain* has always been my favourite ship. A short life because she was lost in the Second World War. She was only completed in 1931, and she didn't really get on to 101 Berth until about 1934 because she was berthed on Itchen Quays in 1933 and 1934. Occasionally she was on 102 Berth. Behind that you had the *Bremen* and *Europa* who would come in for about two or three hours and away they went.'

Empress of Britain launch 1930

Before the war it was possible to go on-board the ships when they were in dock. Bert Moody: 'Before the war you could get on-board a liner easily for a shilling. That surely went to the seaman's charity. I have been on the *Empress of Britain*. Wonderful ship. She was built for two purposes. The Canadian service, and she was the biggest ship to sail on the Canadian service, and in the

The *Empress of Britain*. (Courtesy of Mick Lindsay Collection)

The *Normandie*.
(Courtesy of Nikki Goff Collection)

winter they would have to find jobs for the ships so they sent them on cruises. They used to do round-the-world cruises, leaving December coming back about early May. That was when world cruises lasted for about five to six months and they really did cruise, spending about two or three days at each port. The *Empress of Britain* was unusual because she was a four-screw vessel, but when she did several of the cruises she operated as a twin-screw ship. One of the engine rooms was shut down making it more economical. The liner *Mauretania* also used to cruise.'

The reason the *Empress of Britain* would undertake the cruises is because it was not possible to get to Quebec along the St Lawrence River during the winter months as it would be frozen over.

With the development of the Old Docks came the great age of the ocean liner that started in the early 1900s and reached its height in the 1930s with the launching of three of the most luxurious ships ever built. They were the *Normandie* of France and the *Queen Mary* and *Queen Elizabeth* of the United Kingdom. These large ships were each almost 300m (1,000ft) long and crossed the Atlantic Ocean in just over four days. At that time Cunard's slogan 'Getting there is half the fun!' became a well-known phrase.

In 1935 the French Line transferred its New York and West Indies service from Plymouth to Southampton for outward sailings, but most inward sailings from New York still called at Plymouth. In August the same year the French Liner *Normandie* made a call in the Solent. She was over 70,000 tons and 1,000ft (304.8m) in length. Articles in the local press have referred to her as the 'Liner which never docked.' It is known that the *Normandie* regularly crossed the Atlantic to New York and would anchor at Motherbank, off Ryde, where the passengers and their luggage would be taken by tenders to and from the Port of Southampton. Although it has been said that the reason the *Normandie* would not dock in the port was to save paying port fees, it was mainly to save time.

By 1937 the port's cruising programme had 73,000 passengers, and with easy access to London and the Continent passengers could board a boat train in London and travel the 78 miles (125.5km) to the port, alight direct to the quayside and straight onto the cruise ships.

The RMS *Queen Mary*

It was an important year for Southampton when the new liner RMS *Queen Mary* arrived from the Clyde in March 1936. She entered the King George V Dry Dock for painting and then on Berth 106 for fitting out with furniture, carpets and other carpentry jobs. Edwin Praine was due to join the RMS *Queen Mary* on the Clyde as a member of the crew before she sailed to Southampton, but a mishap with the *Aquitania* where he was a crew member stopped him. 'I was on the *Aquitania* when she went aground on the Brambles, so I missed it!' He did join the RMS *Queen Mary* in Southampton and took part in the shakedown cruises around the Solent with local dignitaries and travel agents, down to the Lizard and across to Cherbourg.

Bert Moody remembers the arrival of the RMS *Queen Mary* in 1936: 'I was at school the time *Queen Mary* arrived. We saw her afterwards when we went down to the railway bridge at Millbrook, just beyond Millbrook Station in Church Lane. You could look down on the dry-dock and get photographs. I didn't have a camera before the war so I couldn't take any. I couldn't afford it in those days. That was one of my spots anyway because I am also a railway enthusiast.'

Kenneth Fielder, also at school at the time, remembers the arrival of the RMS *Queen Mary*: 'When the Queen Mary arrived in 1936 she went straight into the graving dock which had been built for her. Now, as schoolboys from Foundry Lane School in Shirley, we rushed down during the lunch hour. At that time, where freightliners are now, there was an old derelict church, and we went to the top of the tower waiting for the *Queen Mary* to arrive. It was at a time when I think we went back to school at 2 o'clock in the afternoon and it got very close to 2pm so we had to go back and missed seeing her.' All was not lost for the boys, however, and when they got back to the school they did get a sight of the RMS *Queen Mary*. Kenneth Fielder: 'From our classroom we were able to see her funnels as she went up river to turn into the graving dock.'

When the RMS *Queen Mary* left the King George V Graving Dock she was turned in the swinging ground and started on her course down the River Test and into Southampton Water, with seven tugs assisting. The tug tender *Calshot* was in attendance off the Calshot Spit at the mouth of Southampton Water to assist the *Queen Mary* in making the turn into the Thorn Channel

The RMS *Queen Mary's* arrival at Southampton in 1936. (Courtesy of Mick Lindsay Collection)

to continue on her way for the start of her shake-down cruises. While the RMS *Queen Mary* was in dock the week prior to leaving on her maiden voyage she was visited by members of the Houses of Lords and Commons, passenger agents, freight agents and shippers, and the remaining days of the week she was open for public inspection.

In was on one of those days that, as a little boy of seven or eight, Norman Sibley's dad bought tickets to go on-board the RMS *Queen Mary* before she sailed on her maiden voyage. He remembers walking around the deck and, with the height of the ship, being able to see all over Southampton; however, the most vivid memory was that he was very close to the funnel just as the ship's horn was blown to warn all visitors to leave the ship. He said: 'The blast of the horn was so loud that it lifted me off my feet!'

The RMS *Queen Mary* left Southampton on her maiden voyage on 27 May 1936, and Edward Praine was a member of the crew at the time. There were still jobs to do on-board, and some workmen from Harland and Wolff actually sailed with the ship to complete them. Edwin Praine found a good spot just under the bridge and remembers the atmosphere at the time: 'There were bands playing on the quayside and thousands of people about, and I don't how we didn't knock some of the little boats sailing out with the ship!' Arriving in New York four days later it was breakfast time. 'We all left the dining room and went up on deck to see the arrival in New York.'

On the voyage across there was a lot of celebration and a free bar. Edwin Praine: 'Everything was free. If someone asked for a whisky they were given a bottle! If they asked for a cigar they were given a box of cigars and some of the goods, especially the free champagne, used to find its way down into the crew's quarters!'

The RMS *Queen Mary* had to slow down on her maiden voyage because of fog and was not able to take the Blue Riband, but she did capture the Blue Riband on her westbound voyage from Bishop Rock to the Ambrose on 20–24 August 1936.

Arrival in New York was a similar sight to Edwin Praine as when the RMS *Queen Mary* left Southampton: 'Lots of little ships escorting us into New York and bi-planes "zipping" around with photographers on board. The quayside was so crowded that you had a job to get off the ship.'

Kenneth Fielder talks of the catering staff on the RMS *Queen Mary* working in the 'Workhouse': 'I know this is a bit controversial, because when you say it diminishes people's wonderful memories of the *Queen Mary*, because, lets face it, she was very special. Because of the number of passengers that boarded her at that time, she was the favourite liner, she became known as the workhouse for the catering crew because her deck crew and engine room staff only worked four-hour watches, with eight hours off. The catering staff would be there for breakfast, lunch, afternoon tea and evening meals, as well as supplying the other crew.'

Edwin Praine remembers the early mornings and late nights on the RMS *Queen Mary*: 'We would work from 5.30am, working at "scrub out", when we would clean all the inside decks, companionways, passageways and the Mall, and the waiters did the floors around the tables in the restaurants. Before breakfast we would muster in our uniform and have our hands checked to see if they were clean. That was expected in those days. Then it was serving breakfast and working until a break between 11am to 12 noon. Every other afternoon you would have the afternoon off, but it was still working right through to 11pm, a very long day. There was no recreation room or bar to relax in, and all we had was the "Glory Hole", where we would have 20 beds in a room in tiers and an 18in locker to keep our belongings in. The only sitting area we had were the two benches either side of a long table. We used to pay the "Glory Hole" steward a few shillings to make our beds and that was out of the £9 we used to get each month. You did save money because there was nothing to spend on the ship.'

The RMS *Queen Elizabeth*

The RMS *Queen Elizabeth* was ordered as Job 535 from the John Brown shipyard on 6 October 1936, which had also built the RMS *Queen Mary* launched the same year. She was 83,673 tons and 987ft (300.83m) long and was launched on 27 September 1938. Because of the outbreak of World War Two during her fitting-out she was painted grey. Once she had been fitted-out she left for her home port Southampton, but while sailing down the Clyde on 3 March 1940 her captain was given secret orders to head for New York. Bill O'Brien remembers this: 'The *Queen Elizabeth* liner was known as the "Pride of the Clyde". She was finished and was due to sail down to Southampton, and all the riggers were waiting on 43 Berth for her arrival. The *QE* didn't arrive, but sailed directly to America instead to mislead the Germans, and the crew was paid a bonus of £30 to sail over with her!'

On 21 March 1940, the RMS *Queen Elizabeth* sailed to Sydney, via Singapore, to meet the RMS *Queen Mary*. She spent the remainder of the war moving troops around the world, carrying as many as 13,000 to 15,000 on each voyage.

The First Hundred Years

A memorable year in the development of Southampton Docks was 1938 when it was the Southampton Dock Centenary, the first hundred years in the development of the port. Southern Railway published the Southampton Docks Centenary Booklet dated for Wednesday 12 October 1938, exactly 100 years to the day since the foundation stone was laid, outlining the major developments of the port during that time. It was also in that year that the *Berengaria* was at first taken to Jarrow to be broken up. The hull was scrapped at Rosyth in 1946.

The RMS *Queen Elizabeth*. (Courtesy of Mick Lindsay Collection)

The RMS *Queen Elizabeth* in her wartime grey.
(Courtesy of Mick Lindsay Collection)

CHAPTER 6
WORLD WAR TWO

In Wartime, Ocean Liners were Requisitioned for War Service

During World War One and Two ocean liners were requisitioned by the government for war service. In World War One famous liners such as *Mauretania, Olympic* and *Britannic* and in World War Two the RMS *Queen Mary* and RMS *Queen Elizabeth* were used for carrying troops and as hospital ships; however, a tragedy was to befall the *Normandie,* a similarly requisitioned ship, at the beginning of World War Two. The *Normandie* had been in New York from 1939 and was never to return to Europe. She was taken by the US Navy and renamed the USS *Lafayette* in December 1941 but was destroyed by fire on 9 February 1942 while being converted into a troopship. As a result of the fire the *Normandie* capsized at her berth in New York harbour, and she was eventually scrapped in 1946.

In 1939 the government had requisitioned vessels from the shipping companies for war service, including the P&O fleet, and many of these ships were lost. The first ship to be sunk in World War Two was the 13,500-ton passenger liner SS *Athenia* with 1,103 civilians, including over 300 Americans, on-board. She was attacked about 250 miles from the coast of Northern Ireland by U-30, commanded by Oberleutnant Fritz-Josef Lemp, thinking the vessel was an armed cruiser. The sinking occurred only hours after war was declared on 3 September 1939. One hundred and twelve passengers and crew were lost as a result of the sinking. Of the passenger ships requisitioned by the government in World War Two the largest liner to be lost was the 42,000-ton *Empress of Britain*, who was bombed by German aircraft off the coast of Ireland.

Empress of Britain **at the Beginning of the War**

Kenneth Fielder tells of his early attempt to become a member of the crew of the *Empress of Britain* in 1939. Just before the war the *Empress of Britain* was due to sail to Canada to bring back the king and queen who had been on a tour of the country. Kenneth Fielder was aged 16 and very keen to go to sea, and he especially wanted to sail on the *Empress of Britain*. While the ship was berthed in the docks he went down to see if he could get a job on-board.

Kenneth Fielder: 'The *Empress of Britain* had just come back off her world cruise, and I went down one evening, just before she was to go over to Canada to bring King George VI and Queen Elizabeth back from their Canadian tour. I got to the bottom of the gangway and Mrs Hill, the laundry manageress, came down the crew gangway. The fellow at the bottom of the gangway said, "This is Mrs Hill, have a word." I went up to her and said, "Please Mrs Hill, I would very much like to go away to sea." She said, "Well young man, I like the look of you" or words to that effect, "There is nothing we can do at the moment, we cannot take any new crew members on because of the IRA effect." (We are talking about 1939!) She said, "Come and see me when we come back."'

Disappointed that he could not get on for that trip, Ken vowed to wait until the *Empress of Britain* arrived back from Canada, and he would then try again. When the ship arrived he got on to the roof of a building overlooking Bargate as the car carrying the king and queen (with the two princesses who he said, 'were dressed in pink') came up the Bargate, through Above Bar to go to the Civic Centre.

Now the *Empress of Britain* was back in Southampton he could go back and see if he could get a job. He describes what happens next: 'Of course I went down as soon as I could and saw Mrs Hill, and she told me I could join for the coming trip. I always remember we sailed from Quebec on the way home and were at sea when Germany invaded Poland, and we were blacking the ship out the week before war was declared. I do know that when the *Empress of Britain* was bringing the king and queen back from Canada the ship was accompanied by one of the battle cruisers, and as soon as a ship appeared on the horizon the battle cruiser made towards it. That is how things affected them at that time.'

Even with the threat of war Ken still has fond memories of that time. They remind him of the beauty he saw in the world around him: 'We were told on our way home by the foreman that we had to work all night to get things up together because it was pretty apparent there was something amiss. I went on deck about 6am just as we were coming past Lands End and there were very low clouds, and the mast of the ship was going through the clouds; it was a wonderful sight!'

The *Empress of Britain* arrived in Southampton and was back at sea on the Sunday morning, the day war was declared. The ship arrived at Quebec on Thursday, 7 September 1939.

While the ship was in Quebec Ken Fielder had an accident and lacerated his arm. Someone had climbed on a drying machine and Ken grabbed the door, but his arm got jammed between the case and the door. He describes what happened next: 'We had three weeks in Quebec and I got my arm jammed in a laundry machine and was sent home at the end of September on the Canadian Pacific liner *Duchess of York*. They sent some crew home on another Canadian Pacific liner, the *Duchess of Richmond*, into Liverpool.'

When Ken Fielder arrived home after his arm injury on the *Empress of Britain* he stayed ashore to recuperate. Although he got on well in his job as a launch seaman, Ken was not happy being ashore, and by July 1940 he was very keen to get back to sea again. He wrote to the laundry foreman on the *Empress of Britain* to ask if he could return as a crew member. Kenneth Fielder: 'When I heard the *Empress of Britain* had arrived back I wrote to the laundry foreman, Percy Beck, and he told me I could come back. We sailed from Liverpool with 5,000 troops on board on my 17th birthday, which was 5 August 1940. Fresh water was rationed and was only available twice a day. We left Liverpool and formed a convoy by way of Freetown, Cape Town and Simonstown and went to the southern end of the Suez Canal where we disembarked the troops, at a place called Port Tewfic. We were there for about a week, and I only had one afternoon ashore, that was all. We took passengers on board to come back to the UK by way of Durban. I always remember when we sailed into Durban because HMS *Royal Sovereign* was there, and my dad had served on her. He had a commission on her in the Mediterranean for 18 months, although I remember that as a schoolboy. From Durban we set sail and we were 100 miles (161km) off the north coast of Ireland. I think it was called Bloody Foreland. At about 9.30am a four-engined Fockewulf Condor found us and dropped seven bombs and hit us with five. I remember when the first bomb went in. "BANG!" She shook like a jelly, so immediately we had to go to our fire stations. I always remember before the explosion that wounded us. I put my hands up to my face and said, "Whoa, Whoa, Whoa!" I had little black marks over my hands and fortunately had a waist-length life jacket on which protected the chest. I had a couple of little scars at the join. She was badly set on fire, and about two days later it was reported that the Germans had torpedoed her as they were trying to tow her in.'

Ken was too close to one of the explosions and was injured with a fractured femur and taken to a Scottish hospital at Ballacmile in Ayrshire until Easter 1941. He explains what happened after the ship had been hit: 'I was fortunate because we lost three of the laundry staff, one of whom I had been all through school with. We went and sat as we were told to by our fire station and were about three or four decks down. We were told to go and lay down so we chose to go and lay down near what was one of the passengers' toilets, but unfortunately my friend lost an arm from shrapnel and failed to survive. I remember that I could look up and see the sky coming through and first of all thought I had bought it! Then I put my head back and felt peace and thought I would like to see my mum again and shouted like heck for help, and help came! Eventually they got us out and up to the ship's hospital which was on the same deck. One of the people that pulled me out was a fella called Arthur Street. We were asked if we would contribute to his experiences, and ultimately he got the British Empire medal. While he was pulling me out he asked me to stand, but I knew my leg was broken because my leg went over at 90 degrees. He was dragging me out and had his arms underneath my armpits and accidentally dropped me and said, "I've just trod on nails" because the cowling had come down. I said, "Yes, they are tearing into my backside" and I had a couple of marks just above my right hip. Amazingly he got me up to the ship's hospital. They gave the "abandon ship" signal because she was so badly on fire. I think I had to go up on to the forecastle to be rescued. While we were on board, about two decks above us was the gun platform and the gun had been hit while we were waiting for the lifeboats. They said they couldn't get us to the lifeboats and they were bringing them around for us. We were lowered down from the afterdeck, and I was tied to the stretcher and ropes lowered us down into the lifeboat. They got us a little way away from the ship, and there was an explosion from the afterdeck of the ship. I always remember a French Canadian doctor that was helping to look after us, and he was bent over me when all of a sudden there was a "BANG!" from up above us and he jumped and they all said "Alright doc?!" The ship was there and smoke was coming out of her and this projectile, a shell, landed about 20 yards from us. I didn't see it coming, but they shouted "Look out!". I was laying down on the gunwhale.'

One of the guns on the afterdeck was hit, and prior to the gun being hit the PO gunner was racing across the open deck to get to the gun as the aircraft came in from astern. The gunner was in the same ambulance as Ken, and it took them from the rescue destroyer to the first hospital. He said that he had a bullet that creased him on the forehead and a flesh wound in the thigh which brought him down. Later in the hospital one of the younger gunners was in the next bed to Ken and said that as he turned to pull another round out of the rack they were hit. All he could remember was his leg just floating in the air. It was broken in five places.

All they had in the lifeboat was iced water until the rescue destroyer HMS *Echo* picked them up: 'They got us up to the PO mess and used it as an emergency operating theatre, then I was taken to the Royal Infirmary, Greenock, and then to Balacmile hospital in Ayrshire. I was one of the first six patients in the hospital, which had been purposefully built in the grounds of Balacmile House. Literally just weeks before I was due to come home, which was the Easter Weekend of 1941, it was declared a military hospital. They were marvellous, absolutely marvellous, and I only finished up with an inch and a half shortage in the right leg and now still wear surgical shoes.'

Kenneth Fielder well remembers the Irish sister who took off the plaster from his leg: 'Certainly some things stand out visibly in your memory. One was the Irish sister who came to me when they took the splint off. I had two pieces of plaster that ran the full length from groin to the ankle and beyond and from the hip to the ankle and beyond. I had two 36lb weights because I was in what they called a Thomas splint, the weights were to pull the leg and it used to pull me up the bed. I would ask them to pull the weight up and I would get back. As soon as they let the weight go it would pull me back up again. She said, "Look Kenneth, we've got to get those strips of plaster off, and I'm going to use this white surgical spirit on it." She said, "This is going to take a long time Kenneth – what do you think if I gave it a yank?" I said, "Well give it a try!" She got hold of it and "RIP, RIP, RIP!!"

She showed it to me afterwards and there was hairs all down the plaster, and she smiled as well. It was 26 October when we were bombed, and I can remember that as clear as day, clear as a bell!'

The *Empress of Britain* was probably the largest passenger vessel sunk during the war years. She was about 42,000 tons. The number of casualties at the sinking of the *Empress of Britain* was reported as 49. The official casualty list of the crew reported at the time was:

Known Dead: S. Miller, storekeeper; A. Till, waiter; J. Watts, wash-house man; J. Allen, assistant storekeeper; A. Powell, laundry boy; J. Wilkin, laundry boy.

Missing: E. Redmond, chief engineer; A. Atkinson, barber; J. McPherson, assistant butcher; S. Bradley, junior fourth engineer; N. Reading, lounge steward; J. Roberts, ordinary seaman; C. Lyons, junior tenth engineer; J. Allen, waiter; M. Mackrell, boiler attendant; J. England, engineer's writer; J. Ainsworth, waiter; A. Jeames, boiler attendant; W. Weston, second barkeeper; D. Britton, fourth baker; A. Knight, greaser; C. Moreton, third barkeeper; A. Russell, greaser.

Wounded: H.H. Davies, chief officer; H. Arnold, second storekeeper; P. Beck, laundry foreman; S. Keay, first officer; L. Casswill, waiter; K. Fielder, laundry boy; G. Potts, second radio officer; E. Meyer, waiter; J. Delaney, laundry boy.

With two laundry boys killed and the laundry foreman and two laundry boys injured, it appears that they were all very close to one of the explosions. Kenneth Fielder acknowledges that he was fortunate to have survived, although he is very sad at having lost his friends.

World War Two in Southampton
At the start of World War Two the docks were placed under the control of Allied Command. During this period Southampton Docks dealt with the movement of 4,300,000 military personnel and 3,900,000 tons of stores and equipment.

Red Funnel Paddle Steamers were Requisitioned for War Service
Some of the Red Funnel fleet had already served in World War One, namely the *Solent Queen, Her Majesty, Balmoral, Bournemouth Queen* and the *Duchess of Cornwall* (previously *Duchess of York*). Many returned to service again in 1939, mainly in the roles of cross-channel troop ships, anti-aircraft duties and minesweeping. Cyril Duro was working for Red Funnel on the *Vecta* at the beginning of the war. 'At the outbreak of war the *Princess Helena* was kept in the service, running between Southampton and Cowes. They took the *Balmoral* down to Plymouth. What happened after that I don't know.'

The Evacuation from Dunkirk
The British Expeditionary Force was deployed to France at the beginning of World War Two, but was forced back to the Dunkirk beaches by the German attack that started in May 1940. It was important to rescue as many troops as possible off the beaches and back to Great Britain and the evacuation, coded Operation Dynamo, came into force on 26 May. Naval vessels were immediately dispatched to the area but came under intense aerial attack. A large number of ships and civilian boats of all sizes were requisitioned and involved in the evacuation of the BEF from the beaches of Dunkirk.

Red Funnel vessels were also involved in the Dunkirk evacuation, including the *Princess Elizabeth* and *Gracie Fields*; however, despite making a number of trips to the beaches the PS *Gracie Fields* was hit by dive bombers and sunk. Cyril Duro had worked on the *Gracie Fields* before the war: 'The *Gracie Fields* took up the navy flag and was sunk at Dunkirk. She had a bomb right through her funnel!'

The *Vecta*
Red Funnel's first screw vessel was the *Medina*, put into service in 1931. She was followed by the *Vecta*, using Voith Schneider propellers, built by John I. Thornycroft and launched in July 1938. She was 190ft (57.9m) in length with a beam of 30ft (9.1m). Cyril Duro remembers joining her as a member of the crew. 'In 1938 I joined the *Vecta*. She was a Voith Schneider twin-screw of the German design. The engineer on board at that time was German, and course at the beginning of the war he was sent back to Germany.'

The MV *Vecta*. (Red Funnel)

The *Vecta* also took part in the Dunkirk evacuation, although it has often been reported that she had broken down on the way to Dunkirk. At that time the excursions had stopped and they were just making trips over to Cowes. Some of the crew who were RNVR had already left the *Vecta* to join the navy, but Cyril Duro was a member of the crew at the time and remembers actually reaching the beaches.

Cyril Duro: 'We finished up going on the *Vecta* over to Dunkirk. There wasn't a grand plan because of the numbers of vessels involved, and the captain had to make the decisions. It was up to him. When we got over to the coast of Dunkirk there was one of the little boats that came out with a Frenchman saying that the British troops were further along the beaches. We were getting up where the troops were when Mr Spence, the chief engineer, went on the bridge to say that the ship had developed engine trouble. They didn't really understand these Voith-Schneider engines. If they had spent another year or so with the Germen engineer then they would have known more about the engines. When the chief engineer turned he slipped, fell and broke his leg. We were really lucky to get out of there safely and made our way back to Dover. From Dover we were sent back to Southampton.'

Between 26 May and 4 June 1940, 338,226 men were rescued from the Dunkirk beaches, including 120,000 French and Belgian troops.

Bombing of Southampton Docks

The docks were targeted by German bombers, and 23 sheds and warehouses were destroyed or seriously damaged, and the Solent Flour Mill also received a direct hit on one side of the building. On the weekend of 30 November to 2 December 1940 the docks came under intense bombing, and all areas of the dock were affected, with quayside sheds 103 and 104 completely destroyed. Both the Red Funnel paddle steamers *Her Majesty* and the *Duchess of Cornwall* were sunk at their moorings in Southampton in December 1940. The *Duchess of Cornwall* was refloated, repaired and returned to service. The port had been closed to ocean-going passenger ships in 1940 as it was considered too dangerous for the merchant ships bringing important cargoes to the country, and other ports were used instead.

The tug *Canute* was also sunk by German bombs on 28 December 1940. In a German bombing raid on the Thornycroft yard at Southampton, destroyers *Norseman* and *Oppertune*, under construction, were badly damaged with the *Norseman* almost split in two by the bombs.

The International Cold Store on fire after an air raid on 13 August 1940. (Courtesy of Bert Moody Collection)

Another casualty of the bombs in 1940, and a building that was very important for storing food for distribution across Great Britain, was the International Cold Store at Berth 40, which was destroyed and burnt for two weeks. Ken Fielder talks about this: 'The International Cold Store was bombed during the war and blazed for days because of the butter.' There is a story that a machine gunner, who was on the top of the cold storage building, saw a German bomber flying out after a raid. He decided to fire a few rounds at the departing aircraft, but the German airmen were not pleased about this and turned back and bombed the building.

Working in the Shipyards in the 1940s

When Ernest Gay started his apprenticeship at Camper & Nicholson's in 1940 the mine sweepers, MTBs and landing craft started to arrive at Southampton, and he was engaged in making the commando dorys. Ernest Gay: 'You remember the book and film of *The Cockleshell Heroes* that paddled the skiffs? We made all of them.' These were the Cockle Mark 2, a canoe designed to carry a crew of two, including their stores. It was also designed and made to be loaded through a submarine's forward torpedo hatch and was 5m (16.4ft) long, 72cm (2ft 4in) wide and 28cm (11in) high, but only weighed 36.5kg (80.5lb). The canoes were named after fish: *Coalfish, Crayfish, Conger, Cachalot, Catfish*, and *Cuttlefish*.

The actual raid was named Operation Frankton. Under the leadership of Major H.G. 'Blondie' Hasler on 7 December 1942, 10 men in five canoes were launched off the submarine HMS *Tuna* in the Gironde estuary in the Bay of Biscay. They were to paddle some 75 miles (120km) upriver to Bordeaux to attack German merchant ships berthed there. On the night of 11–12 December only two canoes had made it to the harbour and they placed limpet mines on four of the ships. With the exception of Major Hasler and Marine Billy Sparks, who was his co-partner in the canoe, all of the men on the operation were either drowned or captured and executed. Major Hasler and Bill Sparks eventually escaped to Spain and returned to England in April 1943. They successfully sank one ship and the remaining ones were seriously damaged.

Ernest Gay: 'During the war we were in the home guard and never got any time off for the next day. You were up all night, and that was hairy. They had a system where if the sirens went somebody had to go on the roof and at any sign of activity press the button and everyone would go to the shelters.' It was Ernest Gay and Harold Cook, two 17-year-old boys, who had to go on the roof because no men would do the job! Although Ernest Gay completed his apprenticeship in 1945 he remained at the yard until 1950 but had to leave because of a shortage of work.

Ex-mariners Return to Sea

Bill O'Brien, who had spent many years at sea sailing on many of the famous liners, was working ashore at the beginning of the war but decided to go back to sea: 'When the war started I was working at a holiday camp in Seaton, Devon, as a waiter and came back to Southampton to train as a seamen gunner. This I did at Bristol on 4.7 and 12 pounders and then joined a cross-channel boat from Southampton to Cherbourg and Le Havre carrying army equipment. This was a coal-burning ship.'

At the beginning of the war many people were keen to leave Great Britain for the US, and Bill tells the story of how one docker on the quayside suddenly became the owner of a very expensive car: 'One man in his rush to catch a ship drove up to the dock in an expensive car, left it on the dockside and told a docker he could have the car as he wouldn't be needing it any more!'

During the war many of the liners and cargo ships were requisitioned for the war effort, and many of the crew who were not called up sailed on the vessels in convoys. Quite a few of these sailors originated from the ships that sailed in and out of Southampton. Harold Lloyd was the first mate working in the railway in Redbridge, but before that he had to go for his medical for the army: 'I went down the board of trade and went up to Liverpool. It was an outfit called the T124X, and if the number was T124 you could get out anytime, but when they put the X on it you were there for the duration of the war, which I didn't know at the time, but I accepted it. I went to the Far East and was stationed in Ceylon, and then we were sent on to an ex-cargo ship that used to carry race horses. There were three decks that were loaded with mines which were laid outside the harbours on a loop. These mines could only be blown up from the shore. I was out there for three years, and when we came back I wanted to get back into the merchant navy. The first ship I went on when I returned was the *Aquitania*, a Cunard White Star ship, and from there I went on to the Royal Mail Lines.'

The *Arandora Star*. (Courtesy of Bert Moody Collection)

Many ships were sunk during the war, and Kenneth Fielder remembers one particular ship that visited Southampton: 'The other line that I particularly recall was the Blue Star Line. The *Arandora Star* was one of them, but she was torpedoed on 3 July 1940 by the German submarine U47 about 75 miles (120.7km) west of the Bloody Foreland and sunk with a loss of 805 lives.'

The 15,500-ton *Arandora Star* had left Liverpool on 2 July 1940 with German and Italian internees and German prisoners of war on-board. They were being deported to Canadian internment camps by the British government because of the fears of invasion following the fall of France and the evacuation of the British army from Dunkirk. It was 6.45am on 3 July when the *Arandora Star* was torpedoed by the U47 and sank within an hour. It is believed that U47 thought she was an armed merchant ship because of her grey wartime livery.

The Queen Mary in the War Years

As many as 15,000 American servicemen were carried across the Atlantic at one time, and it was during one of those crossings that the RMS *Queen Mary* collided with a British cruiser, sinking her. The German U-Boat captains were very keen to torpedo and sink the *'Queens'* who were bringing the American servicemen across the Atlantic, but they had been unable to do so because of the speed of the liners. The captain of the RMS *Queen Mary* was under orders not to stop the ship for any reason because of the risk of being torpedoed. She was sailing close to the coast of Ireland and zig-zagging to avoid the German U-Boats. One of her escorts, the British light cruiser *Curacoa* of about 4,200 tons, found herself on a collision course with the RMS *Queen Mary* after swinging towards her on the zig-zag course. There was no time to avoid the collision and the RMS *Queen Mary*, who was steaming at 28.5 knots, struck the cruiser amidships and sliced her in half. Of the crew of 440, 338 were lost.

'Youngsters Living in the War Years'

Living in Southampton in the early war years was very exciting for youngsters. Colin Hall remembers seeing the dug-outs and machine-gun-posts being positioned on strategic pieces of raised ground behind bushes and on street corners and the camouflage-netting that was stretched over anti-aircraft gun emplacements. He remembers especially the practice invasions demonstrated by the LDV (Local Defence Volunteers), the fore-runner of the Home Guard, when they: 'Practiced with artificial "fog" exploding from canisters along the streets to hopefully confuse the expected German parachutists when they landed. Everyday was a day of expectancy. Gas-masks were issued, propaganda posters were everywhere telling the community more "what not to do" should the Germans arrive. The BEF (British Expeditionary Force) was on its way to France towards that "last-ditch stand" at Dunkirk and the schools were evacuating the children out of the main towns and cities for their safety into a more rural environment.'

Colin Hall could remember the dock area continually being targeted, especially the 'Supermarine' aircraft works on the River Itchen, the King George V Graving Dock at Millbrook and the Marchwood ammunition dump on the opposite side of the River Test from the dry dock. During the increasing frequency of nightly air-raids families had to spend more time in the air-raid shelters they had erected in their back gardens.

For Colin Hall the whole Millbrook and Redbridge water-front area was the playground for him and his school friends. The Millbrook area was chosen as the main route for the Canadian divisions heading towards the docks, which was their embarkation point. King Georges Avenue, where Colin Hall lived, was called the 'Maroon-Route' and was the main supply route for the Canadian forces, especially their heavy tanks.

The Mulberry harbours were constructed in the area for towing over to the Normandy beaches, to provide a sheltered landing site for the military equipment. At the same time the Pluto (pipeline under the ocean) pipeline from Fawley to the Normandy beaches was put in place to provide fuel for the Allied forces.

In 1943 the Marchwood Military Port was the site of No. 1 Port and Inland Water Transport (IWT) Depot Royal Engineers (RE). Situated on the western shore of the River Test, opposite the New Docks, the unit had the task of preparing and launching the 'Beetles' and 'Whale' units that were to be towed to Normandy for the Mulberry Harbour in the D-Day landing in 1944. The 'Whale' was the floating roadway, supported by pontoons called 'Beetles.'

Colin Hall remembers the early stages of Mulberry floating harbours being constructed. Large logs were strapped together to become massive rafts, the docking-areas for the ships serving the landing. This work was undertaken by Canadian lumberjacks, especially brought in because of their experience in rolling logs on the Canadian rivers. However, some of the more adventurous schoolboys used to swim out to attempt to roll the logs as the lumberjacks did while they positioned them before lashing them together, but the boys were chased away for their own safety. Colin Hall: 'For adventurous youngsters it was a highly dangerous thing to do, especially if you fell between the moving logs and got trapped underneath.'

Colin Hall had left school shortly after his 14th birthday in 1944 and followed the family tradition of working in the docks. This tradition went back to beyond the times of his grandfather, who was a dock worker in the latter days of sail and early days of steam. His father and his brothers, along with their sons, had also followed the same route. Colin Hall: 'So it was an accepted thing to keep the name "Hall" alive in dock-land over the years, as was the case with many other "dock-bred" families.'

The *Empire Orwell*. (Courtesy of Mick Lindsay Collection)

Ken Fielder has memories of the French onion sellers arriving at the Town Quay before the war and the changes introduced in the run-up to D-Day: 'I think it is also important to remember that during the war, in the build up to D-Day, the Town Quay was altered to introduce slipways where there were no slipways before. Before the war the French onion sellers used to berth there and go around with their onions over the handlebars of their bikes. That became an annual event and they used to berth right up by the quayside a few yards from the road. I do remember between the Town Quay and what is the main part of the old docks, you could see people with mud flats on. They were boards tied to their feet to stop them sinking in the mud while they were digging for bait, ragworm. They would sell about 10 worms for 3d.'

The port was used for the invasion barges that were berthed about 10 deep from the quay out into the River Test. On occasions, to avoid the German aircraft seeing the barges, they would put a smoke screen over them. Ken Fielder: 'I remember that one of the buildings in the New Docks was used for the making of anti-submarine nets, and ladies used to work there. I also remember there was a searchlight on the end of Hythe Pier.'

Colin Hall's apprenticeship in the docks began in the period shortly after D-Day. This was a very busy time for the Railway Service cross-channel passenger and cargo vessels that had been requisitioned as troop carriers and hospital ships for servicing the initial landing forces. His job as a boy dock-worker 'apprentice' in the sheds and offices was to help keep the stevedores working 'down the hatch' by supplying them with their 'baccy, beer, and bread' to ensure the quick turn-around of ships between the port and the landing beaches was kept constant. 'Running' for the crews was also part of that job, with the delivery of their mail probably the most important function as far as they were concerned.

He describes the old 'railway' ships, including the *Hantonia*, *Isles of Jersey* and *Guernsey*, along with vessels from GWR, LNER and LMS Railway companies queuing-up to get into the docks. The ships were either in troopship grey or in hospital-ship white with their distinctive red cross emblazoned on the sides and decks, 'to hopefully avoid deliberate attack from the enemy as they transported the wounded back for hospitalisation and treatment of their wounds.'

Colin Hall and the other shed-boys made sure they were down at the quayside to see the homeward-bound troops off. More important to the shed-boys was the gathering up the coins, gum, cigarettes, boxes of 'K' rations and souvenirs that were thrown onto the quay-side by the troops. He was at that time working at the Docks & Marine Offices on the corner of the old No. 1 and 9 Berths on the edge of the Outer Dock. This was his 'reporting' point and the centre of activities in the post-war cross-channel trade.

Colin Hall's elder brother Dennis was also employed in the Southern Railway Docks Commercial Department, which due to the risk of materials being destroyed in the bombing was temporarily moved to Embley Park near Romsey. Their offices were housed in the family home of Florence Nightingale, the nursing heroine of the Crimean War.

During Colin Hall's apprenticeship days many of the old mates of his father made themselves known to him, so he was made to feel quite at home in those early days in the environment which was to dominate his life for many years to come. Work was between 'office' and 'ships', and he was at the beck-and-call of everyone.

TROOPING AFTER WORLD WAR TWO

Don Archbold remembers the port at the end of the war: 'In 1945, when the war was over you had loads of ships coming into the port, especially from America, with the Lease lend cargo which was helping to supply this country with food which we hadn't had during the war. Also the passenger ships started, and gradually as time went on you had the big passenger liners coming into port. At the end of the war the *Aquitania* was responsible for carrying German prisoners of war and also taking the Canadian and American war brides to join their husbands in their home country.'

Trooping continued after World War Two, and some of the troopships' names included the *Empire Orwell, Empire Halladale, Empire Fowey, Devonshire, Oxfordshire* and the *Nevasa*. The *Oxfordshire* was eventually sold in 1964 to the Sitmar Line, renamed the *Fairstar* and used to take emigrants from Southampton to Australia.

The Korean War 1950–53

Troop ships such as the *Dunera* and *Empire Orwell* sailed from Southampton in 1950s for Korea. It took about six weeks to arrive at Pusan, Korea. October 1953 was a time of celebration for the returning prisoners of war on the *Empire Orwell,* who were transferred from the ship to shore by the tug tender *Calshot.*

Although trooping had resumed after World War Two, air transport began to take over in the 1950s, and the last troopship to arrive back in Southampton from the Far East was the Bibby Line's *Oxfordshire* in November 1962.

The return of prisoners of war from Korea. (Courtesy of ABP)

The *Canberra* returns home from the Falklands. (Courtesy of Jim Brown Collection)

The Falklands War

It was thought that trooping by ship had ended in 1962, and servicemen were transported by air from then on; however, in April 1982 Argentina invaded the Falkland Islands in the South Atlantic, and the British government, led by Prime Minister Margaret Thatcher, immediately ordered a task force to be assembled to liberate the islands. The port of Southampton and the naval port of Portsmouth became central to those preparations, with two aircraft carriers, the HMS *Hermes* and *Invincible,* accompanied by the assault ship HMS *Fearless* and escorts, sailing to the Falkland Islands on 5 April 1982.

Southampton-based cruise ships *Canberra* and *QE2* sailed after work to prepare them had been undertaken at the Vosper Thornycroft shipyard on the River Itchen. The shipyard staff worked day and night to put three helicopter pads on the *QE2* that would be carrying troops. The *Canberra* had been on a world cruise when it was requisitioned, as was the educational cruise ship SS *Uganda* (call sign '*Mother Hen*'), used as a hospital ship. When the task force eventually returned the shoreline was lined with thousands of people welcoming them back.

Marchwood Military Port

There is still a military presence in Southampton with the Marchwood Military Port and as home to the Royal Fleet Auxiliary's ships. The city was heavily involved in the 1982 Falklands War and has a continuing role in re-supplying the military forces overseas.

Marchwood Military Port, known today as the Sea Mounting Centre (SMC), is situated on the western side of Southampton Water, opposite Southampton Docks, and is the only military port in the UK. It is operated by the 17 Port and Maritime Regiment RLC (Royal Logistics Corps) whose job is loading and discharging ships that supply units serving overseas.

The port has three main jetties. The largest jetty is 721.7ft (220m) long and 108.2ft (33m) wide and can accommodate vessels up to 16,000 tons. The jetty also has two 35-ton cranes mounted on rails, Ro-Ro facilities, railway lines and a port licence to handle ammunition and explosives on the largest jetty. The second jetty was built during World War Two and is 623.3ft (190m) long, has rail access and can accommodate vessels up to 8,000 tons. The third jetty is 383ft (117m) and used to berth smaller vessels and military landing craft.

PART 2

CHAPTER 7

THE DOCKS AFTER WORLD WAR TWO

BRITISH TRANSPORT COMMISSION 1948–63

At the end of World War Two there were disputes over working conditions in the ports, and the Labour government introduced the NDLS (National Docks Labour Scheme) in 1947 with the registration of dockers and fall-back pay when work was not available. In the same year the Labour government introduced the British Transport Act, and the transport industries were nationalised in 1948, with Southern Railway becoming British Railways and the docks being taken over by the British Transport Commission.

By the end of World War Two, liners such as the 83,673-ton RMS *Queen Elizabeth* were entering the dock. The original passenger and cargo sheds in the Ocean Dock were single-storey buildings and were expected to service the world's largest passenger liners, but they were proving too small and this was causing problems for the number of passengers, luggage and cargo passing through. A decision was made to provide a new terminal which could cater for the larger liners using the docks, and plans were prepared to build a two-storey terminal on the east side of the Ocean Docks at Berths 43 and 44. The design of the new building would solve the accommodation problem by providing a two-storey structure, with the upper floor used for passenger reception and Customs and the ground floor for access to boat trains, cargo, baggage, motor cars and the quayside offices. In preparation for the building of the new terminal the bomb-damaged dock sheds built in 1911 were demolished, and from 1946 the building of the new terminal started and was completed ready for its opening in 1950.

Ocean Terminal

In 1950 the new Ocean Terminal in Ocean Dock was officially opened on 31 July by the British prime minister, the Rt Hon Clement Atlee MP. The building was constructed in Art Deco style and was 1,270ft (387m) long, 120ft (36.5m) wide and had a railway platform that could accommodate two full-length trains at once. The RMS *Queen Elizabeth* was the first ship to use the new terminal.

An aerial view of the Ocean Terminal in Ocean Dock. (Courtesy of ABP)

The RMS *Queen Elizabeth* berth at the Ocean Terminal. (Courtesy of ABP)

The Ocean Terminal – inside the First Class Customs Hall in the early 1950s. (Courtesy of Bert Moody Collection)

The passenger accommodation on the top floor consisted of two reception halls with refreshment buffets. One was the First Class Hall and the other the Cabin Class Hall. Each hall had a telephone bay with operators on hand and 12 individual bays where passengers could telephone anywhere in the world. Other amenities included a flower shop, bank, bookstall, writing room and iced-water fountain. Adjoining the passenger accommodation was the Customs Examination Hall. Travel Agencies, Railway Booking Offices and telegraph and cable companies were represented. The public address system relayed announcements and music. A press room was available, and even the BBC had its own room. To board a ship there were telescopic gangways situated at the first floor level, electrically operated and able to be moved to the doors of the liner. On the ground there was a large area for cargo that included ship stores, a Customs cage for bonded baggage and staff offices.

Once the baggage was taken from a liner's hold by a quayside crane it was landed on the upper floor baggage platform and then transferred by trolleys to the Customs Hall. Once the baggage had been cleared by Customs the passengers could make their way by lift, stairs or an escalator to the railway platform or road platform. If the passenger was to be collected from the road platform the passenger's car was called from the car park. Alternatively, they could be picked up by a taxi.

Norman Sibley joined Streamline Taxis as a driver after suffering a serious accident and remembers working from the Ocean Terminal. Norman Sibley: 'When working the Ocean Terminal you would drive around and join the queue of taxis and eventually get around meeting the passengers and their luggage, taking them to their destination and then rushing back and joining the queue again. It was the same procedure for the Terminus Station.'

To work the docks the licensed taxi driver needed two licences. One licence was to get in the docks and the second licence was a docks licence. Norman Sibley: 'Streamline Taxis was run by the May family, and Pop May used to run a taxi service when it was a horse and carriage. They were successful because they used to be ahead of the others by checking when the ships used to arrive and be there to meet the crew and passengers. The *Daily Echo* was a good source of information for the times of the ships and which berth they would go to.' They also used to go to 50 Berth to take passengers to and from the flying boats.

To get to each floor there were passenger escalators, stairways and lifts for passengers and baggage. On the opposite side of the road there was a transformer station, and from the transformer house there was a footbridge that gave visitors access to the visitors' balcony. The transformer house is the only surviving part of the Ocean Terminal left in the docks today.

It was a popular job unloading and loading the passengers' baggage in the Ocean Terminal. Ron Williams: 'Loading baggage was sent up escalators when the ship was alongside, and the gang on board would sort it out in alphabetical order. The bedroom stewards all had their trolleys and would take it to the cabin. Nine times out of 10 the luggage was in the cabin before the passengers came aboard because you were loading hours before they boarded.'

Ron Williams remembers overhearing an interview conducted for a radio broadcast: 'We were stood waiting for a train to come in and there was a woman, an American woman, interviewed in the Ocean Terminal. She was asked to give her impression of it. The interviewer asked, "What do you think of this Ocean Terminal madam?" She said, "I think it is wonderful, you can't even feel it move!" She thought she was on the ship!'

The 'Whelks'

The stevedore working on the ship did not have the opportunity to gain tips when loading and unloading passengers' baggage. It was the quayside docker who gained the tips – if he drew the 'whelks' when the gangs booked-on at the foreman's office. Colin Hall: 'There were several devious means for getting that particular perk when it was due to be drawn from the hat, with a wink and a nod or a pre-planned sign from the foreman or shop steward who were supposed to ensure that the draw for jobs was fair and square!'

Terry Adams remembers the 'whelking', which was carrying the passengers' baggage: 'One week we would get the "Big-uns" and you would get the "whelks", carrying the passengers' baggage. That season would go from about March to September. That was the first year in, but after your second, third and fourth year you stayed in longer. After four or five years you got your black book, and by then that was different because you were making money then. That was in the days of piecework, when you got what you worked for. If you wanted big money you worked hard, if you didn't you just went on the soft jobs. It was hard work, but it was lovely. I wouldn't swap it. I would do it again.'

As with many of those interviewed who said that if they had their time over again they would still opt to work in the docks, Terry Adams agrees: 'If you asked 10 dockers they would say they would do it again. If you were sick you would try to go in, the men would sit you down, get you out of the way and carry you. You would try to carry a man when you were on piecework, some you couldn't because you had the eight men and they were set out.'

For the porters, tips were always welcome, and they would usually be able to identify a 'rich pickings'. But that does not always hold true. As Ron Williams found out: 'I always remember once we were doing a ship in the Ocean Terminal, and there was a guy there and he had an old army overcoat on with a rope round it and a trilby, and he was really scruffy. Nobody would go near him, especially the boys with the trucks. He stood there and looked fed up. I went ashore to see how it was going and I said, "You still here then mate?" He said "Nobody wants to touch my luggage." So I said to one of the boys, "Hey, what about this man here?" "Oh, OK" the porter said and he filled his truck up with the luggage. When the porter came back he said to me, "There's no more like

A postcard showing an earlier view of the *QE2*.

him about is there? I just got two fivers off of him!" The porter said that the man had his own fleet of cars down below and they were all saluting him. I never found out who he was, but I know he came off a Russian ship.'

The tips received from the transatlantic passengers who travelled in the first and cabin class were generally very good as these were the passengers who, when changing over to air travel, would be travelling in the first or upper class. They were, as Colin Hall says, 'especially good at flashing their dollars around!'

The opportunity to get the best tips often went to the shed 'perms' who would work at the end of the baggage terminal in Berth 43–44 shed that dealt with the first and cabin class passengers, but the 'temps' were generally confined to the other end where the tourist class passengers' baggage was handled. Colin Hall: 'It was considered a bit of a scramble to get a bob or two, as there was definitely not much paper-money seen with these once-named "steerage-class" passengers.'

One of the dockers' nicknames was 'Oncer', and he gained this name while loading baggage on one of the Queen liners. A passenger had asked him what the standard charge was for tipping porters. He had replied, 'A Oncer, (£1),' but the passenger questioned the shed supervisor about this, and consequently the docker was reported to the National Docks Labour Board and almost lost his registration book and job as a result. Of course, the dockers immediately nicknamed him 'Oncer' after this incident.

It was in the 1960s that the popularity of transatlantic ocean travel declined by the transfer of passengers to air travel to arrive at destinations in hours rather than days. By the 1980s the ocean liner heyday was over, and in December 1980 the *QE2* was the last ship to dock at the Ocean Terminal before it was closed. From 1950 to its closure in 1980 many passengers had embarked and landed at the Ocean Terminal, including the rich and famous. These included royalty, politicians, world leaders, film stars, musicians and sporting heroes.

The demolition of the Ocean Terminal. (Courtesy of Maurice Allen Collection)

Queen Elizabeth II Terminal, 2008.

Ocean Terminal Demolished in 1983

The Ocean Terminal was demolished in 1983. Bert Moody knew the inside well: 'I've been inside the Ocean Terminal. A lot of people wanted it preserved as a museum. Wonderful idea, but so far as the dock people were concerned it would have been in the way of the development of the port. It was not being used and no ships were coming in. There were the container ships, but there were also labour troubles. You didn't see a ship because the shipping companies would not put them in here.

'The information I got from the experts was that the cost of keeping it going was such that no insurance company would take it unless massive repairs were done to the building. The insurance companies just wouldn't accept it. It was a prefabricated building, and prefabricated buildings don't last and are not made to last. It is a pity as it was a nice building. It was superb for handling passengers and all that.'

The Ocean Terminal was replaced by the QEII Passenger Terminal at Berth 38–39 and was opened by Her Majesty Queen Elizabeth II in 1966. The terminal mainly serves the Cunard Line. The first liner to use the new terminal was P&O's *Iberia*. Further refurbishment was undertaken in 2003 in preparation for the arrival of the new RMS *Queen Mary 2* in 2004.

CHAPTER 8
POST-WAR DOCK LABOUR

From the BTC, BTDB to ABP

Getting employment in the docks was always going to be difficult for many dockers, especially when having to attend the NDLB 'Pool' each day to get work. The following lament by one London docker will give an introduction to the tales of the Southampton dockers in the following pages.

'The Pool Man's Lament.' The Curse of Casual Labour
by J. Maynsbridge, Millwall Docker in 1952.

Down at Millwall one gloomy morn,
Stood a docker, grim and forlorn,
Like a jungle-cat, with muscles tense,
Waiting for the call to commence.
At a quarter to eight, he sprant at the gate,
But alack and alas, he was too late,
For drenched with dew, tired and worn,
Men had waited since early dawn.
Six days by the gate, and along the wall,
They fought like tigers, around the call,
With tooth and claw, and eyes abright,
They fought and struggled, with all their might.
The chosen few were radiant and glad,
Those that were left were gloomy and sad,
For to each man there the truth was plain,
That a 'bomper' would be his only gain.
The moral of this simple ditty,
Is a docker's life is not so pretty,
On four pound eight to live and eat,
Frankly brothers, it's got me beat.

However, down at Southampton when the dockers did not get work and their books were stamped they would refer to it as being 'bumped'!

The Red and Black Books

As a result of the introduction of the National Docks Labour Scheme in 1947 registration books were introduced. A temporary docker was issued with a red outer-covered book, and this made it easier to identify them from the registered dockers, who had black books. The outer plastic cover of the book had a window cut into it to display the registration number of the docker. Inside were pages that were numbered with each day of the week and marked with three shift periods, 8am–12 noon, 1pm–5pm and 10pm–6am, to record the shift the docker had worked. There was a voluntary overtime shift from 5pm–9pm to cover working on the passenger liners. At the end of each week the weekly pages, which recorded the number of shifts worked, were torn-out. The periods worked were stamped in red ink, but if the docker did not work they were stamped in black. The identification colour helped when recording the hours worked for assessing pay. Colin Hall: 'The "infamous" black stamp was known as a "Bump", and many a docker's wife knew with a heavy heart that when they saw their husbands putting their bikes away so early in the day or shift period, as it usually meant, "Sorry love, bumped again." However, the books were stamped whether a docker worked or not.'

For a temporary docker it was essential to get their black book as soon as they could, become a registered docker and, most importantly, gain more regular work. Colin Hall: 'It became a great occasion among the temps when one could say, "I'm due for a black book next year!" The usual period of holding a temporary book in those days was three to four years, although some had managed to get in earlier through a "wink and a nod" from someone who could pull a few strings. The trade union usually vetted these promotions rather stringently, but they had also been known to "look the other way" on certain occasions!'

Life as a 'Temp' in the 1950s

Ron Williams had started working in the docks in the early 1950s. He was the last of 15 children and his dad was a river man, a boat builder. At first he worked on the river with his dad and had his own boat at the age of 14. When he was old enough he had to do his national service and went to Malaya. That was where he met his wife, Beryl, in Singapore. She was in the WAAFS. Money was short, and Ron Williams found out that they were spending more than he could earn on the river so he went into the docks. 'To work in the docks you could have a three-day card; spend six years as a temporary dock labourer with a red book, but when you were a registered docker you had a black book. You had to do 10 years as a registered docker before you could apply for a foreman's job.' When Ron started work in the docks, however, he found there were a lot of dockers who were in their late 70s and early 80s still working because there was no pension fund or anything. Ron Williams: 'In the old days for the old boys there was no such thing as payoff, compensation or anything like that. If you were off sick you got no money and even when I went in there it was the same. I think the first time it was brought up was with the immediate gang you worked with: if anyone was sick you all put half a crown in the hat to try and make his money up. He didn't get wages he just got sick pay, which was only a bit of what he was earning.' The first payoff for these elderly men came when the bosses offered them £100 for them to leave their employment. Ron Williams and all the other young dockers were struggling to get work and were advising the older dockers to take what they offered so that they had a chance of a job.

It was 1955 when Colin Hall became a temporary docker. When he had spent his third year as a red book temporary docker he was desperate for any work to beat the 'breadline' but again found it difficult to get work because of the quiet periods within the South African fruit imports. This was the period in Southampton Docks when the South African trade (which was one of the highest sources of income for the dockers) was at its quietest. The fruit imports were now between the citrus and deciduous and the soft-fruit or stone-fruit seasons, culminating in a slacking-off of 'labour intensive work' in the port during these quiet periods between the fruit seasons.

The Big Liners, Source of Survival for Temps

Colin Hall: 'These "big-uns", however, were a way of life and the means of survival for many dockers. That is, apart from the thousands of local men who were employed as crew members and those in the ship-building industry from Harland & Woolf and J.I. Thornycroft, who were the ship repair companies in attendance at the annual "lay-ups." Those dockers with a temporary book were almost completely reliant on these "lay-ups" to keep them going until the NDLB called them back at the start of the busier times of the shipping year.'

The Cunard 'lay-ups' were when the *Queen Mary* and *Queen Elizabeth* went into dry dock for their annual overhauls. For the temporary docker the annual 'lay-ups' to refit and paint the ships in the winter months was a time when they could get much needed work. For those weeks the 'casual' workers were employed to do all the 'rough' jobs such as external painting and cleaning jobs, or acting as mates to the other tradesmen working on the ship. Colin Hall had a few periods of these: 'Bottom-of-the-barrel jobs, from being a rough painter balancing on a "bosun's chair" or on pontoons over the sides of the vessel, to eventually becoming a "coppersmith's mate" which was a little better.' He thought that laying on top of the boilers to run in new copper piping for the 'watertight bulkhead stone doors' was the 'nearest to hell I ever wanted to be.'

To get these jobs it was necessary to belong to the TGWU (Transport and General Workers Union), and it took Colin three days to get his TGWU shipyard worker's 2/29 branch union-card: 'To get picked for any temporary work on the "lay-ups" one had to parade daily in two lines opposite the old dock gate on the old "mead" to suffer the scrutiny of the works foremen and the trade union shop steward, who strutted through the centre to make their daily choice.' He describes what happened: 'Firstly it was the shop steward who would only look at people who had a TGWU 2/29 branch shipyard worker's card, and then it was the foreman's turn to see if you looked fit enough – or whether you had bought him a pint or two in the Canute before getting on parade.' The work period could be for one shift or perhaps longer, depending on the circumstances. 'Then it would be back to the "line up" for a hopeful next "lay-off" job or two.' To Colin Hall and all the other 'temps' this was certainly a 'hand-to-mouth' existence, but there was no other choice if they wanted to work. In order to establish himself as a stevedore he adapted to the 'work at anything' attitude.

Colin Hall knew his father, a senior foreman, could have 'pulled some strings' to get him in sooner, but he had refused to do so. He explains his father's reason for doing so. 'It was not only for him to keep his own good name untarnished and to keep secure his credibility as a senior-foreman who gave no favours, but as he explained, "to do it yourself will establish your own position in the docks, and you will also learn that this side of life is by no means a bed of roses, but if you do stick it out you will eventually appreciate everything that you have achieved a lot more."'

To Colin Hall these golden words were to stay with him throughout his working life and certainly proved to be correct, as whatever achievements he did make in the industry were proudly all established through his basic hard work and willingness!

The 'Perms'

The storage sheds at the quay aprons were manned by permanent staff following the traditions of the Southern Railway Company who owned and managed the docks. Colin Hall: 'These "perms", as they were called, were in the 1950s on loan from the NDLB but allocated to the sheds for manning the day-by-day services, such as maintenance and cleanliness of the storage areas. They were also available to hold key positions when the cargo went through its transit period in the sheds. These "cream" jobs were often frowned upon by the "pool" dockers, but little was said in the long run, as they themselves were ill-prepared to do many of the jobs such as sweeping and maintaining the shed-spaces, which were "day-work" paid jobs anyway, as against the more lucrative "piecework" jobs which were available on the pool. There were sheds where the "perms" did very well, especially the two Union Castle Line Inward & Outward berths as the work there was constant, being under the tightly scheduled mail-boat service.

Colin Hall's father was the senior foreman in charge at the 'outward-bound' mail-boat at 104 Berth, and Colin thought that he would give this 'perm' job a try. His father Arthur, although still adamant not to use any influence to pull his son into one of these 'plum' jobs at his particular berth, sent him to 107/8 shed. That was where the less frequent liner service, which included the United States Line, Holland American Line and Norddeutsche Lloyd, whose liners the *Bremen* and *Hanseatic*, still offered a regular liner service to the world.

Ray Strange decided that he wanted to follow the family tradition of working in the docks. Both his brothers were already in the dock industry, and his father had been a docker. The age limit for joining the Southampton Docks was 21, but in the London Docks it was 18. Ray Strange: 'I went to the port employers for an interview and was advised not to come into the dock industry. However, a TGWU officer who knew my dad was on the interview panel. He said to the rest of the panel, "No, no, you can't do that!" He told me to come up the trade union office the next morning, and he would join me up with the union. He was going to let me in anyway! So in April 1951 I went in as a dock worker, whereas the lads who weren't dockers' sons came in as temps in the fruit season and then were paid off. Good friends of mine eventually did get in and are still good friends.'

Ray Strange: 'My brothers had joined the docks when they came out of the army, and they used to "bump" very regularly at £4 a day, probably a little less than that when they started, but when I went in it was £4 a day if you didn't work all week. That was a fall back.'

There were problems with that, and Ray tried to explain to the trade union officer that it was possible to get less than £4 a day: 'I explained to him how you wouldn't get it. Cunard used to sail at 11.45 in the morning, so we got half a day's pay, went on the pool and either got another job or bumped. Cunard then changed to sailing at 12.45 so you got a morning's pay and a dinner hour which didn't equate to a day's pay. So if you got three of those through the week you could finish up with less than £4 a day.' Try as he might he could not convince the union official. Ray Strange: 'He could not see that once you had a dinner hour you couldn't attend the pool!'

From 1951 to the 1960s he attended various training jobs and progressed in his work; however, he was interested in the working of the union and always attended the union meetings on a Thursday night at 7pm. He wanted to become a shop steward and was eventually voted in by the union members at a mass meeting. He remained a shop steward until he retired in 1985.

The NDLB 'Pool' in Canal Walk

The NDLB call-stand, or the 'pool' as it was more widely known, was in Southampton's Canal Walk in the heart of the old-walls' precinct within a couple of hundred yards of the dock's main gate. It was fronted by the administration offices, with the Booking Hall at the back of the building. The main entrance to the hall was on the side of the building and was used by the dockers to enter and leave during the 'booking-on' period. Colin Hall: 'The emergency exit at the back of the hall was usually kept closed to stop any late-comers sneaking in, or to stop those having more devious intentions to "slip in and out unnoticed." The control-point was the large counter just inside the main door, where those delegated for specific jobs would hand in their work books to be later stamped to verify their employment for that shift. That was also where men were collectively bundled into gangs for those operating at the same job, either ship or quay.'

At the pool, the morning 'hopefuls' would park their bikes against the walls and on the kerbs around the building, which was gradually building up quite a crowd as the weekend overtime periods loomed up. There was always the hope for a possible Sunday's work and the chance of 'double-time' to start the week. Colin Hall: 'Despite the hundreds of bikes that were left outside the pool and around the sheds in the docks there was never any record of a bike being stolen!'

Once the labour was sorted out and sent to the various ships, those destined to work in the Old Docks (Eastern Docks) could arrive at their place of work within minutes. It was, however, more difficult for the New Docks (Western Docks) gangs as they had to travel a much longer distance to get to the vessels along this lengthy dock extension.

The New Docks had eight working berths at that time, with each berth large enough to moor ships as big as the *Queen Elizabeth* alongside. As there was no available 'laid-on' transport to get the men to the ships, it was up to each man to get to the ship as quickly as possible using whatever means available in order to start work on time, before the best, more lucrative hatches and jobs were gone. Colin Hall: 'It was all done as fairly as possible I suppose, but there were still many "dodges" cooked up by some of the gangs and foremen involved when booking-on labour for particular jobs or hatches!'

Booking-on in the cargo sheds for quayside operations took place at the window of the foreman's office. Ship's hatches, or particular operational tasks, were drawn out of the hat from pieces of paper with the number of the hatches, or the jobs such as 'hooking-on' or 'landing' the hoists of cargo on the quayside, marked on one side.

Colin Hall: 'Usually a shop steward would be in attendance in the office to guard against any "hanky-panky", but strange as it may seem they very often seemed to land themselves in the plum jobs anyway! Not that there was any fiddle, of course, but it can probably be termed as being the "perk of the job"!

The shipside draw-systems were similar but took part in the open shed or on the quayside. Colin Hall: 'A notorious fiddle on the Cape-boats, that took a long time to be found out by those on the losing end, was the "disc in the bag" trick. This happened when the foreman making the draw favoured a certain gang to get one of the best hatches. Their system was to have a cloth bag with numbered thick wooden discs inside, with each disc identifying the number of a particular hatch. The best hatch which was more financially lucrative would then be held in a corner of the bag by the foreman, who would only release it when his chosen gang made their draw, which was obviously the disc between the finger and thumb of the foreman. But like all devious things, it is usually found out by somebody talking when they are personally dissatisfied by the arrangements, such as being left out of the gang for some reason. These sleight-of-hand tricks may sound petty, or even funny, but they certainly were not funny when the difference between picking a certain hatch could mean, under the piecework system, the chance of a very high week's wage or a hatch with little piecework prospects and less overtime chances!'

A docker had to be fit and able to work as hard as the rest of their gang to get the best out of the piecework system. Colin Hall: 'The piecework system did enable the dockers to earn well in excess of their basic hourly rate, but one had to be fit and able and work within a gang of eight men like an automaton without let up until the "hook" finally stood still at the end of the shift.'

A humorous description of life inside the pool is given by Colin: 'Inside the pool, the "early birds" are already there, lined up on their usual spots in the hall. The system was that the old dock and shipside (stevedore) preferences stood along the wall facing inwards on the east side of the call-stand, while the quay-side dockers stood facing them leaving an aisle gap of about 2m wide for the PLO (Port Labour Officer) Eddy Head to patrol and make his choice of men and gangs in respect to the work in hand.

'He always made a pre-selection trip, walking down the aisle, puffing away at his pipe, nonchalantly eyeing-up what gangs there were available to fill the morning needs and perhaps mentally leaving some chosen few to "bump" in the morning and bring them back in the afternoon so that they could be picked-up for a weekend job!

'To the dockers it was almost a battle of wits to try to gauge what was the best thing to do, come in late and hope for a "bump" or take a chance and stand there in your usual place hoping that Eddy or Springhill Jack would take pity on your honesty!

'Another "dodge" on the Old Dock side was to see if Eddy Head's son was on the stand, for he was like a "Queen-Bee" with all his mates squashed around him, knowing that "papa" would certainly make sure that his own nipper would fall into the right job. Blood is thicker than water, they say, but with Eddy it was like treacle! On the New Dock side it wasn't so bad in that regard, as the other PLO Springhill Jack usually had to do what Eddy prescribed anyway, and his selection choice was done at the speed of a gazelle, just rubber-stamping the pre-planned selection all-round.

'The temporarys stood at the back end of the hall on the Old Dock side but could, of course, be directed anywhere, which was usually completed after all the regulars have been sent to work. Night work was a favourite to send these "take anything" apprentices on, and as they were paid during the week-night shifts at time and a half there wasn't too much trouble in finding plenty of "take me please" looks on their faces.

'Most dockers had their favourite jobs which they always tried to get for either suiting their pockets, or their lifestyles. With the night-shift gangs it was definitely the latter, as not only were the pressures all around you less prominent at night but there were also more choices. This was due to very many normal dockers honestly admitting that night work wasn't for them, so the "owls" had it almost all their own way.

'Regular night-work gangs were considered an almost weird lot, as they fiercely guarded their choice for operating nights only, for which Eddy Head was extremely grateful anyway as it gave him constant availability of labour for operating within the hours which few dockers would consciously choose to work in. Consequently, the earning capacity of these "night-hawks" rose considerably if they had a run on piecework operating vessels, or even on their standard hourly rate of time and a half with, of course, extra double time on weekends and holidays.

'Like the temps, the checkers and the scooter drivers, these night-shift gangs stood unofficially on their own in the pool, which really served everyone's purpose, and they were also, of course, distinguished from anyone else by the "shades" they wore to protect their eyes.

'So the morning pick-up scene was set. Gangs huddled together in their usual places, with each gang member standing in the same position as always, frightened that they wouldn't otherwise be identified when the decision was made to pick-up the labour for the job which they hoped would be going their way. There were others, of course, who liked to gamble on getting a certain job which they knew was due to be manned. These characters, such as one called Shifting Sands, who drifted up and down the back of the lines standing in their set places and waited to pounce into a particular gang of his choice when the time was ripe. Eddy Head was of course aware of this, and often these characters were left stranded at the back to receive a consolation "bump" after everyone else had been picked-up. Sometimes he did take pity on them by rewarding their all too obvious efforts to pick their jobs with a cushy job like over-the-hatch (hatchway-man), tidying-dunnage or something of that nature.

'In fairness to Eddy Head and his counterpart Springhill Jack, it was not easy for them to always suit everyone between 2,000 dockers or more, as they all wanted the best for themselves anyway! In trying to achieve this, the PLOs needed to have a good memory, a crystal-ball and expert knowledge of each and every man within the gangs, and so they very often didn't satisfy everyone in spite of their efforts.'

There were the quays at the old Empress Dock where Eddy Head, the allocating officer at the NDLB call-stand, would send his old-standing regulars in the twilight of their docker careers. Colin Hall: 'This was, after all, an easy-working strip of the docks where the Channel Island boats berthed, with the cargoes being lightly packaged seasonal products of Jersey potatoes, cauliflowers, tomatoes and, at Christmas time, boatloads of mistletoe to service the British public's Christmas celebrations. While working these old railway vessels from earlier years the wage returns were still on the piecework system during the 1950s to 1960s, and so it was a lucrative job to get, whatever the season. At that time there was no pension for the dockers, only the old-age pension, so any extra money would come in handy for any savings one could make for a retirement party.'

Getting Work as a 'Temp' from the 'Pool' from 1960

It was Terry Adams's father-in-law who introduced him to working in the docks in 1960, but he soon found out that the work was not so easy to obtain when you were a temporary attending the pool: 'It was pretty grim, because we would only get the work that was left over. Some weeks you would pick up a job, not a cream job, but it was nice. Most weeks you would be just above the bump. You had some bad weeks when you were down on the bump level and that paid only £6 odd. Rent was only 17s 6d (87.5p) in a council house so everything was a lot lower. A pint of beer was 11d (4.5p), but we didn't do too bad because my wife did sewing and when people started moving in to Thornhill everyone wanted curtains.'

Terry Adams talks about how he found a typical day as a temporary when he would join the pool to try to get a day's work: 'As a temporary you stand at the bottom end. You had four lines for the New Dock and the Old Dock. If they ran out of labour up the Old Dock they would bring the New Dock men in before we ever got in. All the regulars went to work before we went to work. If there were a couple of "not so good" jobs we got them!'

It was important to get to the pool early so that you got a good place in the line: 'If it was a Monday morning you had to be there by 7.45am or the PLO would shut the door at the back so we couldn't get in. You were only allowed in the back door if you were a temp. The PLO was either Bernard Chapmen or the ones that came before. I don't remember Eddie Head, but they said he was a fair man, but I don't know because I was never under him. He was gone by the 1960s.'

The temporary work was certainly not secure for Terry and some of his friends. If they did not get a job in the morning and were bumped they would stay fairly close to the docks so that they could go back to the pool and hope to get allocated to a job for the afternoon. Terry Adams: 'If you got allocated you went to the job. If you got bumped you went to the Edwin Jones's parks and played football, 20-a-side. I always knew it was Monday when the docks had started up and the temps were in because you would see them playing 20-a-side round the parks. You would go back dinner time and nearly every Monday go back at 8pm to hope to get on a "big-un". The *Queen Mary* would come in one week and the *Queen Elizabeth* the next week. If you got a "big-un" you would go home at 1pm and then at 8 o'clock at night you would go down to book on your jobs, whatever they were. We would be back at 12 or a bit later and we would do all the baggage for the passengers when they came off in the morning. If you had a good position you would do the baggage and then go home. If you were doing stores you would be there all night. It was good if you got on stores because you were back the next night so that gave you two nights' pay, so you didn't mind.'

The Advantage of Being in a Good Gang

If you were in a good gang, and the PLOs knew and trusted them, then more work would be available for the gang. Terry Adams: 'The PLOs knew the gangs, and if he wanted three gangs we would be picked, because we were the Old Dock No. 1 gang. Then there was the New Dock No. 1 gang and so on. You needed good equipment. I know two of them up at the New Dock had their own truck and used to take the wheel off it at night so that it wasn't used by others! Once you picked up a gang you stuck to the gang. I was in an eight-man gang, but there are only two of us left now. You still went to the pool when you had the NDLB. When you picked up a job with the gang you followed the job right through. You didn't go to the pool again till it was finished. We could be loading 36 Berth and, say we were No. 1 loading gang, we would stay there until the last bit of fruit went off the deck. You would do, more likely, a full week there.'

Bicycles were used mainly by the dockers to get to the different parts of the dock they had been allotted to work, but they were also to make sure their gang got the 'good' work. Terry Adams: 'We all had bikes, and the man with the fastest bike booked you on in the pool. You had to book a gang of eight so you got the man with the fastest bike to get to the pool to get you on. It was funny because all the rubbishy jobs were left to last. That was the system, you took it and that was what it was.' However, it was not easy cycling around the docks, and men often fell off their pushbikes, especially when getting their wheels stuck in the railway lines!

Colin Hall: 'The perks in this particular section of 107–108 Berths came mostly from the overtime to cover the "odd-hour" arrivals and departures of the calling vessels, and this consisted mostly of handling passengers' baggage when the passengers arrived in the sheds for Customs and Emigration and also when they disembarked. The "Whelks", a tipping arrangement between passengers and porters, was the icing on the cake but with obviously no set rate, for this otherwise "part-of-the-job" service the chance of receiving a reward was entirely at the good will of the passenger.'

'The perms, however, were usually in the best position to be able to isolate the most probable chance of receiving the best tips as they were in close contact with the top travel agents, who in turn had been hired by the top-paying passengers to look after their interests in the formalities of moving through the authorities and the handling of their personal effects. In these cases it was usually the agent who "settled-up" the porterage, with the perm receiving more for that one job than those from the pool received throughout the whole operational period. Once the vessel had left the berth the perm had to work many extra hours cleaning, sweeping and preparing the shed for the next ship's arrival, which might not be for another week or so.'

Timber Cargo

Ron Williams spent 10 years unloading timber ships at Town Quay and at Howard's Timber, Northam Bridge, from 1954 to 1964. He did not always work at the Southampton Docks: 'You were picked up at the Docks Labour Board Pool, and wherever you were sent you went! I've been down to Poole unloading outside the Jolly Sailor for Sydenham's Timber Yard. You would go down by bus in the morning, unload the timber and come back at night. If we were short of labour in Southampton they would see if there were any men available at Poole, and they would bring them up to do the quick jobs like baggage jobs from the *Queen Mary* and other liners.' The men who came up from Poole were only temporary because they had their own work to do down at Poole and also at Weymouth.

There was plenty of varied work in the docks, and the men were never short of work. Ron Williams: 'It could be at Town Quay or wherever the ship was tied up, whatever type of timber. If it were lumber cargo for piles it would be 40 or 41 Berth, one of the big open berths. Railway sleepers, decking, we used to unload everything. If there were no timber ships you went general cargo, which could be unloading cars. At one time dockers used to go out to the British American Tobacco factory in Millbrook to unload tobacco that had been brought from the docks in lorries. You could be sent anywhere. On general cargoes it could be anything. The American ships used to come in with the PX for their troops, their equivalent of our NAAFI. We used to unload that for their various camps. Cars, whatever there was we unloaded it. Whatever would fit in a ship was put in. There are photos of railway locomotives being loaded to go to America.'

To unload timber many dockers wore a shoulder pad, and when Colin Hall worked in the timber shed he underwent the learners' introduction of establishing a layer of hardened skin under the thick leather pad strapped to the shoulder and around the chest for carrying lengths of cut timber. His leather pad was given to him by his Uncle Harold, along with his 'hand hook' as was the tradition within dockland families, prior to his uncle moving to a more 'age related' position in control of the customs and excise 'cage' at the cross-channel boat's berth at Berth 22–23. The shoulder pad was mostly used in those days at the Old

Berth 40 being used as a timber berth in 1929. (Courtesy of ABP)

Docks' timber shed, where lengths of timber were stored to customer's marks and bills of lading. They were loaded onto rail trucks or road vehicles by carrying the measured lengths on the shoulder and placing them onto the transport as per delivery requirements. Due to the piecework era the unrelenting 'getting on with the job' was the name of the game regardless of splinters, for which the advice given was: 'No time for first-aid, you've got matches, burn-it-out!'

It was hard work and was often made worse by the low number of dockers who would be employed to unload the timber ships. Ray Strange: 'The manning scales were always very low on the timber boats, and they were hard graft, especially the Archangel timber from Russia. They used to stow it on deck when it was snowing and when it got here you had a job to move it because it was ice packed. You could see their old fag ends because they used to roll their fags in newspaper! A timber merchant once told me that sometimes when they were thawing it you could find a bullet, probably from the war when the Germans were in Russia.'

There were times when the shipping companies tried to avoid paying the dockers a day's pay. Ray Strange explains the situation of working on the deck of a timber boat when it was raining hard and being told by the employers: 'We don't want you to get wet and we don't want our cargo to get wet, go on home and come back at 1pm. We would then ask if we would be paid, but the employers would say "Oh no!" We would say, "Ok we'll see you tomorrow morning at 8 o'clock", that's how we used to drag that one out. If the employer paid us off then we would get a day's pay.'

Getting Clearance to Board the Ships

Once a ship had docked the stevedores would have to wait on the dockside until given clearance. Ron Williams describes what happens the moment clearance is given for the dockers to board: 'We weren't allowed on board until the yellow flag came down. That was clearance, but the yellow duster meant the doctor was still on board. When the duster came down we were the first up the gangway. The first place you look for is the working alleyway which is the main thoroughfare for the workmen, the union room and stores. You went through there to go to the hatches and cargo holds. When you went past the Indian, Lascars quarters you would see dozens of bike frames being painted. They used to come ashore and buy a Raleigh bike, one even bought an old postman's bike and was made up because he had a rack on the front. You'd see a Singer sewing machine, and if you had a bike and a sewing machine your wife was in business.'

Loading the 'Big-uns!'

Ron Williams: 'I used to load the *Queen Mary* and *Queen Elizabeth*. They carried cargo as well; mail, cars, gold and silver. You could go three or four days loading the Christmas mail from the US to England and England to the US. You had two holds for'ard in the *Queen Mary* and the Pig and Whistle, the crew bar. You went aboard across the Pig and down in the lifts and there was cargo space down below on the after deck. On the *Queen Mary* in one of her hatches, I think it was No. 2, they used to lower a platform down to half a hatch and you used to load mail and money in there.'

At other times when the 'Big-uns' were in port Colin Hall describes what it was like working on a night shift. 'The temps and the regular night-shift gangs were those who were usually picked for the overtime jobs on the big liners. These were the twilight-gangs who didn't want to do anything strenuous, but were happy to grab the jobs on a "one-night-on, one-night-off" basis should the circumstances be right. This was especially prevalent with the stores gangs who could be employed the whole three nights when these huge "Cunarders" were in port. The amount of stores loaded on each trip was tremendous, with usually two store gangs working day and night, with also the 'wet' stores for the Pig and Whistle to keep the crew and passengers happy on these unique Ocean Liners.'

The stores were loaded via the side access of the vessels. Stores were transported up portable electric conveyors between ship and shore, with the packages being lifted onto the wooden-slatted belts and then lifted off at the other end and transported into the storage spaces on the ship by hand-trucks or the ship's four-wheeled trolleys. It was very much a stop-start operation, as every package had to be checked for quality, amount and the order of use on the voyage, especially with the perishable products, which on these top-class vessels meant that only the very best would be accepted. 'Although these store gangs were not piecework paid, the overtime involved was enough to put some jam on the bread, and the chance of an early night was the other sweetener to satisfy some of the layabouts!'

Ray Strange remembers working on the *Queen Mary* or *Queen Elizabeth* when they came in and they would be asked: '"Where are you?" We would reply, "In No. 2 hatch, what have we got?" Maybe it would be a 100 ton which would take about two nights to get rid of. Day work money of course, not piecework money!' However, when the American cargo boats came in there was a different story. 'We would be discharging them, and we found out that the men who swept out after we had finished were getting more money than us and ours was more hard graft. We kicked up about that and got it onto piecework.'

When the 'Big-uns' were due to sail the klaxons would sound to warn that the liner was due to sail. Colin Hall: 'I wonder how many people there are today who can remember the signalled three blasts on those giant klaxons, which could be heard clearly all over the town, to alert the crew members in the Juniper Berry, the Royal Standard or the Coach and Horses in East street and other public houses in the docks area that the ship was due to sail in an hour's time?'

When Piecework was Introduced

During their time with ordinary cargo ships the labour was casual, and dockers would attend the pool twice a day to get work. They were paid a daily wage on the days worked, regardless of the amount of cargo they were loading or unloading, but then piecework was introduced. Don Archbold was very philosophical about its introduction. When his boss asked him what he thought about it said 'No trouble, lets just have a go.' The first ship they got was a Ben Line ship. All the dockers were watching him to see how it was done. 'There was no problem and we worked out the different types of cargo, so much for this cargo and so much for that cargo. We worked out how much tonnage was on the ship and that was piecework.'

The piecework system was on many occasions the cause of disputes, mainly because of the attitude of many to earn as much as they could, while they could. After the way dockers had been treated in the past by the employers one can understand their reasons; however, the piecework system was in effect more popular with the shippers and employers because they got more cargo moved more quickly, achieving in the end greater profits, but for those officials of the trade unions who could see beyond the immediate situation they knew that it was not the best deal for their members. Colin Hall: 'Those "right-thinking" trade unionists, who really had the interests of the dockers at heart, fought against the piecework system with its "quick-fix" methods for putting bread on the table. They concentrated their efforts into trying to educate the men into rather pushing for a realistic basic wage, with pensions, sick-pay, etc, to ensure that they and their families would be looked after over the long-term.'

Terry Adams talks about his experiences on the piecework system: 'If you got the fruit boats, the "R" Boats we called them, that was when the fruit season started and you got a hatch with 60,000 grapes on the top deck, the next deck down you might have 20,000 apples and the next deck down 20,000 pears. The more of that fruit you got out the more money you got. It wasn't good pay, you had to take, say, about 10–12,000 apples out to get a decent day's pay. It was all down the hatch, all roller work on to a board. It wasn't just pick it up and put it down.'

Working as a docker was very demanding due to the shift work and the fact that the work was ongoing 24 hours a day. Some preferred to work only nights and some just days. Colin Hall: 'Apart from the physical side, the constantly changing circumstances and resultant adjustments, which must often be made within the time constraints in the shipping world, is the basic driving force which creates tensions and extreme efforts far above the considered levels of normality. In the cargo-handling world ships arrive and depart on a 24-hour basis, and the stevedore has to facilitate these requirements.'

The diverse background and environment that the men work under was the core principle for commencing most negotiations by the trades-union officers, as it not only brought into focus the often hazardous conditions, but would also determine how the work was to be achieved within the constraints and the trade demands to complete the job as speedily as possible. These time factors were usually covered at the pre-planning meetings prior to the vessel's arrival, with usually the trade union representative (shop steward) also in attendance to ensure that the basic interests of the men were being attended to throughout the duration of the job. Safety is always the prime principle behind any negotiated settlement and the pre-planning of operations, which required careful decisions borne from long and sound experience from the shop steward, with a determination to ensure that everything in this regard was securely in place.

Colin Hall: 'It must, however, be counted that with the greed of piecework in those days, with its financial rewards being the considered key motivator for these disputes, it is no wonder that when the piecework system was done away with relative "peace" in the other sense became the order of the day.'

Size and Work of the Docks Labour Force

Due to the large amount of cargo coming in there was a requirement for a large labour force. At the time the dockers were paid piecework, so the incentive was the more cargo they handled the more they earned. Harold Lloyd: 'I enjoyed every minute, every day, every year, but when they cut the piecework out, that was when things started going haywire. They couldn't care less. In piecework you got paid by the tonnage. The bosses didn't want to get rid of the piecework, they loved it because they knew they would get more done. I used to look forward to getting to work, especially when we were on piecework. You had the comedians, and there was one bloke who, when we were unloading oranges, spent the time telling jokes instead of working and at the end of the day he would say "How much did we earn today!?" I told them that they were crazy because they were laughing at him and doing all the work and he was doing nothing and was getting paid for it. At the dock gate you would have the offices, and if you had been working on a banana boat you could ask how much you earned the previous day and they would tell you. You could then work out how much you had earned in the week.'

To load, unload and distribute the goods to different parts of the country it was necessary to have a large work force in the docks. Harold Lloyd remembers, 'There were a large number of dockers working in Southampton at the time. You had loading gangs, discharging gangs, porters loading lorries to take goods to different parts of the country, fruit, apples, oranges and all kinds of fruit. All the fruit was taken through Port Health. They would check the condition of the fruit and come with thermometers and open up a case to check the fruit, and they also measured the thickness of the oranges. Some people used to come down from the markets, like the London markets, and if there was one orange out of a box, they paid a £1 for the box. When the fruit season started the Cape boats would come into the Old Docks as well. Some would come in and unload and load again to go out, but the fruit boats just came in with the fruit and went away again empty.'

The Port Health maintained a strict check on meat and fish before it was distributed. Harold Lloyd, 'With the meat boats that came over, the Port Health was there and they would look at the meat before it was distributed. With the frozen prawns that came over in container ships the Customs would say, "Open that and take out 12 boxes." They would then inspect them. Sometimes Customs would let us have them after the boxes had been opened, and sometimes they were given to the seagulls!'

PX Stores

It was decided to use 108 shed for a regular service of old Lykes Line's vessels to bring the PX stores for the American forces stationed in this country. Colin Hall: 'This was like Christmas every day for these permanent dockers at 108, with the vessels arriving and departing as fast as they could to move the goods around. The families of the US forces in Brize-Norton and other airfields and US bases in England were also moving backwards and forwards to the States, as the personnel were discharged and replaced when the de-mob sessions set in. This meant that their personal effects, which were then cased in ply-board containers of standard size, usually 8ft (2.4m) x 6ft (1.8m) x 4ft (1.2m), arrived by road transport onto the quay apron and were either put into the shed or directly shipped onto the vessel, if one was alongside at that time. Whatever the situation, the unloading, stacking and loading the vessel was, of course, under the piecework system, and as these cases were relatively light in structure and internal weight they could be very speedily handled, with sometimes four being slung at one time.'

The cargo was handled under the piecework system, and goods which were calculated as having a 'stowage-factor' of above 40c.ft to the ton fell under the 'space measurement' tonnage rate. Although not so high a rate as for 'deadweight' cargoes, the goods could be moved much faster, and therefore the earning capacity was high. This was good money for the stevedores and the perms in the shed, who received and assembled the cased goods prior to loading.

Shed 108 and part of the passenger shed at Berth 107 were usually full of cartons, boxes, and crates. The perms' job of sorting these mountains of packages in the sheds into tiers, to be sent to their respective destination bases, was under a special handling rate, which also took into account their accepted honesty, which could be really stretched to the limit at times!

This period in the late 1950s was the time when the 'Barbie' dolls were first introduced, and due to their flimsy packaging they were often littered around the shed floor, along with her first wardrobe, jewellery and cosmetics etc. Eventually the volume of work necessitated that they open up another berth to assist in handling the PX cargoes. So Berth 34 in the Old Docks became the reserve area for mostly household goods.

An example of the onset of disputes concerning piecework rates is given by Colin Hall involving the men working on Berth 108 in the New Docks, where at that time the PX stores were discharged. The men were unloading a large consignment of canned beer that had been stowed in the two deep tanks, but due to the small access at the top of the tanks the time taken to get the cases out seriously affected the agreed piecework rate. Colin Hall: 'The result was that the gangs in the hold were complaining heavily, due to the small packages and the length of time being used to discharge the small hoists, which meant that they were losing money in relation to the piecework tonnage rate which covered these cargoes. The men threatened to stop work unless something was done about it.'

Colin Hall, who was then a shop steward, was called to deal with the problem. He tried to reason with the employer, but the employer's representatives at that time were well known for their unbending manner, especially as most issues revolved around financial matters to which they always reacted negatively! After a number of fruitless attempts to get a meeting arranged it was necessary to inform the official trade union representative and port employers' association, but the union representative had already left on a long weekend with his family. The shop steward had no option but to report the lack of progress back to the men who then immediately walked off the ship, informing him that he had better be there when their night-shift was due to start to carry the dispute forward until 'somebody listened!' This was not successful, however, because when he arrived to meet the night shift he was met 'by an unknown sea of bright young faces of apparently 'temporary' dockers, instead of the regular 'night-hawks'. After listening intently to his reasoning, they were then politely told what to do, as they had not had a job for nearly a week. They were glad of the opportunity to do anything, but with the 'treasure trove' of thousands of cans of 'Budweiser' and 'Schlitz' beer it was too much to expect of them to now make a considered retreat from the job!

Colin Hall retreated as there was no more he could do, but the 'dispute' was seen as unofficial and 'was forgotten as quickly as it had started, but with unfortunately a red flush appearing on certain people's faces, and a black-mark against their records!'

The unloading of PX ships was not always popular with some of the dockers. Terry Adams: 'Then there was the PX, they were different altogether. They were joyless ships. You would be on a ship, and all of a sudden the mate of the ship would look down and ask, "What's the matter, you are all quiet down there, the beer no good this time?" No one was singing, and in those days they always had beer on, Budweiser, but we still used to get the cargo out.'

Ingenious ways were planned to create a 'bar' for refreshments. Terry Adams: 'When you were on the quay you used to stack everything in lines. In the middle there would be a square and the stacks all round, and there would be the bar and you could go and have a beer, piece of Christmas cake, plum jam, anything. The yanks had everything, and there would be the dockie sitting there with a Budweiser and a big cigar!'

The dockers knew that piecework would come to an end, especially with so much cargo being palletised, even though there had always been trucks and the old-style fork trucks; however, even the dockers realised that if you put everything on the pallets

Working on the quayside. (Courtesy of M. Beckett Collection)

it would be easier to move around the sheds with fork trucks. Previously the dockers would take the cargo off the sling as it came off the ship and take it into the shed. From the shed floor it was loaded onto a lorry, but every move was more of a time factor. Goods on a pallet could be moved more effectively and more efficiently. The dockers seemed to accept this quite well and many of them had to learn to drive fork trucks, but an added incentive was that they got more money for being a fork-truck driver!

The Union Castle ships in Southampton

Another perm's job was assisting the cooper in the wine bay. Jimmy Leach, the resident cooper at the time, came from Liverpool, had learnt the trade as a boy and had been especially brought in to manage and service the barrels of South African import wines and brandies. Colin Hall was able to learn a few things from Jimmy Leach about repairing wooden casks and how to arrange consignments for Customs inspection, which gave him another set of skills to carry with him.

The job for the perms in the wine bay was to lay out the barrels according to marks and consignments in perfectly straight lines with their bungs facing up which were then checked visually for any leakages or damage. Colin Hall: 'These straight lines were measured accurately using a length of white chalked string, which was stretched taught over the shed floor to indicate where the consignment marked-end of the barrels would be, then plucked so that the string came forcibly into contact with the floor, which then created the straight line.' Casks were held in place (chocked) with wooden wedges, allowing enough room for the Customs officer to walk all around each cask and check for the general condition of the cask.

On the morning of the inspection the bungs were removed, and the perm on duty 'would carry-out this duty using a "flogging-hammer", which is a slim/flat wooden hammer-head, fixed to a long, flexible cane handle [2ft 6ins in length] which was operated by striking either side of the bung several times until it sprang-loose.' They were then laid alongside the bung-hole until the excise duty officer examined the cask for contents measurement, followed by a sample dip to test for quality and alcohol content.

This was an opportunity for those working in the wine bay, led by the cooper and his assistant, to 'sample' the best sherry. The Customs tended to turn a blind-eye to this as long as it did not get out of hand!

Colin Hall recalls an amusing story of a scooter driver who would lean against a cask and in his hand have an end of a long plastic tube which he inserted into the open cask. The plastic tube went up his overcoat sleeve and out of the neck of his jacket and he would suck away at the contents in the cask!

The 'Jungle Juice!'

Terry Adams talks about the 'Jungle' (sherry) on the Cape boats: 'They used to tip it out into a bucket. Two buckets, one for the quayside, one for the shipside. I've been up at 202 Berth on a wet night with 13 men and a big bucket of "Jungle". You would see one of the men standing up on the bales of wool stacked up very high, dancing away, naked!'

Getting home was not always easy for a docker who had been on the 'Jungle'. 'They used to have railway wagons and put them up in the sidings and there was one bloke that had too much to drink. The gang put him in one of the wagons on the straw at about 5.30am, and when they came back that night he was still there asleep!'

The gang would try to look after a docker if he had had too much to drink, but getting home was not always easy after being on nights! Terry Adams: 'If one of the gang got too drunk they would shove him in a corner and make him go to sleep. They used to look after him, get him out of the way, and then when we finished work they would get him home. We didn't have cars, just bikes, but we still saw him home. Mind you, the number of times men fell off their pushbikes through drink was nobody's business. The worst thing when riding your bike in the docks was going in the railway lines and messing your wheels up.'

Unloading the sherry and wine from the ships was not always an easy task, but the ship-board operations of the stevedore were helped by liquid refreshment. Colin Hall: 'Usually the "chambers" at No. 3 hatch on the mail boats were the favoured stowage positions for the barrels, due to the added security of the "lock-up" arrangements. This was, of course, no problem for the experienced stevedore, for it just needed a couple of the lads to keep the hatch watchman distracted and the ever present "gimlet" was put to use to bore a couple of holes, and by using a fire-bucket you could quickly decant enough to keep them all happy until the end of the shift!'

Imported wines and sherry.

However, getting the barrels of wine out of the hold was difficult in those days because they were heavy and because of the amount of room the dockers had to move around in. Ray Strange: 'In the dirty rooms, No. 3 hatches, they carried South African wine, but there was a chamber door too narrow to roll them so you had to upend them to get them out. They were about 3cwt a piece, and they used to put them in the dirty room or somewhere awkward, and they would have cartons over the top. You knew you would get nothing for that, but you had to clear that to get down to where the cash was, and that wasn't great. That's the homewards.'

Colin Hall: 'There was an unwritten law, which was that "the job must go on normally" otherwise, not only would their piecework earnings be affected, but it would raise the alarm for the "law" to intervene – which no one wanted. Secret stores of bottles were plentiful around the shed at 102, and it became a game to outwit the Dock's police by continuously changing hiding places. Very often, it became so complex that one would forget where the heck it was this time!'

Sadly, drinking while at work or before starting work did result in some deaths. Harold Lloyd: 'I know of about five dockers that were killed, mostly with drink. They were on the night stand and reported at 8pm to 6am. They would turn up "boozed up", and along the quayside one fell over. He was taken by the tide from the Container Terminal to Hythe, and it was three days before they found the body. His mate was also a "boozer", and he kept his money in a leather pouch around his neck, and they found him down there as well. There was another one who had been drinking brandy, they had opened some brandy in the cargo ship and had been drinking it. Then he wanted to go for a swim, so he went round to the dry dock and rode his bike round and undressed and they never found him. That was until one day a container ship's captain reported to the police that there was a body floating in the water, and it turned out to be him. There was another one who had been drinking in a Shirley pub while he was off duty. He tied himself to his motorbike and rode down to the docks, straight over the side where he used to work. They found him about four or five months afterwards after searching everywhere for the body. Eventually some of the army divers from Marchwood found him still tied to his bike. I saw his bike with the rope still tied to the handlebars. He must have had some trouble at home or somebody had upset him or something like that. He was a bit of a loner anyway and didn't mix well.'

A certain amount of turning a 'blind eye' went on about what happened in the docks, but for anyone trying to take goods out of the docks then they were in serious trouble. 'If you got caught taking goods out of the gates then that was your job. If you were a temp with a red book then your feet didn't touch the ground. You just had to forget it. If you were a black book, well the union might fight a bit for you.'

Jim Brown: 'It was well known that if you slipped the docks policemen half a crown inside the dock pass he would let you through. All the dock workers and crews knew that. We in the "real" police knew it went on and were upset because we never accepted anything from anybody (other than cups of tea in cafés), as we felt it reflected on us. One very strict and conscientious BTDB PC once checked a Customs officer and found a load of stuff. There was then a "war" between docks police and Customs, with each checking the other for some time!'

Dockers' Perks

It was possible for the agents to be given some boxes of fruit that could be sold on cheaply to the dockers. However, not everyone played by the rules, and there were some men who would try to get more than they were entitled to. 'You had a lot of fiddles, not everybody is honest. For instance, at the time the grapes came in they were packed in a wooden box, and at each end was a strip to keep the lid on, and they were packed in straw. The shipping agents would be given about 20 boxes a day, and 20 men could buy a box for £1. If they were not satisfied with the box they just undid the lid, took the straw out, pushed the grapes up and got another box and filled up the one box, so they had two boxes of grapes in one.' This also happened with avocado pears (which were dear to buy at the time) and apples. 'They were in trays, and the men would lift the trays and cover the box with avocado pears, put the apples on top and put the trays back on again. They were greedy about it, and the police cottoned on to it and that was that.'

A similar thing happened with the Fyffes banana boats. Harold Lloyd, 'The ship would come in, and at that time the bananas weren't boxed, they were on stalks. Fyffes allowed the dockers to buy a bunch of bananas or a stalk, but some of them weren't satisfied with that, they wanted to take the bunch or stalk, and when they were found out it was stopped. They even stopped giving them to the hospitals as well. All the fruit that was yellowing went up to Millbrook where the Container Terminal is now and was buried there.'

Other Cargo

Harold Lloyd: 'Then of course you had the wool and skins that came off the ship. When it arrived it was in its raw state. The skins were made into leather and then sent back to South Africa! The wool was baled up, and the same happened. You had snake skins and you had frogs which they sent over to France for eating.

'In one shed you had all the mail, about 5,000 bags of mail, then the fruit and then the wool and skins. The sheds were two-storey, so there was the fruit on the lower deck, and on the top deck all the wool and skins were unloaded. When the fruit came in it was marked M&S, which was Marks & Spencer's, or BHS for British Home Stores.'

Learning how to unload the cargoes was a skill for the young men joining the gangs. Some had other ideas of how to do it! Harold Lloyd: 'When they brought in the dockers' sons to work in the gang I was a charge hand on the Cape boats and had some young chaps with me. We opened the hatch and it was loaded to the top. They said that they would go and get a fork truck. I told them that you don't get a fork truck here you handle every box! The crane would drop a big board down, and you would get about 40-50 cases on and lift it out. When you had cleared a square, you dug in. That was when they thought they would get a fork truck to go in; however, after a while the cargo became palletised and then you cleared a square and could send a fork truck down and clear it out.'

The cold stores were in Millbrook at the other end of the dock, and it could be dangerous unloading some of the cargoes, especially frozen meat. Harold Lloyd: 'There was a lot of trouble on the refrigerated meat boats berthed at the cold store. A lot of the meat was in cartons, and you could easily slip up and break your leg there. The system was to clear the square in the hold, and as you were walking around on it all the time you could easily slip up because of the ice. It was also very hard work. Gangs would be loading the meat from the cold store onto lorries to go all over the country.'

Ron Williams: 'The Union Castle would bring a ship such as the *Windsor Castle* in on a Monday morning to 102 Berth, and she would have eight gangs on the ship for eight hatches. There would also be eight gangs on the quay to meet them. You start unloading, and you would also have a gang come on for the night shift from 8pm to 6am. Five to six days are taken unloading that ship of its cargo, which could be fruit. All that fruit used to have to come out of the hatch, onto the quay and into the shed to be sorted, and then there would be gangs loading it on railway trucks and lorries. They were called the loading gangs. It used to take a week to discharge that ship. Then she would move up to 104 Berth and start loading. It would take another week to load it, night and day, and she would sail from 104 Berth smack on time at 1pm Friday lunchtime. The next one was in again on the following Monday. In the meantime you had one in unloading, one up at 104 loading and another sailing. The one loading would work all the weekend. It would start filling up from Saturday morning or Saturday night onwards till it sailed the following Friday. Deck cargo, animals, horses and railway trucks would be on deck. It was fascinating, and I used to love it working all the different cargoes. You used to look forward to doing it.'

'Jumbo' Cargo

There were some strange cargoes that the dockers would have to load on to the ships. Colin Hall relates the story of one gang of dockers who had been responsible for loading a heavy locomotive on to a P&O ship with the floating crane earlier that week.

P&O *Canton*. (Courtesy of Mick Lindsay Collection)

The PLO Mickey Hart, who had a very good memory and a dry sense of humour, remembered this and met the gang. Mickey Hart said to the gang: 'Another P&O job for you lot at 106 Berth, you're just the gang for the heavy-lifts.' After booking-on at the berth with the stevedore foreman, they asked what cargo was to be loaded and were told: 'You have to ship five elephants on the fore-deck.'

Despite the number of very experienced dockers in the gang, no one had ever shipped elephants before. They discussed how they could accomplish the task: 'What gear are we to use?' They realised that horse or cattle boxes are either too narrow or did not have enough doors. They considered slings with belly-bands and wondered if there was a special rig made for the job. Someone joked: 'Maybe we should break-out the "Jumbo" derrick!' The foreman was puzzled and admitted that, in all his time in the docks, he also had never shipped elephants before. 'Go and have a cup of tea lads, and I'll find out the elephants' individual weights, so we can work out whether to use rope or wire slings with belly-bands and spreaders, which will probably do the job OK.' said the foreman.

They were surprised when a quarter of an hour later they went back to the P&O *Canton* and saw the five elephants standing on the fore-deck nuzzling straw. 'How the heck did they get on board?' they asked the foreman. 'Which crane did you use and who landed them on deck?' The foreman burst out laughing and said, 'That Chipperfield's Circus bloke over there just walked them up the crew's gangway and along the deck. He put them in a line and hitched them up trunk to tail, with the smallest elephant at the front, and simply walked them up the open-topped gangway like entering the circus ring, with no fuss at all'.

They gang returned to shore and were amused at the very harassed checker on the quayside who was refusing to sign for the elephants because he had not counted them aboard. It materialised that the 'Chipperfield's Circus bloke' was Colonel Bill, better known as 'Elephant Bill' of the 14th Army Elephant Company in Burma during World War Two.

Sometimes cars were loaded into the Union Castle ships, and to do that the car would be driven over a frame and lifted up by crane and lowered into the hold. Terry Adams: 'In the Cape boats you would have one or two cars in the square. That is the hatch where you look down, the last square in the hatch as you look down. Everything had to come into the square. As you took your hatch boards up for each deck square there was a ladder right down each deck. When discharging the cargo you would start on the top deck and take your hatch boards up, lift the beams and then on down to the next hatch. When loading you started on the bottom deck and worked your way up, replacing the beams and hatch boards as you completed loading each cargo hold and then start loading the next hold.'

Money also used to be loaded on the Union Castle ships: 'We used to load money on the ships on Fridays. It used to come from the printers, paper money all in boxes from somewhere in Hampshire. We were told that it was no good opening one of the boxes because the money was only printed on one side and the other side had to be printed out in South Africa. What they used to do is send the plates for the printing on the next ship.'

Ray Strange well remembers the hard work involved in working on the Union Castle ships: 'There were the homeward bounders, they were hard graft. If you were shipside and the foreman had a cloth bag with numbers in there, from one to seven, for the hatches. I know for a fact that the best ones were held by the checker foreman. Anyone would know that he would have hold of that one because it was a good hatch. The best hatches were two, three, five and sometimes possibly six because you were always there after a Sunday. If you got two, three or five you knew you were in for a Sunday. If she was dry docking they would pretty well have everyone in because she would dry dock early on a Tuesday morning. She would come in on a Friday in those days so therefore you had to discharge that ship night and day to get her in the dry dock. Sometimes she went in dry dock with cargo still in her, because you couldn't do her in time.'

Unloading the fruit ships was popular because the fruit was paid on tonnage, but the payment was different depending on the type of fruit. Ray Strange: 'You would have to do about 22,000 cases of grapes to get a reasonable days work. Oranges were OK because you were paid on tonnage. They were 100lb (45kg) boxes and you could discharge 2 ton a time so you could earn money on those. As you came down the fruit scale, lemons were paid the same as oranges, but they were in half cases and were awkward to handle and carry because you had to take two cases so you couldn't shift those as quick. Eggs were the same price as oranges, down to plums and peaches which were paid at rubbishy prices.'

By the time the men reached the lower holds there was some of the not so pleasant cargo to move, but the more unpleasant it was to move the better you were paid! Ray Strange: 'Then down to the lower holds and you would get into the skins. Wool didn't pay well, but skins did. You used to try to hold off the skins till Sunday when they were two for one, to get the weight! Invariably they would stow skins and wool with cartons on top, if you can believe it. That meant you had to get rollers down, Yo-Yo's we called them, to clear your cartons so you could get to the wool, break it all down again, let the wool go and then set it all up again to get at the cartons to clear them. They paid next to nothing!'

The outward bounders were more popular with the dockers, although they were still hard work. Ray Strange: 'The outward bound was a better job altogether because it was space tonnage. With the cased car, say a Hillman, which was the biggest we could handle in size but not necessary in weight, what we didn't want was dead weight. These were the tractors which they sent in twos. They would weigh about 3 ton or more, and you had to roll them back to the bulkhead. If you landed them in the square you may have to move them about 30 to 40ft back up against the bulkhead. We used to do that like the Romans, with steel pipe rollers underneath. Push them, bring the pipe from the back put it in the front and so on. We used to get two at a time to rush it on a bit. Ferguson Tractors were not too good for us, and we used to get paper going out to South Africa. It was all shapes and sizes that was dead weight, with two of us having to lift them up, and they were 3cwt (152.4kg). On the outward bound if you got the right cargo you could earn a few bob.'

The docker's job was a dangerous one, and Ray gives one example of how dangerous it could be: 'Another of our jobs was loading copper, which used to go on the lower deck or bottom deck. Each unit used to weigh about 80lb (36.3kg). We used to get two of those because it was quicker than one and they were taken out in eights, eight in each chain. It was a dangerous job because chains don't lift too well and if the copper hit a combing and the load drops you don't know where it is going to land. It broke one old docker's leg. The dockers' job was second to the miners' as a dangerous job.'

For most dockers, getting on the Cape berths was well sought after, and Colin Hall was fortunate to be transferred to the 'Inward-Cape' Berth 102 when a vacancy arrived. The Cape boat berths were the most sought-after due to their regular piecework services, but it was a matter of waiting for someone to literally die before you could get in.

The perms' piecework jobs at this berth were plentiful but were mostly involved with 'laying-out' import cargoes in the sheds according to marks and consignments. On a vessel's arrival there was the system of keeping the flow constant while blending-in with cargoes from other hatches in the spaces allotted. It became a work of art, requiring good co-ordination with the 'layer-out' in the adjacent hatch.

The sheds at the Union Castle 102 Berth were two-storey, and hatch cargoes could differ. For instance, baled wool and skins were unloaded and stored on the top-floor storage-area at 102, and during certain times of the year, when shiploads of wool and skins were being imported in large quantities, it became a specialist's job to keep separate the dozens of importers' marks from the different hatches, which could often evolve into a storage nightmare. Colin Hall soon became adept at working out a system, however, and was eventually given the task of 'loading-away' the receivers' consignments.

Gold Missing from the *Capetown Castle*

It was in February 1965 that £100,000 of gold ingots went missing on the *Capetown Castle*. Ron Williams was a stevedore working shipside on the day that the theft was discovered: 'I was on the *Capetown Castle* when the gold went missing. It didn't go missing from Southampton, it was already missing. They stopped everyone going off the ship. What happened was that they were unloading the gold and the last bloke came out carrying the box. There was a box with two ignots in as big as wall bricks. Every one was numbered and you showed it to the officer, he would shout it out and there would be the checkers with three or four officers writing the numbers down. Then one says, "That's the last one." "What do you mean that's the last one? There's no more in there!" "Oh, we are so many short – nobody move." No good searching us, you couldn't carry one of the bricks in your pocket. They went out and checked the railway wagons, where it was put. There were police dogs, everything out there. They counted it up, it was definitely missing. When the lads went down the next day and went into one of the fruit rooms they found the empty boxes. One of the crew that "waited the hold" and some other guys had gone in through the air vent. They took the grill off and pulled the gold out and when they put the flap back up they plastered it over with tape and painted it. When they found the gold it was cemented in the mast house because she was going to the breakers that trip, she was finished. They found so many bars of it cemented in with quick-drying cement and the rest of it was in the kids' sandbox on deck.'

Another ex-docker remembers the missing gold from the *Capetown Castle*, although he was in South Africa when the robbery was discovered. Harold Lloyd had left the docks and had gone back to sea, sailing on the *Windsor Castle* as chief laundryman and was in Cape Town when the *Capetown Castle* was unloading in Southampton. The CID travelled to South Africa to interview Harold Lloyd because he had been a stevedore in Southampton: 'They asked me how far the gold could be carried. I told them that it was only a few feet. I was also asked how the gold was loaded onto the lorries, and I told him we had a big table as they came in, the gold was put on the table and then it was laid out on the floor of the wagon.'

The gold had been loaded in Cape Town and was stolen on the way over to Southampton. While it was being unloaded from the species room the checker on board announced that the last box had been unloaded, but the quayside checker said there were still more boxes to come. The moment it was discovered that some gold was missing the alarm was given and the dock gates shut. At the same time there was a meat boat in and as the dockers were going down the Docks Road they saw the dock gates were closed and quickly got rid of all the sausages, meat steaks and legs of lamb they were carrying on to the roadside before getting to the gate! This story was verified by a number of dockers who saw the meat which had been thrown under cars after the cars had been driven away!

The *Capetown Castle* gold story follows that when a foreman looked at his hatch he saw a bump outside of it, and in all the time he had been working on his hatch he had never seen such a bump on the deck. Of course, the deck was green and the hold was green and the bump was painted green. They broke it open and there was the gold. The thieves had gone ashore and got some cement and cemented the gold into the deck and painted it green, the same colour as the deck. Harold Lloyd: 'They also found gold in the bilges. Apparently they put a small fellah through the vents, and he dropped down and broke open the cases. They found all the broken cases down in the lower hold.'

Asbestos

When Ron Williams started in the docks his wage was £3 8s 8d (£3.45) a week, and that was for unloading any cargo that was in the holds of the ships. His concern at the time was the kind of cargoes they were handling, especially the skins and the asbestos which they were handling without any protection.

As Ron says: 'Today you would have to have special suits and masks. In them days all you had was overalls. My biggest fear was anthrax from the wet skins of hides that you unloaded from the Cape ships. When you opened the hatch up the smell was awful. Where the hides had been jammed down you had to get down there and put ropes around them and send them out ashore. I used to worry sick coming out of that, but with the asbestos the bosses told us that it wouldn't hurt us – until one day one of our lads had an operation and took a lung out and they said it was asbestos related. I think that was the first time it had been recognised. In the US they knew about this prior to the war! In the 1930s people were dying of it. I had a mate whose wife died of it through ironing his clothes, but today it is in sealed containers. So if there is nothing wrong with it why is it now double wrapped in sealed containers?'

Other dockers have talked about the smell from working with skins. When they arrived home and walked in their wife would say, 'You've been on skins!' Early on some dockers would wear aprons made of sail cloth when handling skins.

Among the various cargoes carried on the Union Castle ships were the end hatches that were reserved for bags of asbestos to safeguard against any contamination of other cargo in the main hatches. The bagged asbestos was placed in the lower-holds of the cargo hatches and were relatively light (approx 25kgs) so the cargo nets could be filled to capacity without fear of overloading. Again with piecework operation the dockers wanted to get as many bags as possible into each net. Colin Hall explains: 'With the result that when the loaded nets were lifted through these small hatchway openings in the end hatches, it was like a champagne cork being pulled from a bottle.' Bags were sometimes torn at the edge of the hatchway, sending a 'snowstorm' of asbestos fibres down into the work area.

Colin Hall: 'On emerging from these hatches, the stevedores looked like "grey-ghosts" from the spilled asbestos dust and fibres.' However, extra payment had been arranged through 'dirty-cargo' circumstances, but in the early days no protective clothing or equipment such as overalls or dust-masks was made available for the men. They were completely exposed to the dust inhalation, and they were even forced to take their contaminated clothing home with them, inadvertently exposing their families to the asbestos dust.

Ray Strange: 'They did eventually give us masks, but there were the dangers to the wives with the washing. If you knew you were working on it the next day you used to put your clothes in the hall and put them on again the next day; however, there was documented evidence that one worker's wife, who shook out her husbands overalls in the garden on a regular basis, subsequently contracted the fatal level of mesothelioma. A more recent example was reported in the *Daily Echo* on 30 November 2007, of a 70-year-old wife of a Southampton stevedore who had died from mesothelioma. It was confirmed by the coroner that death was as a result of exposure to asbestos. Each evening from the late 1950s the wife would wash her husband's work clothes and overalls after he had arrived home after unloading asbestos from the cargo holds. The husband, like many other dockers who had worked on asbestos, describes the bags breaking and looking like it was snowing.'

Ron Williams talks about his experiences of the difficult conditions when unloading the bags of asbestos: 'The Cape Line Union Castle was when we used to unload the asbestos. The cargo was so light and worthless to us, and the only way you could get it out was to get as much as you could in the hoist for them to take it out. When it was going out the hessian bags it was in would rip and it would come floating down and you would be smothered in it. For days afterwards someone would go up and start sweeping because it was dust everywhere. There was absolutely no protection whatsoever.'

The dangers of unloading asbestos in the early days was unknown, hence it was only wrapped in a single cover of hessian, so that even when an experienced stevedore used a hook on the bag it would often split and the powdery asbestos would start to float around.

At the time the dockers were working on piecework, and the more they unloaded the more they earned. Ron Williams explains another hazard of working with asbestos: 'We were on piecework at the time, and you didn't stop to go to the canteen because by the time you got over the road to the canteen the whistle had gone and you started work again. That was even before you got in the door. There was always a queue, with lorry drivers and everything. So each gang of a dozen had their own tea boy who would take his bucket up. They had special boilers on so the tea boy could fill your bucket with scolding water. He would make the tea and wash up the cups, bring them back and lower it down into the hold. By the time that tea in the bucket got to the bottom of the hatch there was a film of asbestos on it. You would dip your cup in the bucket for your tea, and it too would come out with a film of asbestos on it.'

Ray Strange: 'I was involved with asbestos for 25 to 30 years, and the conditions were terrible. If you had copper they would store asbestos on top and then skins, anything heavy on top. They would put it in thin hessian bags, and the weight would split the bags, and sometimes the crane driver would catch them on the combing and split the bags. Once they were split you were working in it all day. There was a foreman in No. 1 who was a proper "heart and soul madam", and he would start cleaning the hatch while we were still working down below and he would be brushing it down. We complained from day one. The kids in South Africa of 10 and 11 who were digging out were dying of it.'

Crew Members and Shipyard Workers also Exposed to Asbestos

The asbestos started to be double wrapped, but that still did not completely get rid of the dust. Ron Williams: 'In the 1970s they began to put it in two bags, and you still had to go down with a vacuum cleaner to suck it up and you had a mask on – a bit late by then! We think, all this time later, if there was nothing wrong with it why is it now in sealed containers? The people who unload it at the other end are dressed like astronauts, with masks and breathing apparatus on their backs. The worst cases who have caught the disease were the laggers. On the merchant ships every pipe was lagged with asbestos. That had to be taken off and renewed on a refit, otherwise a pipe busts and that's it.'

The dangers of working with asbestos were not only of a concern to the dockers, but to crew members on board ships and also the shipyard workers. Gordon Brown, who worked as a butcher on the *Queen Mary*, would help with other workers when the liner was in the dry dock for anything up to six weeks for the annual lay-up: 'We worked on the chain gangs and worked with the laggers as well. A lot of us have got pleural plaque, which is asbestos related. I've got that and all my brothers-in-law have got it.'

Working on the Quayside

Colin Hall: 'On occasions, small plastic dust masks were issued "on request" when the dust got too thick. The quayside operations were equally as bad, as the bags were loaded into box wagons by hand and forced up to the roof of the enclosed truck to ensure a capacity load. This led to the dockers getting an equal share of the dust and contamination from the porous and sometimes split bags.'

Terry Adams was one docker who worked on the quayside when the asbestos was unloaded from the ships: 'When I got my black book I became a quayside man, and I was in the gang loading cargo off the quay onto lorries and railway wagons. Asbestos used to come in a sack as long as a mattress and it weighed about 25lb (11.2kg). You could pick it up easily and do what you liked with it. If a Cape boat came in they had about 400 of these sacks on board. They would tell us that there were 10 railway trucks for the asbestos to be loaded in. We would load some in and then get in the truck and press the sacks down. We would even bounce on them like a mattress, there was asbestos dust flying everywhere and we would take no notice of it. Your hair would be all white. Once you started on it, it was everywhere. We didn't know anything about the dangers to health. We had one or two boys who said it wasn't good for you.'

Taking the asbestos out of the hold was fraught with problems, especially if the sling was very full and the hatch opening was not very large: 'When we used to unload the sacks the boys used to lay the big sling down, chuck it all in, then up and over it went. It would get caught on a rafter, come down like snow and that was another bagful lost. They then put it on pallets, all bagged up and picked it up on a forklift truck. It was packed in bags with red polythene around it. But when we unloaded it, it was ordinary sacking.'

There were still dangers, even when it was put on pallets and moved by the fork lift trucks. Ray Strange: 'They started to pack it in three paper bags, then hessian bags on a pallet board, covered over with plastic. That was alright until the fork lift truck driver went in too high and split the bags. Then it started to go in containers, and we didn't know anymore about it.'

The Transport and General Workers Union Takes Action over Asbestos

Peter Wareham: 'The union officials had to be pushed all the time. If it didn't come from the rank and file they would not take action, but there were some good genuine blokes, such as Bernard Behan, who when we had the trouble with the asbestos stood for a week outside the Union Castle offices. They said it wouldn't affect us. There it was coming down like snow. All you had at the top of the hatch was a bucket and soap. It took us ages with strikes and stoppages.'

The problems associated with the unloading of asbestos did become the concern of the TGWU 2/28 Union Branch. They took up the important matter of health and safety of its members in the mid-1960s over the moving of dangerous or hazardous cargoes, especially asbestos. The members were called to the Thursday branch meeting to warn them that they might have to make an important decision over working conditions. Colin Hall: 'The word was out from the chairman of the day, Reg Behan, that a very important topic would be raised at the branch-meeting that week, which required as many members as possible to attend and might in turn require the dockers to make a vital decision.'

At the meeting the chairman spoke of the importance to the dockers of the Union Castle Line's regular weekly visits to Southampton with the weekly 'Inward' and 'Outward' bound vessels that were berthed for five days, discharging and loading all types of goods. Colin Hall: 'Which kept many men employed both day and night and were without doubt the most lucrative working vessels in the port as far as the dockers were concerned. The men were immediately alert for anything that might affect this "golden egg" in Southampton Docks, and they certainly did not want to make any foolish decisions that could change their working life permanently.'

The union had also carried out an investigation into the dangers of asbestos fibres. The conclusion was made based on medical evidence that asbestos fibres were a potential killer and led to asbestosis. Variations of this disease are from a milder form of pleural plaque to the more advanced stages of pleural plaque that could lead to a fatal malignant cancerous growth.

Colin Hall: 'Sadly many dockers fell victim to this industrial killer over the years, which had been brought to the attention of the dockers by the TDWU 2/28 Union Branch chairman at the union meeting in the 1960s, but for many, of course, it was already too late.'

As the next ship was due the next morning, with three hatches full of bagged asbestos, a decision had to be made. Finally the decision was made to work passengers and mail and to negotiate working other cargoes in the hatches where the asbestos was stowed, provided that the decks containing the bagged asbestos remained closed. Due to the documentary evidence, the TGWU wrote to the Union Castle Line informing them that in view of the medical evidence which now at hand, no more asbestos cargoes in any form would be handled by the Southampton dockers of the TGWU 2/28 branch.

When the news broke nationally it was immediately endorsed by all ports around the country and meant that other industries were now affected. These included the transport industry and the building industry that used asbestos sheets, and the car industry that used asbestos for brake shoes.

Ron Williams remembers one of the times when the dockers threatened to go on strike and when the representations were made from the various industries working with asbestos: 'We threatened to go on strike one time because of those conditions, and we were certain that one of the men had died because of asbestos. We stopped one day and refused to unload it off a ship and were called to a meeting by the union and the shop stewards to be spoken to by people from up the North of the country. These people said that if we didn't unload the asbestos they will shut their factory. They were making brake linings for cars. They really had us over a barrel, and we gave in. We really were gullible.'

Ray Strange talks about when the ban was announced: 'This is the last ship you are bringing in here with asbestos in it. If you bring it in again it will stay in the ship. That's what we had to do. We had a delegation down from an asbestos works up north. There were doctors over from South Africa who said, "You could eat this like cornflakes." They then gave us a bucket of water, soap and old rags to clean yourself up before you went up and eventually you had overalls.'

One of the employers was recorded on a video saying that he did not know what the problem was because if anyone was going to catch anything from asbestos then surely he would because he walked across the ship every day.

Colin Hall: 'Ships with asbestos cargoes already en-route to the UK were now being turned back, and their consignments were put into storage in South African warehouses pending any possible alteration in the present situation, which was never to come. Consignments were nevertheless stealthily shipped for a long period afterwards under licence via containers and plastic-sheeted "sealed" pallets of bags.'

The concern and frustration of many dockers and their families is summed up by Ron Williams: 'Now, 30 or 40 years after I started in the docks, there are possibly nine out of 10 dockers that are suffering from pluerel plaque, an asbestos related disease which the government won't recognise because they say it is not life threatening. I say that I never had it when I went in there, so why have I got it now?'

Details of pleural disease is given in *Asbestos News*: 'Pleural disease is a benign condition that is caused by frequent exposure to high levels of asbestos, a fibrous mineral known to cause serious injury or illnesses such as cancer. When loose asbestos fibres are inhaled they permanently fix themselves in the pleura, the thin lining of the lung and chest cavity, and cause scarring.

'There are different degrees of pleural disease. If the scarring spreads to the chest wall, it is considered pleural thickening, which may cause shortness of breath. Over time, the scarred lining can expand, blocking the lungs and making it hard to breath.

If the scarring is more centralized, it is called pleural plaques. While pleural plaques don't typically have symptoms, the scarred area can grow and become hard and calcified causing breathing complications and lung impairment.'

There are a large number of former workers from the docks who have contracted pleural plaque and have tried to take action against their employers, but one former docker, who did not have the condition, actually received an out-of-court settlement after being in fear of the condition developing. He had already retired but had spent 15 years unloading bags of asbestos from ships and was in fear of getting an asbestos-related illness after inhaling the asbestos dust in the cargo holds of the ships in Southampton Docks. Working in the docks was a family tradition, with his father and seven brothers also working there with him; however, after seeing former work colleagues die of asbestos-related disease, including his own sister-in-law after exposure to the asbestos dust from her husband's work clothes, his worry increased. Although he was suffering from breathing problems he had not been diagnosed with the condition, but he still sued his former employers, Union Castle and Associated British Ports, through his Southampton-based solicitors and was awarded an out-of-court settlement. He is possibly the only person to have a successful outcome to such an action against his employers regarding working with asbestos in the docks.

Accidents

As well as the dangers of dealing with hazardous cargoes, the dockers' job was considered one of the most dangerous, just behind the miners, in terms of accidents. Accidents could easily happen through overwork, tiredness and the 'jungle', which was the reference to the drinking of spirits and beer while working. Some dockers have commented on the problems of cycling in the docks and getting the bicycle wheels stuck in the rail lines that were on the quayside, and some have told tales of some dockers who had either gone over the quayside on their bikes or had fallen into the water as a result of drink while at work.

Colin Hall describes an incident that happened at 4am: 'A crane-driver who had agreed to work the night-shift as extra overtime, after already working a full day-shift, was half-asleep over his controls and, when entering the hatch-way with the last hoist of plate-glass, he misjudged the access opening. He landed the hoist onto the hatch-coaming, whereby the cases became half-balanced on the edge, which slackened off the rope-slings, allowing the hoist to pitch forward down to the lower-hold.'

Working in the hatch square is always dangerous, but this time only four of the eight men in the gang were working below placing the cargo units into position and releasing the slings when stowed into place, and two of those men were injured. Colin Hall: 'It was fortunate that the internal plate glass was of the "shatter-proof" type as had they been a conventional plate-glass type, with perhaps pointed shards flying everywhere, the injuries to the two men would have been far worse.' The ambulance was called and took the two men to hospital. Sadly, however, one of the men later volunteered for a five-to-nine shift at the Ocean Terminal and was walking along the quay towards the berth with his mates, when he just 'walked off the edge of the quay-apron' and disappeared into the black depths. Colin Hall: 'It was obviously a deliberate movement, as there was no sign of a struggle to swim or cries for help, and his body was tragically eventually recovered three weeks later among the reeds at nearby Netley Marsh. It was later understood that he had lost his wife a short while before the incident.'

Mickey Hart, a port labour officer, had two other brothers. One, Tom Hart, who for years was the senior night-shift foreman on the 'homeward-bound' Union Castle vessels, and Jim Hart, who was Arthur Hall's (father of Colin Hall) close friend for many years and also a Union Castle night-shift supervisor on the 'outward-bound' mail boats. Sadly, Jim was killed in the docks during one night-shift when he was trying to climb up the long 'trunk-way' hold ladder in No. 3 hatch during a meal-time inspection on one of the outward-bound mail boats. He miss-footed the rungs and fell to his death in the hatch-square.

Regrettably, the shipping-line argued that the circumstances of him being in the hold at that time were outside the area of his normal duties. So his wife was left without a husband and no pension based on this accident. This became a bone of contention for many who worked the Union Castle Line vessels in those days who felt that Jim's wife was certainly hard done-by in circumstances where there were no witnesses. Colin Hall: 'Just cold and unrelenting "reasoning" is unfortunately what many business hearts are made of, as one can serve his master for many years but when the chips are down the years of dedicated service are swept away as though they had never been there.'

Dockies' Nicknames

Peter Wareham joined the docks 1959 and worked there for 40 years leaving in 1999: 'They called me "Sailor". How that came about was that I came out of the Royal Navy on a Friday and started work on the Monday. I was asked what I had been doing, and I said that I had just come out of the navy and was immediately given the nickname "Sailor".

Most dockers had a nickname, and they would often only know another docker by his nickname. A book of *Dockers' Nicknames* was compiled by George Harley, who was a docker from 1939 until he retired in 1971. These are just a few examples of the names in the book: there was the 'All Electric' (not a spark in him), 'Blanket Brothers' (never took their coats off),

'Cinderella' (must get away by midnight), 'Dr Mo' (old quack), 'Electric Eel' (proper live wire), 'Father and Son' (always together), 'Gravel Voice John' (frog in the throat), 'Horace Hotplate' (keep out of the galley) and so on. ('Gumpy', 'Jersey', 'Sailor' and others were often still seen in the Southampton Dockers Social Club in 2007.)

Harold Lloyd: 'You had one docker whose nickname was "Overcoat Bill", and the reason for that was because he wore an overcoat down to his ankles. Another was called "Slippery Sands" because he would try to slide up to a position where the best jobs were and try to get picked. He was not very successful because the PLO would tell him to go back from where he came from, however, the port labour officer would pick out men for jobs and might send someone as a checker for seven days. If they were not happy and perhaps a bit lazy they would make their way back to the pool to try and get a better job. The PLO, Eddie Head, never forgot a face and would recognise them and tell him he had sent them checking for seven days and send them back again.'

The Stevedores' Tools

Dockers' tools: a hand-hook.

The distinction between stevedores and the general term dockers is that stevedores are experienced shipside workers who could stow cargo in the hold expertly so that it would not shift during the voyage. The dockers on the quay would load the cargo onto the railway wagons and lorries and, although many dockers were called stevedores, in fact there were very few of them.

Colin Hall describes the old stevedoring skills which are still often used today, but in the 1950s these crafts formed the backbone of the dockers' work, with predominantly 'manual-handling' of break-bulk cargoes still being used. 'There were the "hand-hooks", "roller-pipes", "crow-bars" and "bull-roping" techniques, using "snatch-blocks" and "gun-tackles" to move heavy cargo units into and out of the stowage positions. The use of deck-winches was then the only mechanical means for generating force in a ship's cargo hold, as the use of large fork-lift trucks to move and stack freight into the "wings" and "long-ends" was, at that time, still some way around the corner.'

Colin Hall: 'The main tools of the trade for the docker were the hand-hook, the timber-pad, the crow-bar, the hand-truck and other hand-held implements such as lengths of pipe or thick metal tubing, which were placed under heavy-case work to assist in guiding the units into the hold stows. The ship's winches were also often used in such instances, for "bull-roping" these heavier units of cargo, including "snatch-blocks" and "gun-tackles" to further assist in the placing and removing of such heavy units in the holds.'

The skills had been handed down from generation to generation and required adaptability to meet any circumstance, with safety considerations guiding decision making. 'This emphasis on safety was inbred with everyone working in the docks, especially on board ship where each and every vessel had its own structure of cargo holds in the different sizes and shape configurations.'

Colin Hall explains the dockers' hand-hook: 'The hand-hook was carried by most dockers as it was constantly required as a means of leverage and grip when lifting or moving cargoes in ships' holds and storage sheds. In fact it was known as "an extension of the dockers' arm" and a critical means of assistance in handling almost all cargoes.' A skilled docker could use it even when handling cases of eggs or delicate bags of rice, with hardly a dent being made on the surface, let alone the inexcusable hole in the hessian bag. 'Bag-hooks' were available, however, and were encouraged to be used when handling hessian bags. These hooks were a smaller version of the conventional hand-hook, with an oval plate at the end of the handle covered with tiny spikes. These were inserted into the weave of the bags, thereby lessening any chance of damage to the cover and contents when lifting with the hook.

In the casual labour system dockers would attend the pool to try and get work for the day. Those that were unfortunate enough not to get work were told 'sling your hook' (to put the hook over their shoulder and leave). This is the origin of the phrase 'sling your hook,' which is still in use today.

Most dockers went to work with their hooks slung in their waist belts, with the curve snugly fitting around the top of the buttocks, whereas the more flamboyant types would sling them over their shoulders. Important to the docker, the hand-hook was not only a badge of the trade but often a valued part of family history, handed down from father to son. However, there were dangers in using the hand-hook. If a docker was using a hand-hook lacking concentration, or even worse he was was careless, he could not only injure himself but also men working alongside him. Colin Hall remembers a serious injury caused when a docker was cycling home after work with his hook in his waist belt and was knocked off his cycle by a car at the railway bridge over Four Post Hill. Sadly the injuries proved fatal.

The Work of a Foreman

The work of a foreman was important because he was in charge of the whole operation. Ron Williams describes his job as a foreman: 'If I was sent to a ship as foreman you were effectively in charge of the ship, and your job was to book all the labour and make out a draw for the hatches. The blokes would draw a number out of the hat and say "we've got No. 1 or No. 5" or whatever. They had to draw out the hat so there was no cheating. You couldn't say "that hatch is working something so you can go there." There was none of that, you put your hand in the bag and pulled out one ticket. That was the ticket you had, you couldn't chuck it in and say I'll have another one. You booked your men on, so many men to a gang. I would be doing that for the ship, and the man next to me would be doing it for the quay. I would be in charge of the ship overall, and you would have a foreman down each hatch to make sure the cargo was stored properly. The outward Cape boat went to Cape Town, East London, Durban and Port Elizabeth. The smaller ship, the *Reina Del Mar*, was a cruise ship and would call at the Ascension Islands and Tristan Da Cuna and places like that. That was once every six months. You had to send your Christmas cards about April!'

Ron Williams loved his job and the challenge of loading a ship, making sure that every bit of space is used. He talks specifically about the challenges of loading the Antarctic survey ships, who would be away for months at a time, and the importance of making sure that everything they need for that time is loaded aboard. Ron Williams: 'When I became a foreman I used to have the great job of loading the Antarctic survey ships, the *John Biscoe* and the *Bransfield*. On those they would send the gang, and you realised that you were plying for inches because that ship was taking three years' supply. You couldn't lose any space whatsoever. You would force something down to get something else in. Even a sheet of plywood, you'd say "I know where that can go!" Over the top of something there was a quarter of an inch gap. Everyone looked forward to loading those ships because you felt like you were achieving something.'

Once the Antarctic survey ships arrived at the Falklands Islands it would most likely be the scientists who would be involved in the unloading, and the dockers wanted to make it as easy as possible for them. Ron Williams: 'You realised that when that ship got to the Falkland Islands, Port Stanley, all that had to come out was unloaded by the scientists. All the fuel used to come out at Port Stanley. That used to go in the ship first all over the bottom of the ship in 45 gall drums. Aviation fuel as well. We also used to send tons of anthracite out.'

Ron enjoyed the challenges, but also the opportunities to offer advice and ideas on how to gain space. As he says: 'On one trip I was asked by the agent to come up with an idea for gaining some more space. I was down in the hold looking at the drums and went up to ask the chief officer where the anthracite came out. He said it was with the fuel. I asked if we could cut the bags and shake it down between the drums. There was 30-ton of anthracite going, and if it was put between the drums then when the drums came out the coal could be swept up into heaps and lifted out. We gave it a try and we gained 30-ton of space!'

There are some strange cargoes, but nothing stranger than loading an entire village into a hold: 'There was one time when we loaded a complete pre-fabricated village because the original village had disappeared under an avalanche. Everything that was put in this ship was put in upside down! Roofs went in first, then the sides and floors and the skis were put in last. The skis came out first and they built the thing as it came out of the ship. I think that was the most interesting job I had in the docks. It was Berth 47 where they first started, and after that we loaded at the Town Quay.'

Every day was different and every cargo was different: 'You would get together with the first officer to plan where the cargo would be loaded. We were always fighting for inches. You would go down and find something had been moved, and the lads would say they had found a space somewhere else. We filled the ship up to capacity, and when you put the lid on the hatch that was it and then you started on the deck. You filled the deck up with cargo of all sorts, such as boats and anything else they required.'

Everything was planned by measurement: 'You had your rule and measured the ship, and you would then go down on the quay and measure some cargo and think, "that'll go in there and that will go behind it." It was fantastic, I loved every day, fascinating, every day was different, and you wouldn't think you would hear blokes, hard dockers, say, "hang on, if I move that an inch that will go in there." The docks were a fantastic place because you could go there at 8am and the boys would line up and punch you in the nose because they had the wrong job, and at 9am they were lining up to buy you a cup of tea. That was "dockology", you know! It was "I'm a docker, he's a docker, and anyone starts on him they got the rest of us to contend with." The camaraderie was brilliant!'

Ron Williams often wondered what fish the *John Biscoe* might bring back to England: 'We had the *Bransfield*, she was the most modern, but the *John Biscoe*, they cut out the back part to make her into a trawler, because I think they were planning to trawl fish out there to bring back to England because of the depleting fish stocks in the North Sea. I don't know what fish they had out there, but some would probably frighten the life out of you!'

Messengers

For some young men leaving school in the 1950s it was often thought that getting an apprenticeship was a good idea, especially in the time of national service because those on an apprenticeship could apply for deferment. When Maurice Allen left school it was just at the end of national service and he did not have any plans or ambitions, but his dad got him a job in the docks. He says: 'My dad got me in the docks. That was the way it worked in those days. My dad's intention was for me to become a checker because they earned good money. I wasn't ambitious, but it was always good money in the docks, better than other places, and that is what attracted people from other trades.' His first job was as a messenger in the Commercial and Estate Office in 1958 at the age of 15, working in the old Dock House in Canute Road. He was later transferred to the Publicity Office (today's Public Relations department). He found this more interesting because they prepared the monthly *Southampton Docks Sailing List and Shipping Guide.*

The office also dealt with visitors, and staff would give tours of the port. During the summer months hundreds of school children were taken on trips around the docks, given a meal in the canteen and then were taken on a cruise around the docks. Sadly, this does not happen for schools today because of health and safety regulations and port security. The busiest time was at the end of the month when the shipping guide from the publishers. The shipping guides would be put into envelopes and tied up in bundles for the post office, and then Maurice Allen would hand-deliver the local ones to shipping companies, agents and most firms in the dock area. Every department had a messenger boy who would do some filing and general work in the office and, of course, made the tea and coffee. Maurice Allen: 'You couldn't stay a messenger for too long, and they started pushing me to take the exam to be a junior clerk. That was the way up, and progress depended on how ambitious or how good you were.'

The Clerical Department

Prior to the abolition of the British Transport Commission, Maurice Allen had moved to the Staff & Labour Office as a junior clerk in the Outdoor Superintendent Department based in South Western House: 'In those days you had offices scattered all over the place. A lot of them were railway offices. There was still a relationship between Southern Railway and the docks' board, and they used to transfer staff from the railway over into the dock, a sort of unofficial transfer of staff because in the old days the railway ran everything. The Southern Railway had their own hotels and a large marine department.'

In 1960 the British government published a white paper recommending the breakup of the British Transport Commission. This was finally completed by 1962, and the British Transport Docks Board was created to take control of the ports.

The Fawley Oil Refinery

An oil refinery was first established by the AGWI (Atlantic Gulf and West Indies Company) at Fawley, Hampshire, in 1921. It was a small-scale plant, and the main aim of this company was to process crude oil from Mexico into heavy fuel oil for ships.

There were a number of reasons why the site was chosen. The location was near to Southampton Docks, with the opportunity to supply the ocean liners and cargo ships with fuel. It was on the west bank of Southampton Water, near Calshot, the Solent, and had close access to the English Channel and the Atlantic. Most important was that there was land available for development and the area was sparsely populated.

The site was acquired in 1925 by Esso Petroleum Company, and it was in 1948 that Cyril Duro left his job at Northam and went to work for Foster Wheeler's, who were building the Esso Oil Refinery at Fawley. Cyril Duro: 'When I went down to get the job there wasn't a thing above the ground, and they were putting wooden structures down to take the concrete for the base.' Later, after the Esso Oil Refinery had been built and opened in 1951, Cyril Duro went to work at the refinery as a rigger and stayed there for 28 years.

Colin Hall was working as a temp in the docks before becoming a full-time stevedore. To maintain a living in-between the temporary work Colin had to take other employment, and he became a labourer at the new Esso Oil Refinery. He then managed to get more money in the refinery as an oil storage tank cleaner.

Today, tankers berth at the Marine Terminal, which has five deep-sea and four inshore berths, and unload crude oil from the North Sea, Europe and the Middle East. It is turned into products that include petrol, diesel, aviation fuel and petrochemicals. Exxon Mobil chemical manufacturing facility is Esso's sister company and receives feedstock from Esso, where its products are used to make plastics, detergents, textiles, butyl rubber and bitumen for roads.

CHAPTER 9

POST-WAR SHIPYARDS

After the war, work became more difficult for the shipyard workers, and by 1950 there was less work in the Camper & Nicholson shipyard. The management wanted the shipwrights to stop the piecework, and they were warned that if this did not happen they would have to get rid of some men. Ernest Gay: 'They got rid of two thirds of us, and the shipwrights' union had a strict rule that men who were out of work went to the back of the rota. Then you worked your way down until you were working regularly. I went to British Rail to work on the Old Docks & Marine, working on the cross-channel ferries for one year. They didn't do me any favours. In the end, although they wanted to keep me on, the position was that I had to go to the end of the rota.'

Ernest went to work in J.I. Thornycroft Repair in 1951 as a shipwright. What happened was that he went there for a weekend in June 1951 to secure all the equipment and tanks for the Red Devils to go to Cyprus. 'That lasted over the weekend and went on to Wednesday or Thursday. In those days they had a system where if you worked after five o'clock you were paid off, and you had to go in the next morning and pick up your money and your cards. For that you got two hours' pay.'

There were 17 working in the J.I. Thornycroft workshop, and the chargehand came out from the office and asked if any of them could read a plan. Ernest said that he could. The chargehand went back into his office and then came back again to tell the workers they were going to work on a 'C' class destroyer that they were converting into the first atomic bomb vessel. 'The job was to cut down from the forecastle, and I had to go and mark everything off. I asked the chargehand years later if he ever checked it. He said, "Good God, no! You looked like you knew what you were doing so I let you get on with it."' Ernest said that the *Vigilant* was all under cover and when she was driven at sea there was no bridge, only periscopes: 'Something went terribly wrong in the Channel, but we didn't hear what it was.'

Ernest found it very difficult to accept the idle chat in the morning and would go and put his overalls on and go into a small cubbyhole where he could read the plans. In 1957 he was told that the manager wanted to see him and was offered the position of chargehand because the previous chargehand had left to take up a position as shore superintendent for Cunard: 'I was asked to take over as chargehand. That was hard work picking it up because, although I knew my part of the job, I had to pick up everything else. I was the chargehand on the *Creole* and the *Crispin*, which we modernized for Pakistan.'

When Ernest was promoted to chargehand there were problems of demarcation between the shipwrights and joiners, and he talks about the time *HMS Hermes* was in No. 7 Dry Dock in 1957: 'The other big job was aircraft carrier *HMS Hermes*. She came down brand new from Barrow. She went into No. 7 Dry Dock and only just made it, we had to juggle between the buttresses. You would never believe it. You build a cradle under the ship, and when it goes down that side you've got softwood designed to compress at least an inch. That was the first time there was all this trouble with demarcation with shipwrights and joiners. There was Ralph, the chargehand joiner. I said to him that "we are running round in circles, if I do something and it belongs to you, I will do it and give it to you at the end of the day to put on your time sheet. You do the same thing from me." That was the only time I went through a whole job without any arguing.'

One of the jobs was to fit the arrester wires, and Ernest said that he did not have a clue how to do it: 'I had two shipwrights, strong young lads they were. They came back about two or three days later saying it was all done. They were good. You had good men and you had some idlers.'

Fitting Stabilisers to *Queen Mary* and *Queen Elizabeth*

Ernest Gay was a shop steward for a short time: 'That didn't last long, it didn't suit me at all, but while I was there I got seconded to the *Queen Elizabeth*. I went up and did the complete lining-off and the marking-out for the stabilisers. I have wondered how I had the nerve to do that, but you are young and keen. But I have never been so cold in all my life!' From the plans all the work had to be arranged for every trade working on the job. 'One of the first jobs we did from the outside was to ascertain which frames were which and cut two big holes for the stabiliser boxes to go in. I think you only had 1in margin all the way round. There were four stabilizers, for'ard and aft'.'

When the stabilisers were fitted on the *Queen Mary* her first two for'ard stabilizers were fitted successfully: 'We did a lot of preparation work on the *Queen Mary*, but the after two were staggered a little because of the construction of the ship. We did six weeks on nights in the No. 7 Dry Dock. When we were on nights we were told they wanted to lower the Fin box for the mechanical rams. They were resting on stools, and I think then that was the turning point to my career really, the manager Rex Scorey put it on record I was the best manager he had ever had.'

'A Little Tale'

Some of the crew of the *Queen Mary* would stay while the ship was in dry dock. One crew member at the time was Geoffrey Le Marquand. Geoffrey can be seen regularly in the docks in 2008 helping with the mobility team and assisting passengers by taking them on board in a wheelchair. However, Geoffrey has a tale to tell from his experiences on board the *Queen Mary* as a

RMS *Queen Elizabeth* entering the No. 7 Dry Dock. (Courtesy of Mick Lindsay Collection)

member of the crew from 1957–59. Geoffrey Le Marquand: 'When I was on the *QM* in 1959 she went into King George V Dry Dock in Southampton for 10 weeks having her annual overhaul and being fitted with stabilisers. I chose to move out of the crew accommodation and into a first class suit (cabin A133) for the duration, and while in this cabin I pulled out a drawer and wrote my name on the underside. Recently a friend of mine (also *QM* crew) went out to Long Beach to visit the ship, and I told him what I had done. He was able to get into this cabin and checked the drawers by turning them upside-down. Hey Presto!

The Queen Mary in Long Beach, California, Cabin A133.
(Courtesy of Keith Lloyd)

'Geoffrey Le Marquand Jersey CI crew member 1957–1959.'
He took a couple of photos: as the cabin is today and the one
drawer. I asked him why did he not bring the drawer back,
but he told me he was unable to shove it up his shirt without
looking suspicious!'

Oriana and Iberia

At the end of the work on the destroyer series, P&O
increased their activities in Southampton, and Ernest Gay, at
34, was the youngest chargehand shipwright and was put on
the P&O ships. Two of the biggest jobs undertaken at the
time involved the work on the first *Oriana* and *Iberia*. The
first *Oriana* was built in 1960 by Vickers-Armstrong's,
Barrow and was registered to the Orient Steam Navigation
Co. Unlike the earlier Orient Liners which had sailed from
London, the *Oriana* served the route to Australia from
Southampton. 'The *Oriana* came round new from the
maker's yard at Barrow. That was the original *Oriana*, a
beautiful ship. She was the Orient line. That was hard work

Geoffrey Le Marquand, 1950s graffiti artist! (Courtesy of Keith Lloyd)

for about six weeks. She did a mini-cruise for selected guests to go to Portugal and back just to shake down before she did her
trip to Australia. The steel strong backs for the shell doors still had not arrived from Barrow. We did it temporary with timber,
and when she came back the strong backs had arrived, but the night before sailing they were found to be ¼ inch too long. We
worked all through the night, and as we were caulking these things off the F deck was full up with Scottish emigrants, already
in their cabins, kids were crying, everything!'

It was while putting air-conditioning on the *Iberia* that shipwright Ernest Gay was taken ill and spent four months in a chest
hospital. After he completed work on the *Oriana* he was assigned to the *Iberia*, built by Harland & Wolff of Belfast in 1954 and
operating the UK to Australia service. In 1960, during a refit in Southampton, she was fitted with full air-conditioning: 'After
the *Oriana* I went from there to three months on the *Iberia*. We completely air-conditioned her. It was a seven o'clock finish
every night. All those months I never had a hot meal during the day, and I ended up in the chest hospital for four months with
chest troubles. We did the big air-conditioning pipes on the main deck, but down on the Asian crew deck they were small ones.
We had little wooden saddles that carried them. As you were fitting, the other trades would come along insulating them.
Although they said it was foam, we found out afterwards there was asbestos in it. I ended up in the chest hospital, but they made
a good job of it, although I was out for four months. I know I've got scars on my lungs, a condition called pleural plaque, from
asbestos. We didn't know what we were doing in those days.'

Using the King George V Graving Dock (No. 7 Dry Dock)

When a ship was brought in for dry docking it was the responsibility of the dockmaster to ensure the operation was successfully
undertaken. The dock was first pumped dry, and the first job for the shipwrights was to prepare the cradle for the ship to sit on.
(The cradle is a centre line of keel blocks with a line of bilge blocks for the ship to rest on.)

The bilge blocks were built up with wood to form the profile of the ship being docked. Once this had been completed the
dock was flooded and the caisson of the dock opened, allowing the ship to enter. The dockmaster worked with the captain, pilot
and line launches to bring the ship into the dock. Tugs assisted from the rear and men would grab the ropes thrown from the
ship and help in guiding and positioning the ship into the dock. Once the caisson was closed the ship was positioned by centre
line marks on the caisson and the head of the docks and similar marks on the sides of the dock. By the means of sighting along
plumb-bobs, the ship was accurately centred, and as the dock was pumped dry the ship rested down on the cradle in the
calculated position.

When open, the caisson was housed in a recess at the side of the dock, and to shut it an electric winch hauled the caisson
into a closed position. Once the caisson was closed, the pumping out of the water began and the ship settled down on to the
blocks. No time was wasted because, while the ship was slowly resting down on the blocks, painters in floats would be cleaning
the underwater portion of the hull.

The pump house was adjacent to the dock and contained all the machinery necessary to pump water in and out of the dock,
and it was under the control of one engineer at a central control desk.

The *Arcadia* in Dry Dock

Quick thinking by Ernest Gay saved serious damage to the *Arcadia* while she was in dry dock. 'The *Arcadia* was in No. 6 Dry Dock, and the assistant was Captain Kidd. I think he was the first officer on the watch in the war when the *Queen Mary* ran down the cruiser *Curacoa*. It was blowing a bit, the ship was due to go out, and I told them they had a leak and they only had an half an hour. The captain shouted up to them to get the ship down on the blocks immediately. It was already in dry dock when they started up and found the leak. When we got all squared up there was only 9in of water underneath that ship, and if I hadn't anticipated the problem there could have been serious damage to the ship. The managing director congratulated me the next day.'

By 1967 he was appointed senior foreman, was responsible for all the dry dockings associated with J.I. Thornycroft and was responsible for all the shipwrights at the Northam Yard, but by the 1970s there were strikes and difficulties in the docks between the management and the dockers. The Labour government responded by bringing in regulations for the unions. To ensure that any contact with the media was undertaken with confidence the unions gave their shop stewards training to develop their skills when being interviewed on radio and television.

Ernest Gay: 'When I became senior foreman I had some authority. We then had terms of reference for refusing to do this and to do that. The terms of reference said they had to take orders from the head of the department, which was me. From then on to the first one that said they would not do something I would say, "You're off pay!" After that I got the nickname "Off Pay Gay". Nobody ever refused after that!'

In 1972 Ernest worked on the big conversion to the *Queen Elizabeth 2*, which included taking a staircase out, refitting the restaurant, a kitchen and two lifts. 'We'd just about finished everything on board, with everything shipshape and ready to hand over. The board of trade came along and had the plans from the start. We had moved the restaurant and kitchen and put a crew stairway up. The crew stairway was to keep the crew away from the passengers. They said that had to be fireproofed. Next day a newspaper headline said that we would two days late again, but it was not our fault. We were ready!'

Harland and Wolff 1972

Ernest Gay: 'The ship repair was closed down, and we took over Harland's in 1972. The docks board wanted half of it, actually, for Ocean Village. The docks board had planned to close the dry docks years before and had stopped all maintenance. Some managers came down from Scotland, and we knew they would be coming to close us down. We had just finished a big conversion of the *Discovery*, the Antarctic ship that we re-engined, a big job.

'British Shipbuilders said that we were broke so they closed us down. Previously when I suspected that they were going to close down I had asked for redundancy, but they refused because I was responsible for the dry-docking. By that refusal it cost me £28,000 redundancy, and the £4,000 I got left me with a loss of £24,000.

'Everybody was going. We all got called in and were given notice. There were not many shipwrights left and a couple or three platers. There was one job running at the New Docks, and they left me in charge so I could finish it off. Price Waterhouse promised us a reference but we got six months notice instead. I was the last one to leave, and I left about half past two, and by five o'clock Hughes had bought the building and the use of the dry dock. One of our project managers asked me to go down the next morning to see him, and I was told that they wanted me to work for them. I went to Alex Hughes and he gave me an interview, and he said they were paying £9,000, and I told him it was less than I was getting. He told me at the end of the month my salary would either go up or I would go out of the door. He said, "there is only one shop steward here and that's me!"'

In 1975 Ernest Gay was a workaholic and was working all hours, but his wife, sensing that if he continued with his present workload he would be ill, intervened and encouraged him in the game of bowls in which he has become very involved for many years. Ernest Gay: 'I was so wrapped up in my work and came home at about 10.30 or 11 o'clock each night, but when I told the personnel manager that I was doing too many hours he told me that I was only as good as my number two, and my number two was a brilliant shipwright overnight! I took up bowls and that was my saviour. They used to call staff meetings at 4.30pm and we would be there until six. I used to tell them that I had an important game of bowls to play, and they would let me leave. That was how I got out of meetings!'

In 1985 he had been put in charge of the whole yard operation until it was closed by British Shipbuilders in 1987. From 1967 to 1987 there had been 636 dry dockings in Southampton. Ernest Gay joined Thew Engineering as a marine manager in 1987, in charge of the dry docks and dry dockings. During that time he was involved with a further 138 dry dockings until his retirement in 1999, including docking the final ship in the Trafalgar Dock before its closure. At one period as dry-dock manager he had a ship in Nos. 2, 3, 4, 5, 6 and 7 Dry Docks at the same time.

Ernest Gay was involved in the docking of the *QE2* in No. 7 Dry Dock when she was unable to get the planned work done in Germany: 'I was marine manager when the *QE2* had been to Germany to have new props fitted. They weren't working, and a dry-dock was required to do the work. I was told to get No. 7 Dry Dock ready as the *QE2* was coming in. I got it ready she went in on time, no damage, got all the work done and she went out on time, and I was thanked for doing the work. Alex Hughes called me to his office the next morning and put my salary up from £9,000 to £16,000, and after one more year I was told I could have another £1,000.'

CHAPTER 10

POST-WAR SHIPS AND SHIPPING

After World War Two other ships started to use the port. Kenneth Fielder talks about his memories of some of those ships: 'After World War Two we had a couple of Dutch vessels. One was the *Nieuw Amsterdam*, a beautiful vessel, and another that I think was called the *Oranje*. Then Cunard also brought in the *Caronia*. A beautiful painted green hull, the *Green Goddess*, and about the same time there was the *Ile de France*.'

When the *Caronia* entered service in 1948 she was a two-class vessel with first class and cabin class accommodations, omitting what would be either tourist or third class. Most cruise ships today are a one-class, although Cunard still maintains different classes on its ships. It is generally the price the passenger pays for the cabin that determines the restaurant that they eat in. The higher the price for the suite or cabin the more luxurious the dining arrangements, and those passengers in lower grades of cabins will have separate restaurants.

The *Capetown Castle*. (Courtesy of Mick Lindsay Collection)

The Union Castle Ships Sailed like Clockwork

The Union Castle ships docked regularly in Southampton and were very important to the economy of Southampton and to the earnings of the dockers. They sailed every Thursday like clockwork. The service eventually ended in 1977. Many of the ships are remembered with fondness by those who sailed in them as passengers, and they were also a blessing to many of the dockers who relied on their regular services for work, loading and unloading the cargoes.

Some of the ships are very well known and include the *Windsor Castle, Capetown Castle, Athlone Castle* and *Stirling Castle* to name but a few. They used to serve South Africa, calling at Maderia, Cape Town, Durban and Port Elizabeth. The Cape ships used to be away for about six to seven weeks.

The *Edinburgh Castle* and *Pretoria Castle* were sister ships and the first post-war mail ships to join the Union Castle fleet in 1948. They were both 28,700 tons and 748ft (228m) in length and were the first steam ships built by the company for many years. They had taller funnels than the motor ships. The maiden voyage for the *Pretoria Castle* was on 27 July 1948 and the *Edinburgh Castle* on 9 December 1948.

The *Windsor Castle*. (Courtesy of Mick Lindsay Collection)

The Post-war P&O Ships

The P&O post-war ships were refitted and completely air-conditioned: P&O's *Himalaya, Chusan, Arcadia* and *Iberia* plus the Orient Line's *Orcades, Oronsay* and *Orsova*. Each group had similar design and style, and all were between 24,000 and 29,000 tons and completed between 1948 and 1954.

P&O *Himalaya*. (Courtesy of Mick Lindsay Collection)

P&O *Arcadia*. (Courtesy of Mick Lindsay Collection)

Orient Line *Orcades*. (Courtesy of Mick Lindsay
Collection)

Final Years of the Queens

Gordon Brown worked on the RMS *Queen Mary* in the 1950s and also talks about a typical working day on board for the catering staff: 'You turned to in the morning between 6.00am or 6.30am. After breakfast the chef would tell you to wipe her down when the last passengers had their food. You would scrub everything down and take turns. If there were four on the roast, two would go off to freshen up, have a shower, change their checks and whites and maybe have a half-hour kip, then come back for lunch wipe-down at about 2.30pm. From 2.30pm to 4.30pm you could have a sleep. That was the hardest thing to get used to when you first went to sea. Get up at about 4pm and then you were on the go until about 10.30pm at night when the chef would go off duty.'

It was a sad day in October 1967 when the RMS *Queen Mary* left Southampton for the last time as she embarked on her final voyage to Long Beach, California. The *Queen Mary* has remained moored as a tourist attraction and museum at Long Beach ever since.

Bert Moody: 'I was on the Royal Pier in 1967 when the *Queen Mary* went down, and a lovely sight that was. That was my last memory of *Queen Mary* going down.'

After the war the RMS *Queen Elizabeth* went for an extensive refit, and on 16 October 1946 she finally completed her maiden passenger voyage. In the late 1960s, however, due to the drop in numbers of passengers crossing the Atlantic by ship, Cunard started to offer cruises, but despite putting in a swimming pool and air conditioning the RMS *Queen Elizabeth* was lacking in many of the facilities needed for cruising and began to lose money.

The RMS *Queen Elizabeth* made her final Atlantic crossing on 5 November 1968 and then sailed to Florida where she was opened to the public in February 1969. Bert Moody saw the RMS *Queen Elizabeth* when she sailed out of Southampton for the last time: 'The last time the *Queen Elizabeth* sailed out of Southampton was in 1968. I was still working for the railways and had to catch a train for a meeting in Bournemouth on the day she sailed. It was a bit of a murky morning, and as the train went past Millbrook the *Queen Elizabeth* was just leaving and I saw her in the distance.'

The Florida venture was not very successful, and she was then sold to a group of businessmen, renamed *Seawise University* and put to use as a floating university; however, while being refitted for her new role in Hong Kong a fire broke out and the *Queen Elizabeth* capsized, and she was eventually scrapped in 1973. It was concluded later that the fire was a result of an arsonist who was never caught.

It was to be the end of the great liner services of the early 20th century which over time had became important to the life and trade in Southampton. With an increasing number of passengers transferring to air travel as a faster means of getting to their destinations there appeared to be less need for the Atlantic liner services between Southampton and New York. It was the shops, traders and other services in Southampton reliant on the liners' passengers who suffered through loss of trade, especially when Cunard ceased operating the RMS *Queen Mary* and RMS *Queen Elizabeth* on their transatlantic service. Changes began to happen in the development of the Port of Southampton when the management started to look for new profitable uses of the port site.

With the two 'Queens' being retired due to the competition from passenger aircraft it seemed unlikely that another transatlantic liner would be built, but Cunard had other ideas. The decision was made to build a liner that was smaller, which could sail through the Panama and Suez canals and also provide a transatlantic cruising service. This new ship was to be the RMS *Queen Elizabeth 2*, and she would spend the summer on the transatlantic service from Southampton to New York and the winter cruising.

The *Queen Elizabeth 2*

When the RMS *Queen Mary* had left Southampton for the last time in October 1967 another famous ocean liner had been launched a month earlier. At 70,327 tons and 963ft (293.52m) long, with a service speed of 32.5 knots and known only as *Q4* before her naming, she would take over the transatlantic crossing from Southampton to New York.

It was on 20 September 1967 that Her Majesty Queen Elizabeth II launched the *Queen Elizabeth 2*. The *QE2* was built by John Brown & Company, Clydebank, Scotland, for the Cunard Line, Southampton. Gus Shanahan, a qualified shipwright, was sent by Cunard as a standby assistant to the naval architect for 18 months until she was completed: 'I was standby assistant to the naval architect while she was being built, and every day we would have the Lloyds surveyor and sometimes the board of trade surveyor visit. We would go round the ship each day and check the work that was being done. With electric welding on aluminium work the welder would stop to put in a new rod in his machine, but this would tend to cause a fracture in the seam of the welding. We would find these fractures and the welder would have to come back, dig it all out and re-weld it. This did not seem such a problem when using electric welding on steel.'

The day before the launch the final checks were completed: 'On the day before the launch of the *QE2* I went around with the Lloyds and board of trade surveyors to do a complete check while she was still on the slipway. The John Brown's senior draughtsman was also with us. Underneath the *QE2* there is what is termed the "bottom plug". This is a brass plug about 1½ inches round. These plugs are screwed into the bottom where the oil and freshwater tanks are and these can be drained when in dry dock. I had to check and sign that all the bottom plugs were firmly screwed in. There are about 70 plugs in the bottom of the *QE2* so it was quite a job. If anything went wrong after this you would get the blame because you had signed that all had been checked.'

During the build Gus Shanahan arranged it so that he had quite pleasant and picturesque surroundings to live in: 'While I was working on the *QE2* build I had a caravan on the banks of Lock Lomond for 12 months because it was handy to get to the shipyard each morning. In the six-week school holidays my wife and two children came to stay with me.'

A final inspection before the launch of the *QE2* the next day. From left to right: two boilermakers, Gus Shanahan, John Brown's chief draftsman and Bob Patton, Cunards inspector. (Courtesy of Gus Shanahan)

119

The Ship's Carpenter

One of the jobs for the ship's carpenter was to be in charge of the anchor: 'We did the trial run on the *QE2*, and I had to check that the anchor was alright. As the ship's carpenter on board you had to drop the anchor, and sometimes you had to break the cable to detach the anchor, or "hang it" as they call it, so that you could moor to a buoy. This depended on what the port people want. The "chippie" gets involved in all sorts!'

The *QE2* left John Brown's yard in the December for a dry dock in Greenock and then went on to her sea trials. Gus Shanahan: 'We went from there to the measured mile at Skelmore and then down to Southampton. At first the *QE2* had some engine problems and was in Southampton for three months before she sailed for New York on her maiden voyage.'

United States Line in the 20th Century

The United States of America had launched its own ocean liner, the *United States*, in 1951. The *United States's* length was 990ft (301.7m) with a beam of 101ft (30.5m) and a draft of 31ft (9.4m). Her cruising speed was 35 knots, and she could carry 1,972 passengers and 1,000 crew. She was to be the fastest ocean liner afloat. On 4 July 1952 (American Independence Day) the *United States* embarked on her maiden voyage and arrived at Southampton on 8 July, taking the Blue Riband transatlantic speed record for the fastest eastbound crossing of the Atlantic away from the *Queen Mary*, a record which had been held for 14 years.

The speed record was measured from the Ambrose lightship, New York, to Bishop Rock off Cornwall, UK. The actual time was three days, 10 hours and 40 minutes, beating the *Queen Mary's* record by over 10 hours. The average speed for the crossing was 35.59 knots. The *United States* also broke the westbound record by crossing in three days 12 hours and 12 minutes, with an average speed of 34.51 knots. Her captain for the record crossing was Captain Harry Manning.

The liner *United States* also withdrew from service in 1969, partly due to the increased competition from airliners and a consequent loss in numbers of passengers, but also because of a series of strikes by union crew members who caused the cancellation of a large number of voyages. This was the final straw for the United States Lines and signalled the end to the transatlantic passenger services. Today, the US has no major passenger liner service across the Atlantic.

Colin Hall talks about the visit of the United States Liner and a film company engaged in filming at the docks in 1962: 'On one visit of the "Blue Riband" vessel, the *United States*, an American film company were shooting a couple of scenes for a film called *The Iron Maiden*. The actor playing the "millionaire" [the film's central character] was the well-known actor Alan Hale Jr. His father was a well-known actor from the days of the early cowboy films, with Alan Jr being the spitting image of the old man and with the same loud hearty laugh. His sense of humour showed during the "takes" of the scene that involved the landing of his Cadillac on the quayside from the ship.'

The *United States's* arrival at Southampton on 8 July 1952 after her successful maiden voyage. (Courtesy of ABP)

The *Caronia*. (Courtesy of Mick Lindsay Collection)

It was Colin Hall's 'star' performance to carry Alan's baggage to the car and pack it into the boot. On completion the 'jolly millionaire' slipped Colin a ten-bob (10 shillings, equivalent to 50p today) note. Unfortunately, they had to shoot the same scene several times, but try as he did to retain the ten bob note on each occasion, Alan Hale must have had docker's blood in him, as he grabbed Colin on each occasion, and rubbing his finger and thumb together he said, 'Come on, you're not a "star" yet,' to which the well worn note was handed back for 'Scene 20, shoot five'. However, he did receive his 'Fiver' (£5) as wages for the day, which in those days was 'dinner for two at the Ritz!'

Coronation Year 1953

In the introduction to the June 1953 *Southampton Sailing List and Shipping Guide* published by the Docks and Inland Waterways Executive, the Docks and Marine Manager, R.P. Biddle writes:

> Southampton, from time immemorial, has been the Gateway for England's Kings and Queens and a chronicle of Royal occasions at the docks appear in this issue.
>
> As befits this Port, which has been the point of arrival for thousands of visitors coming to this country for the Coronation, Southampton Docks wears a 'Royal Look' for the occasion, and the main gateways, the Ocean Terminal and other reception points have all been specially decorated.
>
> The period of the Coronation Naval Review at Spithead will be an intense activity at the docks, and ships sailing to witness the Review will vary from the large liners to tugs and tenders. In the period 13th to 16th June, 42 special trains will be run from Waterloo to the docks with passengers for the Review. The majority of these trains will be dealt with on Monday, 15th June, within the space of three hours and in the early morning of Tuesday, 16th June, 31 special trains will be dispatched from the docks in four hours. All of these, of course, in addition to ordinary boat train traffic for ships engaged on normal commercial services.
>
> By kind permission of the Naval Authorities, H.M. Aircraft Carrier *Implacable* will visit Southampton Docks from 29th May to 5th June, and during her stay arrangements have been made for public inspections.
> R.P. Biddle'

The June 1953 *Shipping List and Shipping Guide* also felt it fitting that 'In this Coronation month it will be of interest to recall royal occasions at Southampton Docks, which, during its one hundred and fifteen years' history, has been honoured by royalty either by arriving or sailing or visiting the Docks to give the seal of commendation to some new maritime enterprise.'

The *Shipping List and Shipping Guide* lists the first recorded occasion on 27 August 1853, when Queen Victoria, with Prince Albert, the Prince of Wales and

The *Esperance Bay*. (Courtesy of Mick Lindsay Collection)

Prince Alfred, travelled from Cowes, in the Isle of Wight steamer *Elgin*, en route from Osborne to Ireland, up until the most recent occasion on 28 July 1948. That was when King George VI, Queen Elizabeth and Princess Margaret went on-board the liner *Queen Elizabeth* to see the portrait of Her Majesty by the late Sir Oswald Birley to mark the launching of the liner in September 1938.

A new canteen for dock workers at the New Docks was opened on 11 May and the building, situated in Herbert Walker Avenue and near Berth 107, 'embodies the latest ideas in industrial canteen design.'

During the summer 13,000 children from schools in Southern England and centres as far apart as Exeter and Aylesbury planned to visit the dock and undertake a two-hour cruise round the docks and in Southampton Water.

A first visit to the docks by the 15,187-ton Shaw Savill liner *Athenic* brought a cargo of apples and pears from Australia.

The largest ships using Southampton Docks in 1953 included, from the largest the *Queen Elizabeth* at 83,673 tons, with a 1031ft (314.25m) length and a beam of 119ft (36.27m) down to the *Esperance Bay* at 14,343 tons, with a 549ft (167.33m) length and a 68ft (20.73m) beam.

From the *Queen Elizabeth* the order in size continued with: *Queen Mary, United States, Liberte, Ile de France, Nieuw Amsterdam, Mauretania, Caronia, America, Pretoria Castle, Edinburgh Castle, Orcades, Himalaya, Georgic, Capetown Castle, Dominion Monarch, Andes, Athlone Castle, Stirling Castle, Chusan, Alcantara, Asturias, Rangitane, Rangitoto, William Ruys, Flandre, New Australia, Oranje, Carnarvon Castle, Winchester Castle, Scythia, Samara, Antilles, Arundal Castle, Empire Fowey, Empire Orwell, Ruahine, Rangitiki, Rangitata, Italia, Canton, Veendam, Atlantic, Akaroa, Maasdam, Ryndam, Empire Windrush, Arawa, Moreton Bay, Largs Bay, Batory, Carthage* and *Corfu*.

The programme of pleasure cruises from Southampton in June 1953 included the British Railways vessel *Falaise*, whose itinerary was Southampton to Guernsey and St Malo. The *Himalaya* sailed to Maderia, Las Palmas and Casablanca. The *Orcades* sailed to Palma, Barcelona, Naples, Venice, Malta, Gibraltar and Lisbon. Later in the month, the *Himalaya* sailed again on a cruise to Athens, Casablanca and Lisbon, and the *Oransay* sailed to Gibraltar, Villefranche, Genoa, Palma and Casablanca.

The Union Castle Line centenary was also celebrated in 1953. A centenary dinner and dance was held on board the RMMV *Capetown Castle* on Tuesday 17 November 1953 by the Union Castle Line, Southampton. The menu was prepared with each letter of the word 'centenary' being the first letter of the name of each dish on the menu, and in the second half of the dance programme there was the *Centenary Waltz*.

Comparing the emphasis on travelling by sea in 1953 with today, most of the long-distance travel by passengers is by air, and the only service from Southampton across the Atlantic to New York is now undertaken by the *Queen Mary 2*. The numbers of cruise ships now visiting Southampton, however, show the increasing demand for cruises, as many people fly to destinations such as the Caribbean and then continue on a cruise.

By 1954 the Orient Line's 27,632-ton *Oransay* sailed from Sydney across the Pacific to San Francisco and returned. This historic voyage was such a success that other ships followed the example, including P&O's

The *Nieuw Amsterdam*. (Courtesy of Mick Lindsay Collection)

The *Stirling Castle* in 1955. (Courtesy of Mike Edwards Collection)

The *Edinburgh Castle* in 1963. (Courtesy of Mike Edwards Collection)

Orient Line *Oransay*. (Courtesy of Mick Lindsay Collection)

27,955-ton *Himalaya* in 1958. This service became known as the Orient & Pacific Line.

World cruises followed in 1958, first by the *Oransay* in 1958 and then by the *Himalaya* in 1959. In 1960 P&O passenger service merged with the Orient and became P&O Orient Lines, but in 1965 the name returned to P&O. At the time of the merger each company had a ship under construction; the Orient Line's 42,000-ton *Oriana* in 1960 and the P&O Line 45,000-ton flagship *Canberra* in 1961.

New Cargo and Passenger Building for Union Castle Line
Following the bomb damage to the port, new buildings were constructed to handle cargo and passengers, and in 1952 a decision was made to construct a new Union Castle Cargo & Passenger Building at Berth 102. The new building was officially opened on 25 January 1956 by His Excellency Mr G.P. Jooste, High Commissioner for the Union of South Africa. It was a two-storey building, with the lower floor designed to receive passengers arriving on the weekly mail ships from South Africa. The upper floor was used for the storage of wool, skins and other baled cargoes. The passenger reception hall facilities included an immigration hall, telephone area, bookstall, buffet, travel agencies and rail ticket offices. Once the passengers had landed they made their way to the hall, where their baggage had been sorted into alphabetical order for a Customs inspection. Once cleared, the passengers would make their way to the waiting boat train at the rail platform or to the west end of the shed where taxis could be met. The public address system used for announcements or for playing music would also be used to call waiting taxis or private cars from the nearby car parks. Union Castle moved from the Old Docks, where they previously used 35–36 and 38–39 Berths, to the New Docks on 102 Berth.

Sitmar Line-Assisted Passages
In late 1957 the Sitmar Line gained the contract to take British migrants to Australia. The ships concerned were the *Fairsea*, *Fairsky* and *Castel Felice*. If they had two or three days in port the ship would unload passengers, go into dry dock, come out of dry dock, load passengers and head off to sea.

The *Fairsea*. (Courtesy of Mick Lindsay Collection)

The *Fairsky*. (Courtesy of Mick Lindsay Collection)

Don Archbold: 'One of the companies we dealt with for passenger ships was the Sitmar Line, an Italian company, and they had the contract for taking British emigrants out to Australia. They used to load about 1,500 passengers at a time. When they arrived they brought back about 100 passengers and then loaded 1,500. We used to work night and day for that. I remember on one occasion one came in at 5pm on a Saturday afternoon and sailed again at 4pm on the Sunday, and we had done the job. I praised the dockers, and we wrote them a letter of appreciation for their work and that we respected the good job they had done.' Don reaped the benefits of his early experiences when he started work about giving respect: 'I could get more out of those dockers by treating them with respect and can now walk down Shirley High Street and be greeted with "Hello Guv!"'

The ships did not always leave the dry dock before the passengers embarked: 'We sometimes had the ships in dry dock to have their bottoms scraped. On one or two occasions we had to embark passengers in dry dock because they were running late. The worst one we had was on one occasion when the ship was very late, and of course it was left to Southampton to make up the time, and she went straight into dry dock, and we discharged the passengers, embarked the passengers in dry dock and she sailed from dry dock to sea.'

Ron Williams remembers the £10 assisted passages to Australia which was on a one-class ship especially built for those who wanted to emigrate. Ron Williams: 'In those ships they were full both ways. The famous picture that came in the press one time was of a woman running down the gangway, rushing past the master at arms and kissing the floor where she had managed to get back from Australia. I was on that ship. The *Fairsky* was an Italian run ship which was the ex-HMS *Attacker*, an aircraft carrier. The conditions on some of those ships were really appalling in what were previously the old hangers, although they had to come up to certain standards for the port. I heard that when they got to Australia they were housed in buildings like

The *Castel Felice*. (Courtesy of Mick Lindsay Collection)

The *Canberra*. (Courtesy of Ann Wright Collection)

P&O *Oriana*. (Courtesy of Bert Moody Collection)

cowsheds. They didn't think they would have to go to work and thought there would be plenty of time on the beach, but you still had to earn a living. I talked to people that returned, and they said nobody wanted to work outside the cities, but the jobs weren't there. The jobs were out in the outback. The unions were also very strong out there, just like in England.'

In 1960 the P&O Passenger Terminal was completed at Berth 106 in the New Docks, and in the same year the P&O *Oriana* left Southampton on her maiden voyage to Sydney, Australia. The P&O *Canberra* left a year later on 2 June 1961 for her maiden voyage, also to Sydney. By 1969 the P&O ships in operation in Southampton were the *Orsova*, *Orcades*, *Oronsay*, *Arcadia*, *Iberia*, *Himalaya*, *Chusan*, *Canberra* and *Oriana*.

The Beginning of the End for the Union Castle Line
With the sailing of *Windsor Castle* on 16 July 1965, the mail service could complete the passage from Southampton to Cape Town in just 11 days. The familiar Thursday 4pm departures then changed to Friday 1pm departures; however, in 1966 the mail service became jointly shared with Safmarine (South African Marine Corporation). Two of the Union Castle fleet, the *Pretoria Castle* and *Transvaal Castle*, were transferred to Safmarine. The ships were repainted in the Safmarine colours and the *Pretoria Castle* became the SA *Oranje*, and the *Transvaal Castle* the SA *Vaal*.

The *Transvaal Castle*. (Courtesy of Mick Lindsay Collection)

The *Pendennis Castle*. (Courtesy of Mike Edwards Collection)

The Final Years

With the increasing use of the jet airliner and the start of containerisation came the changes in passenger and cargo transportation. With it came the end to 120 years of service linked with Southampton. This was to have a huge impact on the docks and dockworkers. The *Southern Echo* on Monday 19 September 1977 carried the headlines: 'Sad end of a great service'. The newspaper reported that 'by December more than 300 will have been made redundant, including many in the 40–50 age group who had expected to be with the company for the rest of the careers.' It also commented: 'The loss to the Port of Southampton and the city would be immense. After October there will be no work for some 700 dockers, checkers and crane drivers.' There would also be the loss to the ship repair, dry docking and the firms that service the liners with supplies and equipment.

The withdrawal of services started to happen from the middle of the 1970s. It was on 28 May 1975 that the cruise liner *Reina del Mar* left Southampton, bound for Taiwan to be scrapped. The reduction in the mail service started to impact on services with the SA *Oranje* being withdrawn from service. She left Southampton for the breaker's yard on 19 September 1975. One year later the *Edinburgh Castle* made her last departure from Southampton on 23 April 1976 for Durban without passengers, also for the breakers yard.

After the *Pendennis Castle* had arrived at Southampton on 14 June 1976 she was withdrawn from service. The *Pendennis Castle* left Southampton on 7 July for the Far East, where she was laid up until she was scrapped in 1980.

The Union Castle Line's flagship *Windsor Castle* left Southampton for her last voyage on 12 August 1977, arriving back on 19 September. The *Windsor Castle* left Southampton on 3 October for the Middle East to be used as a floating hotel; however, after being laid up for a long time near Piraeus in Greece she sailed on 14 April 2005 for the Alang shipbreaker's yard in India.

On the 26 September 1977 *Good Hope Castle* arrived at Southampton after completing her last voyage in the mail service. Just one month later, on 24 October, the *Southampton Castle* arrived at Southampton, ending the mail service after 120 years.

SA *Vaal* arrived at Southampton on 10 October 1977, sailing again on 29 October for Kobe, Japan. In Japan she was rebuilt before joining Carnival Cruise Lines as the *Festivale*. From 1978 she was based in Florida, cruising the Caribbean until 1996 when Dolphin Cruise Line chartered her as the *Island Breeze*. During the summer she was chartered to Thomson Holidays, returning to cruise the Caribbean in the winter. In 1998, Dolphin Cruise Line was merged with Premier Cruise Line and became the Big Red Boat III, but in 2003 she also went to the shipbreaker's yard at Alang, India.

Both the *Southampton Castle* and her sister ship *Good Hope Castle* were sold to Costa Lines. The *Southampton Castle* was renamed *Franca C*, and the *Good Hope Castle* the *Paola C*. The ships finally departed Southampton for Genoa in February 1978, but both ships had short careers with Costa Lines before being sent to the shipbreaker's yard.

Cruising Takes Over from Transatlantic Services

By the 1970s P&O had bought Princess Cruises, and by 2003 P&O Princess Cruises and Carnival Corporation had merged and today operate the largest passenger shipping operation in the world.

The *Norway* in Southampton (SS France). (Courtesy of Richard de Jong Collection)

In 1974 the French Line's SS *France* was withdrawn from service. The *France* was launched on 11 May 1960 with her maiden voyage to New York taking place on 3 February 1961. The *France* was distinguished by two unusual funnels, which had wings on either side to dispense the exhaust. At the time of launching she was the longest passenger ship in the world at 1,036.7ft (316m) and maintained that distinction until the launching of the RMS *QM2* at 1,132ft (345.03m) in 2005. She was laid up and eventually sold to the Norwegian Cruise Line and renamed *Norway*. The maiden voyage of the *Norway* took her to Miami, where she became a popular liner for cruises around the Caribbean.

Cruising into the 21st Century from Southampton

The only luxury liner to provide regular transatlantic service today is the *Queen Mary 2* which took over from the *Queen Elizabeth 2* in 2004. When ABP opened the improved cruise terminals and developed a third cruise facility in 2003, this included the Queen Elizabeth II Ocean Terminal which was refurbished in preparation for the arrival of the new RMS *Queen Mary 2* in 2004. The terminal consisted of a larger embarkation lounge and waiting area, larger luggage handling area and an overhead passenger gangway. The new facilities were opened on 3 October 2003 by Mrs Pauline Prescott, wife of the Rt Hon John Prescott MP (the deputy prime minister).

The *Queen Mary 2* passing Calshot.

When the RMS *Queen Mary 2* sailed into Southampton on Boxing Day 2003 it was a dull wet day, but it was quite an exciting time for the people waiting for the liner at Calshot when the *QM2* gradually appeared through the mist as she came through the Thorn Channel. On 8 January 2004 she was named by Her Majesty Queen Elizabeth II, and on 12 January 2004 the *Queen Mary 2* sailed from Southampton on her maiden voyage to Fort Lauderdale, US.

It was on 16 April 2004 that she made her maiden transatlantic crossing to New York, and on 25 April she made her historic eastbound transatlantic crossing in tandem with the *QE2*. For Cunard the tradition of transatlantic travel still continues today, starting in the spring and ending in the autumn (avoiding the rough Atlantic weather). The world cruises follow this for the winter months. Most liners today are used as cruise ships to the Mediterranean, the Caribbean and other vacation areas.

Today Cunard and P&O Princes Cruises are part of the Carnival Corporation. Carnival Corporation, based in North America, is a global cruise company and extends to North America, Europe and Australasia. The cruise lines incorporated in the Carnival Corporation also include cruise ships from the Holland America Line, Seabourn Cruises, Windstar Cruises, Aida Cruises, P&O Cruises, Ocean Village, Costa Cruises and Swan Hellenic. As well as Southampton being the home port for Cunard and P&O Cruises, Royal Caribbean International, Fred Olsen Cruise Lines, Saga Cruises and Thomson Cruises also use the port. 2005 was a record year when 702,356 passengers passed through the port. The previous record was made in 1955 with 689,000 passengers passing through the port. This was prior to the impact that air travel was to have on ocean travel in the future.

Time is Money!

As with all ships, there are normally two main operation departments on board to sail the ship. These are the deck and engine departments. The officers and crew on the deck departments deal with the overall operation of the ship and are responsible for the navigation, communications, maintenance and safety. The engine room department are responsible for the operation of the main engine propulsion, other plant and machinery and electrical generators. Unlike the cargo ships, which sail with a smaller number of crew because of the modern technology, the crew on a cruise ship include not only the deck and engineering officers and crew, but also all the crew to meet the catering and hotel services, such as laundry, galley, restaurant, bedrooms and entertainment.

Due to the commercial need to cut costs and make money the phrase 'Time is Money' is important to the shipping companies, so cruise ships spend as short a time as possible in port. When cruise ships arrive in the Port of Southampton they usually arrive at the dock between 5am and 6am. During its time in port a ship has to disembark over 2,000 passengers (each usually having two bags amounting to over 4,000 pieces of luggage), make the beds, clean the ship, load tons of food and drink, take the garbage off and take on tons of fuel. The passengers for the next cruise will embark and yet with all that activity the ship leaves again at 6pm the same day. The *QM2* carries 2,500 to 3,000 passengers, and yet the same process has to be completed as for a smaller ship and the *QM2* still leaves the port the same day.

Royal Caribbean International *Freedom of the Seas.*

The Mega Cruise Ships

With larger cruise ships being built with capacity for 5,000-plus passengers, the companies are aiming to cater for the interests and leisure needs of all ages, including on the ships things like theatres, swimming pools, night clubs, casinos, ice skating, rock climbing walls, water sports, fitness suites and golf courses. One reason why passengers new to cruising prefer the larger cruise ships is because these ships cut through the waves better that the smaller ships, giving a smoother ride. More experienced passengers may prefer the smaller ships because of the smaller numbers of passengers and the advantage of getting to know the officers and crew when on repeat cruises.

When the 151,400-ton *Queen Mary 2* was officially launched by the queen on 8 January 2004 she was at the time the world's largest passenger ship afloat and also the longest, widest and tallest passenger ship ever built. That was until the *Freedom of the Seas* left the Aker Finland shipyard and arrived at Southampton on 29 April 2006, before sailing to New York for her naming ceremony.

The *Queen Victoria.* (Courtesy of Richard de Jong Collection)

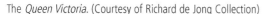

Royal Caribbean International *Independence of the Seas*. (Courtesy of Richard de Jong Collection)

At 154,407 gross ton, Royal Caribbean International's *Freedom of the Seas* took over as the largest passenger ship afloat, carrying 4,370 passengers; however, the *Queen Mary 2* is 1,132ft (345.03m) in length and the *Freedom of the Seas* is 1,112ft (338.9m), so the *QM2* is still longer in length by 20ft (6.9m).

The newest Cunarder, the 90,000-ton *Queen Victoria*, arrived at Southampton on 7 December 2007. She was named *Queen Victoria* by Her Royal Highness The Duchess of Cornwall on Monday 10 December and left on her maiden cruise on Tuesday 11 December 2007.

The new Royal Caribbean *Independence of the Seas* arrived at Southampton in April 2008 and commenced her service, taking cruise passengers out of Southampton for the summer. After the summer season 2008 she sailed to Miami, Florida, for the winter cruise season.

Working for P&O

Chris Wright, who is now P&O's manager of fleet maintenance and purchasing systems, gives an insight into how he became interested in a career at sea and his early experiences: 'My time at sea goes back to holiday jobs and working on tugs through knowing various people up around the west coast of Scotland. Then after leaving college and completing A levels I spent a year out working as assistant harbour master at Lymington. I had quite a lot of links with the sea and then towards the end of college P&O came looking for electrical and electronic engineers and they were promoting a life at sea, which seemed interesting, and I ended up getting a job as a trainee electro-technical officer. That lasted for a year and I started as an electro-technical officer. I thought I would do it for two or three years to get experience and travel around the world.

'I was based in Southampton and started out on the *Canberra* in the late 1980s, and I think the first trip on the *Canberra* was the refit in Bremerhaven where they were re-engining the *Queen Elizabeth 2*, and then we went on a Christmas cruise and then a world cruise. So it was a "baptism of fire" into the world of voyaging. At the time cruising was fairly new, certainly to the public in the UK, because the line voyages which the *Canberra* had been built for had been effectively stopped with the advent of the jumbo jet. So the company turned to cruising.

The *Sky Princess*. (Courtesy of Ann Wright Collection)

'At the time the Port of Southampton was going through a difficult time, including trouble with the RMT union and the dock workers with strikes and all sorts; however, the cruising kept going, although P&O did have the Princess fleet out in North America. We all wanted to work on the Princess ships as it was much more fun. Instead of sailing in and out of Southampton, you could be sailing in and out of Florida and Mexico – much more interesting. From the *Canberra* I then worked on the *Royal Princess* in Alaska, and between the two ships I saw Alaska, the Caribbean and the Mediterranean.

'Over the years I have worked my way up through the ranks. I spent a long time on one ship which was at the time called the *Sky Princess*, now called the *Pacific Sky*. It was 1984 and it was one of the last steam-powered passenger ship. It is still sailing and will do as long as it makes money!

'When I left Sky I was seconded on to a new build project for P&O which was the *Oriana*. She was built in Pappenburg, in Northern Germany, which is 30 miles inland! The shipbuilders had already built a number of large cruise ships, and *Oriana* was build number 636, starting from small river boats and working their way up to the large cruise ships. I was out on that build for about seven or eight months before the ship went into service. To see a 69,000-ton ship carrying 2,000 passengers and 800 officers and crew being built in a shed is quite a sight! It is a real shame that by that time, around 1993–94, the UK was incapable of building a ship of that size on a schedule. I don't think we even had the technology or the facilities to build on a schedule in this country, so we had to go to Germany.'

The New P&O Cruise Ship *Oriana* Arrives in Southampton

Her Majesty Queen Elizabeth II named the new P&O cruise ship *Oriana* in 1995. Chris Wright: 'When the newly built *Oriana* sailed into Southampton for the first time there was a lot of excitement because it was the first new passenger cruise ship to come to P&O for a very long time. It was very large, very modern and very unlike its predecessors in the way it was built. The technology meant it was the first ship with no mechanical connections between the bridge, engine and steering. It was all electronic and done by computers.'

Chris Wright: 'When the *Oriana* sailed down the River Ems from Pappenburg, Germany, it was estimated that there were at least 100,000 visitors to the area, just to see the ship. To enable the ship to sail down the river power lines over the river had to be pulled taut to get the ship underneath and part of the river had to be dredged.'

'The *Oriana* had the biggest swimming pool at sea and a waterfall that dropped over four decks through the atrium, which were things that people had never seen on a ship before. It had a theatre with 700 seats with a clear view of the stage, a revolving stage, and it really was a boost for Southampton. Since then, the only ship that has made a similar impact coming into Southampton was the *Queen Mary 2*.

'The *Aurora* and various other ships joined from the Princess fleet, with the *Ocean Princess* renamed as the *Oceana*, but nothing that made such an impact on the public when sailing into Southampton as the *Oriana* and *Queen Mary 2*; however, there are no new facilities on board the *Queen Mary 2*, other than the planetarium that has not been provided before in other ships. It is just the scale of it, it is just so massive.'

The *Oriana*.

The *Arcadia.*

Size of the Ships Today

Today the size and scale of ships appears to be ever increasing. The *Oriana* accommodates 2,000 passengers, with a maximum of 1,000 cabins. The *QE2* takes 2,500–3,000 passengers but has much more space for them.

The newly built *Arcadia* takes 2,500 passengers but is not as big as the *QE2*. This is not always the answer to all passengers' needs and requirements, and there is a call for having smaller ships similar to the ships of yesteryear. P&O's answer to that is to bring in the *Royal Princess*, built in 1984, which was to be called the *Artemis*.

The *Royal Princess* can carry about 1,200 passengers, but is not small (it is about 45,000 tons) in comparison to the old 30,000-ton cruise ship such as the *Island Princess*, but it is small compared to the 80,000–130,000 tons of the *QE2*.

The Atmosphere On-board Different Ships

Chris Wright: 'The atmosphere on every ship is different. Every ship has its own character, and all the various companies that operate them try to generate the same feeling on board all their ships so that passengers know what the atmosphere will be like and what the facilities will be like. With P&O, however, they have deliberately gone the other way and have allowed each ship to develop its own character, its own feel. The advertising for the *Arcadia* says "this re-invented cruising" and has a more contemporary feel to it. The *Oriana* is much more classic with a slower pace on board. The *Aurora* is meant to be a little more contemporary than *Oriana*, but actually on-board the look of the ship is slightly darker, with a sort of 1930s or 1940s feel to the ship. It is just the facilities on board. What they promote on-board and how it evolves encourages the different passengers staying with that ship.

The *Artemis.*

The *Island Princess.* (Courtesy of Mick Lindsay Collection)

'For passengers on cruise ships for the first time, the itinerary is initially very important, especially for those taking cruises to the Mediterranean, the Caribbean and to Alaska. After this, passengers experiment with more and more cruises, and then they discover the ship that suits their needs and repeat cruises on the same ship again and again. They like the feel, the atmosphere and the facilities and become well known to the crew by coming back again and again. So many passengers that have been on a lot of cruises tend to stay with one ship or one type of ship because they just like that feel.

'At the naming ceremony of the *Oriana*, the Queen named the ship, and it was a "spark" to the cruise business. The catchphrase for many of the passengers on the first few cruises was always "It's not like *Canberra*!" Everybody loved the *Canberra*. The *Canberra* was built in 1961 and by 1995 when the *Oriana* arrived she was very "tired". The *Canberra* really only kept going because of the name being boosted after the Falklands conflict. All the passengers who had previously been on *Canberra* compared the *Oriana* to that. When we hosted tables for dinner we had passengers quite often commenting that: "it wasn't like Canberra at all, not the same atmosphere."'

Plenty to do When On-board

The vacation itself may not be the world's cheapest vacation but cruise passengers will not get that kind of value for money anywhere else other than cruising. To go on a ship for 14 days, visit different countries over that 14 day period, enjoy the quality of the accommodation and food eaten every single day, the entertainment with the shows in the theatre, the show lounges, cinema, day-time activities, bands, discos and all the rest. It is the best way to see the ports. When berthed at the port, coaches will take the passengers to visit places of interest in the locality. Going on these tours enables the tourists to get a good taste of a place and to see what it is like and whether they would like to go back there again. A lot of cruise passengers use the cruises to find places they wish to return to for a holiday and then try a cruise somewhere else.'

With the advent of the 'Grand Class' ships, which are larger than the Panamax, meaning they cannot use the Panama Canal, the planning of the cruise itinerary for these larger ships is limited only to the ports that can accommodate them, and these ships have to stay on a very fixed itinerary. Ships such as the *Adonia* and *Oriana* can go through the Panama Canal and transfer from the Caribbean to the Pacific and then up to Alaska. The smaller ships such as the Minerva ships from Swan Hellenic go to places that some cruise ships have never been before, and they go out of their way to visit new ports each year to give the passengers a taste of something different. There are cruises that will go up to the edge of the Arctic Circle or around the Cape off South America. The only thing that will stop a cruise ship visiting anywhere is war!

In America there are the four-day party cruises, where many of the passengers are aged in their 20s, to the seven-day family or retired cruises. The longer two-week cruises up to Alaska cater mainly for the retired, who are usually the only people who have the time to do that length of cruise. The world cruises are lengthier, and the majority of the passengers are retired.

Chris Wright: 'The other thing that is changing is class. The original ships that started cruising were mainly a two-class and even in some cases three-class ships. The cruise ship *Canberra* was a two-class ship, and those passengers in the forward section of the ship were in the upper-class section, and those in the aft section of the ship were the second class or holiday class, where you shared facilities. Cabins did not have their own showers or toilets. Second-class passengers had to go down to a block of showers and toilets in the alleyways. That has now all changed, as all cabins have their own facilities, and some of the top suites are on two decks, containing grand pianos and jacuzzis. It is a matter of what you want to do on your cruise. There are passengers who want an extremely expensive cabin and look out their windows and those who prefer a cheaper cabin that they just want to use for sleeping in at night. There have been for years more and more ships providing outboard cabins with balconies as well. The new cruise liner *Arcadia* has a lot of balconies, which is planned for because the company wants to sell more cabins at a premium rate. The *Oriana* has about 1,000 cabins and carries 2,000 passengers, averaging out at about two people to a cabin; however, a lot of cabins that normally have two occupants have bunks up in the deck heads so that they can be brought down for children. Some cabins may then have two people in, and others may have a family.'

For passenger safety it is not the number of berths or bunks a ship has that is important but the number of passengers. A ship is governed by the passengers certificate which says that 'this ship is safe to carry [number of passengers]'. This means that there has to be enough lifeboats and life-raft places and lifesaving equipment for all passengers on-board.

The *Aurora*

Today it is very rare for a ship to have a major breakdown, with all the modern propulsion units, engineering equipment and modern electronic technology, but the P&O *Aurora* did have a serious major breakdown. The *Aurora* was due to set out on a 103-day round-the-world trip in January 2005 but was held up because of persistent engine propulsion problems.

The ship undertook days of repairs and tests by sailing up Southampton Water and into the Solent, but the problems still persisted. This was a very unusual occurrence, and the *Aurora* motor failure was considered to be the first time that this had happened in memory. Taking into account the hundreds of ships and years of experience of the industry experts, to have such a major component part of the ship fail in such an unmanageable way was almost unheard of. It is not unusual for ships to have components fail that could stop the ship for a week, but for a problem of this scale to happen to a ship is very unusual. The failure was that the ship had diesel electric propulsion, so the diesel generators generate power and the propulsion motors are then driven through speed controllers and filters to control the speed of the ship. Each motor contains two half-motors, so in one box you have two electric motors on one shaft. In the days of the cruise ship *Canberra* those motors would have been two separate machines in one box, but with all the modern technology in manufacturing techniques the way of making the motors efficient and cheaper is to make the them inter-wound. So the problem was that one half of the motor failed, and it failed because the copper wire was worn through, and it blew up and caused serious damage to the other motor in that unit. If the motors had been separate, as in the past, the ship's master could have explained to passengers that they could not maintain the speed they normally would have done, but they could have provided a limited cruise itinerary instead. The first thing P&O did was change from a world voyage to a grand voyage. This would mean that they would have to drop certain ports and plan what ports they could visit on the speed that would be available. When they tried to achieve that speed they discovered the other half of the machine had been so badly damaged and was causing such serious vibration that they just could not maintain a suitable speed, so P&O had to abandon the voyage completely.

The *Aurora* was taken to Bremerhaven, where the shipyard cut the bottom of the ship out under the main propulsion motors, dropped the motors out to the bottom of the dry dock and took them to the manufacturer. The manufacturer was at the time in the process of building motors for a new ship, and the company could use these motors for the *Aurora* and then build new motors for the other ship. The new motors were fitted, and the ship then went on sea trials and is now back in service. At the time of the breakdown about 380 passengers left after a few days, but those passengers who stayed on board for the two weeks were very happy with the way they had been treated and all got their money back.

Chris Wright: 'It cost P&O a lot of money in refunding the cost of the holidays to the passengers, but it is important to the company and its name that all passengers are happy. They cannot be allowed to go away dissatisfied.

The *Aurora*.

'As far as my job now is concerned I left the *Aurora* and was seconded into the office for a project to roll out the new maintenance and purchasing computer system for the fleet. About 18 months ago I took over as the manager of the fleet maintenance and purchasing systems. At the start it covered 18 ships and now covers 27 ships and rising because we have had a lot of Princesses built and ships coming in from Carnival, Princess Group and P&O Australia group, moving ships from here and there and putting them into different brands because the whole thing has expanded. I expect that a lot of this will end up as a corporate level within the Carnival Corporation. It is going on for about 80 ships now – it is massive and is the world's largest passenger operation through all its different brands. In all the years of having worked in and out of Southampton and around the world I can see that Southampton is really starting to move along again. It is still some way behind some of the ports we visit in the rest of the world but has a lot to offer. On an industry show in Miami a contingent from India put on a lunch and were promoting all the different ports in India for ships to come and visit, and here we are in the UK thinking "Wow, what a lot of money there is in cruising" and yet we have things to offer that nobody else in the world has got.

'I actually did a cruise on a small cruise ship before they got rid of them, the *Island Princess*. That sailed from Dover around the UK stopped in at Ireland, north of Scotland, the Orkney Islands and then back down the east coast. It was packed full of Americans who were convinced they were Scottish or Irish, and they loved it, the quaintness, they loved it. Yet there was one little ship going around the UK. I think if you're close to London, Edinburgh, Glasgow or Dublin, they are just crying out to attract these ships, and the only thing that puts paid the cruising market around the UK is the weather. This is shown to be the case when working out of Southampton, as ships have to be very fast. This is because you can't waste time getting from Southampton down to the Mediterranean to get the sunshine as quick as possible. The advent of fly/cruising is something that has come along quite a number of years ago and is expanding, and we have ships that are permanently based in the Mediterranean and the Caribbean. You get on a charter flight, join the ship, spend the two weeks on a cruise and then fly home again. We are learning, we are expanding and as we get more ships we can customise them to these different markets as well. With a corporate business we have Aida, which is German, and Costa, which is Italian, and the only ones that haven't caught on to cruising in a big way is the French.

'There are a lot of ships operating out of Scandinavia because they want to get away from Scandinavia while the rest of the world want to visit it, although it is incredibly expensive. You can go out and spend £50 on a lunch. Places to go are the Caribbean and now out to Fiji, and places like that are developing and changing, adapting and coming on line. There are more specialist ships, too. When you look at the German market layout it is totally different to the UK. Uou could not sell a cruise to a large number of Germans for a P&O ship, nor could you put a British family on an Aida cruise. It is totally different the way it works. It is developing all the time. Marketplaces are opening up everywhere. Take Australia for example. They have a population of 18 million even before we send cruises down there!

'As a ship leaves the berth at Southampton the passengers are drinking champagne on the deck, celebrating their cruise and waving farewell to their families on the quayside, while listening to the marine band playing down below. Whereas, in Australia they have *Waltzing Matilda* blaring out and the passengers are all wandering around barefoot with cans of beer. A totally different world!'

CHAPTER 11
THE DEVELOPMENT OF TUGS

In 1736 Jonathan Hulls, a British inventor from Campden, Gloucestershire, patented a steamboat with a paddle wheel at the stern, powered by a Newcomen engine steam engine for towing. The patent stated that the aim was to move: 'ships and vessels out of and into any harbour, port, or river against wind and tide or in a calm.' He tested his steamboat on the River Avon, at Evesham, but without success.

It was Robert Fulton from Pennsylvania, America, who built the first steamship. He had originally wanted to be an artist and had gone to Paris to study, but he then turned his attention to engineering and inventions. After spending time in England in 1786, he visited Birmingham where he studied Watt's steam engine. He had a model made to his own specifications and shipped it to America where he built the paddle steamer *Clermont*. In 1807 the *Clermont* sailed the 150 miles from New York City to Albany, making history in 32 hours at an average speed of 5mph.

The first actual tugboat built was the *Charlotte Dundas,* powered by a Watt engine and paddle wheel, which was used on the Forth and Clyde Canal in Scotland. It was in 1801 that William Symington was hired by Lord Dundas, a governor of the Forth and Clyde Canal, to build a steam tug. A model of the vessel was made for Lord Dundas, who named the steam tug *Charlotte Dundas* after one of his daughters. The first trial of the *Charlotte Dundas* was on 4 January 1803, with Lord Dundas and a few of his relatives and friends aboard. After some modifications a second trial was held in March 1803. This time the *Charlotte Dundas* towed two barges, one of 80 tons and the other 50 tons, the 18 miles along the Forth and Clyde Canal to Port Dundas, Glasgow, in 9¼ hours.

By this time the usefulness of steam tugboats was being recognised for towing sailing ships in and out of harbours, especially in adverse wind and weather. This was quickly noticed by the sailing ship owners who realised that the early paddle tugs could ensure that their sailing ships were not held up, and so they could keep their cargo schedules on the trade routes by being able to get their vessels in and out of the ports more quickly. This was the start of the towing industry, and good prices were paid for a tow. Subsequently, towing vessels became a highly competitive trade; however, in the early days the steam tugs were mainly confined to assisting sailing ships in and out of the docks, often just until the sailing ship could fill its sails and make headway. The early steam tugs were also not very powerful, especially when towing against the tide. Once steam ships came along, the steam tugs' role changed to helping the larger ships through deep water channels into the port and assisting in their berthing. These tugs were very reliant on the amount of coal stocks they could carry to keep their steam engines going, and they would sometimes have to borrow coal from a ship they were towing.

Side paddle wheels were known to cause damage to riverbanks from their wash, and they were eventually replaced with stern paddle wheels. From about the 1850s screw propellers started to be used instead of paddle wheels.

The Southampton, Isle of Wight and South of England Royal Mail Steam Packet Company

Services to and from Southampton and the Isle of Wight were important for passengers and trade, and in 1861 the Southampton, Isle of Wight and South of England Royal Mail Steam Packet Limited Company was registered. The new company was formed through the amalgamation of two companies, the Cowes-based Isle of Wight Royal Mail Steam Packet Company, who started in 1820, and the Southampton-based Isle of Wight Steam Packet Company, who started in 1826. Today the company is better known as Red Funnel. Both companies merged because of the competition from the Southampton, Isle of Wight & Portsmouth Improved Steamboat Company, who introduced two paddle steamers into service in 1860. This company developed serious financial problems, however, and was eventually taken over by Red Funnel in 1865. Red Funnel's first seven paddle steamers were led by the *Medina,* the largest, dating from 1852. The remaining paddlers were the *Gem* and the *Queen,* and the *Sapphire, Emerald, Ruby* and *Pearl* whose four colours represented the four triangles of the Red Funnel house flag.

The Alexandra Towing Company

The Alexandra Towing Company began working in the Liverpool Docks in 1887. At the time the company were using the tugs *Flying Tempest, Flying Whirlwind, Turbot, Flying Breeze* and *Flying Kestrel*. They began to establish operations in other ports, and one of those was the Port of Southampton, when in 1919 they followed the Cunard Line's move to the south coast. Their tug tender *Flying Kestrel* moved with them at the same time.

It was the Southampton, Isle of Wight and South of England Royal Mail Steam Packet Limited Company (Red Funnel Line) tugs *Albert Edward, Hercules, Vulcan, Ajax, Hector* and *Neptune* that were present at the departure of the *Titanic* on Wednesday 10 April 1912. It was the tug *Vulcan* that saved a near collision between the *New York* and the *Titanic.* The *Titanic* left the White Star Dock and was passing the *New York,* moored alongside the *Oceanic* at Berth 38, when the suction from the *Titanic* snapped the mooring ropes of the *New York*. The stern of the *New York* began to swing out towards the *Titanic* and it was the quick

The tug *Vulcan*. (Courtesy of Bert Moody Collection)

thinking of the tug *Vulcan*'s master Captain Gale who managed to get a line aboard the ship and pull her away from the *Titanic*. The *Vulcan* was built in 1893 and remained in service with Red Funnel right up to 1957.

Early in World War One there was a need to increase the number of tugs in Southampton to manage the number of troopships sailing to France and the hospital ships returning with the wounded. Here is an account of one person who worked on the tugs in World War One: 'I had my brother in there as a deck-boy. He advised me to come into that because the money was good and it was one of those jobs where it was looked upon as a necessity for the war effort. They used to carry a master, a mate, two able seamen and a deckboy, two firemen, a greaser and an engineer. Why there was two firemen was because tugs were fired by coal, and therefore it used to take a lot of hard work, cleaning flues and moving ashes.

'During the war, the First World War, they had a system whereby if they wanted you in a hurry they used to send a telegram. You'd hear a bang on the door late at night, you know, and perhaps you'd been ordered in for 10 o'clock in the morning. About 10 o'clock at night you'd hear a bang on the door, get a telegram "Steam for 3am", so you had to be ready to go somewhere, it could be anywhere. I mean to say you might have to go and tow a disabled ship in, or it might be just berthing a ship or taking one out. You never knew what you were going to get. Well if variety is the spice of life you certainly got the spice of life! Believe you me. You never knew what was coming. It could be a coal-barge. It could be an oil barge. It could be anything. It could be a transatlantic liner. You never knew what you were going to get hold of.

'The most depressing part of it always was the night time, seeing so many men going out and singing and cheering, really enjoying themselves, and the next morning you dealt with hospital ships coming back loaded with wounded. You got so used to it. It began to be mechanical.

'It was amazing the work that was done. All round the dock it was done, night-time as well, because time was money to shipping people. The more trips a ship got in the more money she was making.' (*Oral History Unit, Southampton*.)

Tug Tendering Work in the 1930s

During the 1930s the tugs working the Port of Southampton came from two tug companies, The Alexandra Towing Company and Red Funnel. The Alexandra Towing Company tugs were the tender *Greetings,* tug tenders *Romsey* and *Flying Kestrel* and tugs *Brockenhurst, William Poulson, Wellington* and *Sloyne*. The Red Funnel tugs were the tug tender *Calshot, Clausentum, Canute, Vulcan, Hector, Neptune* and *Sir Bevois*. In the 1930s and 1940s the tug tenders *Calshot* and *Romsey* often transported world-famous celebrities, including film stars and politicians, to and from liners anchored in the Solent. These trips involved the sailing to and from Cowes Roads to service the liners that had anchored to take on cargo, provisions, passengers and their luggage and sometimes cars.

An account of the arrival of the tug tender *Romsey*, and what it was like to work on her is given by another Southampton tugboatman: 'We were tied up alongside 47 Berth in the Ocean Dock and up comes this, well, what I call a "white elephant" because she was all white, painted like a yacht! And, "Oh!" they said, "here she comes". I said, "Who? Where? What comes?" They said, "This is the new *Romsey*." I said, "What, that abortion!" Little did I think I was going to spend five years in her.

'The idea of the tenders was the fact that a lot of big passenger ships used to anchor in Cowes Roads to save time on the voyage, particularly the German ships like the *Bremen* and *Europa* and all those coming across, because it saved them coming up to Southampton which saved them docking dues and so on. The tenders used to go down, pick up the passengers and the baggage and the mail and bring it back to Southampton, discharge it in Southampton and the ship would go on her way.

The tug *Sir Bevois*. (Courtesy of Mick Lindsay Collection)

The tug *Paladin*. (Courtesy of Bert Moody Collection)

'There was quite a nice passenger deck, although she was a tug. Everything was dismantled and the towing hook and everything was covered up, so that if they wanted to charter her for a party or anything like that, that was all taken out, stowed away out of the way. There was a nice big, open deck. If they wanted to have a dance they could, and there was a nice sheltered deck the fore-end. In the winter we used to put canvas screens round that so as to keep the weather out, so that the passengers could get in under there.

'I suppose as a dual-purpose job she was really successful. From a tugboatman's point of view she was not the ideal tug, because having a passenger deck built above the main deck and the hook on the passenger deck puts the centre of gravity out. But she was very efficient and very effective. There's no doubt about that. And she was utilised on all the big ships.' (*Oral History Unit, Southampton.*)

The tug tender *Calshot* was often seen servicing many of the famous ocean liners, including the *Queen Mary* and *Queen Elizabeth*, *Mauretania*, *Olympic*, *Bremen* and the French Line's flagship *Normandie*. It was not uncommon for the Red Funnel paddle steamers to act as tenders. These included the paddlers *Gracie Fields*, *Princess Elizabeth* and *Lorna Doone*.

Some shipping companies would not pay the port fees, which included docking fees and charges for taking water and all the facilities that went with it. They wouldn't pay for that, but would pay for a tug to bring the supplies and passengers down to the ships that anchored in Cowes Roads. All they had to pay for then was stevedores and the tug. It was mostly the tug tenders *Calshot* and *Romsey* that used to service the ships that anchored in Cowes Roads, and Don Archbold, who was working as a ships agent for Keller Bryant & Co Ltd, had the experience of tendering the vessels in Cowes Roads: 'Another thing we used to do was tender work. That was when I did the *Calshot* with the passengers, when it had open sides! The *Calshot* was a big tug, but also she had two saloons down below where we used to put the passengers. The Red Funnel steamers also had another tug, the *Paladin*, and when we were busy sometimes we used the *Paladin*. She was slightly different because she had a more covered inside.'

When tendering the liners the job was mainly taking passengers, their luggage, mail and provisions to the ships and returning with the passengers bound for Southampton, but when cargo ships anchored off the port the ships agent would have the daunting task of climbing the pilot's ladder to board the ship. Don Archbold: 'We used to go down to a ship anchored in Cowes Roads and take the passengers and their baggage off and bring them back to the port and vice versa if the ship was outward bound. Some of the cargo ships used to anchor off the port and the ships agent would have to climb up and down the ladder at the side of the ship.'

Don gives an example of a typical day when tendering the ships: 'There was one company called the Holland Africa Line, and they sometimes didn't have a lot of passengers, maybe about 50 or 60, and it would be too expensive to bring the ship up to the port, and so it used to anchor in Cowes Road. At 6am we would have the *Calshot* laid on. The stevedores would arrive at 6am as well, and we would put the gear on, such as nets and boards for lifting the baggage and any cars, because some ships used to bring cars on them. We would sail down to Cowes Roads, lay alongside the ship and the men would stay on the tender, but the ship's crew would then load the baggage over to the tender for the stevedores to stack it, and then the passengers would come aboard. We would take Customs and immigration officials down with us, which saved a lot of time for everybody. We would come back to Southampton, unload the baggage to the shed, disembark the passengers and they would pick up their baggage and off they would go.'

Ron Williams was one of the dockers who would also travel down to Cowes on the tug tender *Calshot*: 'We used to go on the *Calshot* to Cowes Roads and tender the ships. Every year at Christmas there was one ship arrival, and that was the *Batory* of the Polish Ocean Lines. She used to tie up in Cowes Roads, and the tug would go down, take the passengers down and if there were any passengers for England they used to come back with us on the top. It was good pay, but it was always done by volunteers because it was Christmas Day. On the tender you used to have a gang for the ship, when you got down there, and a gang for the tender. There were six men on the tender and about eight on the ship to receive the baggage, mail or provisions for the ship and make sure it was all stowed safely. Of course you had the foreman on the ship, and you used to take cars down on the deck of the *Calshot* and bring any back. There could be up to six cars on the deck, and the last car was left in the gear that strapped round the wheels and the spar-spreaders, to make sure it was secure so that it could be lifted out first.'

The dockers who went down on the tug tenders to Cowes Roads used to enjoy the work, but they did find difficulty in pronouncing the names of some of the ships. Ron Williams: 'We used to call one of the ships the 'Olden Down Boat' because her name was *Johan van Oldenbarnevelt*. Well, most of the lads couldn't say that. They were tender jobs. They were nice little jobs because it took us an hour to get down on there on the tender.' While on board the tender to and from the port, the dockers would be on deck.

Sometimes the tug tender would go down with 100 passengers, and more times than enough it was VIPs and film stars: 'We went down to pick up Dick van Dyke and the artist Graham Sutherland, the artist that painted Churchill and his wife. He came up on the same job. Cary Grant and the others were mainly on the *Queen Mary*. Most times you never saw them as they were off through the VIP area. They would not see their luggage and didn't go on trains but would have a car waiting.'

Ron remembers going down to Cowes Roads to load hovercraft on to a ship: 'We went down to Cowes Roads and lifted two of the biggest hovercraft ever made over on the IOW. We lifted them on deck. They used to have special ships built for heavy lifting up to 80 to 100 tons. What they would do was flood the ship on one side to counteract her going over.'

Terry Adams was very grateful to the skipper of the tug tender *Calshot* in the way he used to time their arrival back at the docks: 'We used to go down on the old *Calshot*. The skipper was always good to us, because if we ever went on a tender and got back to the docks at 1.05pm we got another hour's pay. We would go down in the morning to do one of the Dutch boats, and if the skipper berthed us by 1pm we didn't get the extra hour. So the skipper used to slow down so that we got our hour's pay! The mail was one of the biggest things we would take down, and we used to lose some in the water. It would come out on the ship's derrick, and she would shift over and "plonk", a mail bag might go in the water. We would try to fish it out, but were not always very successful.'

Ray Strange remembers the tender work and the skipper of the tug taking time to get back to the dock so they could get the hour's pay. He says it was: 'A good job, but it didn't pay a lot, but we used to tender the ships in Cowes Roads and take passengers, mail, baggage and the odd car on the *Old Calshot*, and it was a day out. It was a nice day out, providing it wasn't rough of course!'

The *Gatcombe II*. (Courtesy of Bert Moody Collection)

Getting the extra hour did not always happen, however, because of one particular dockers' foreman. Ray Strange: 'There was one foreman, who, if you picked up your tender at 107 Berth and you got on down the river and we were "poodling" to get back past 5 o'clock, he would drop us at 43 Berth to save paying the hour. All our bikes were at 107 Berth! I don't know if he got a medal for that. Some were good lads who had worked with you and had gone on, and they knew the job. Then

The *Calshot II*. (Courtesy of Bert Moody Collection)

you got the younger element who had never done it, and quite frankly I don't know why they took them on because they knew nothing at all.'

Other tugs would also act as tug tenders, including the *Paladin* and *Gatcombe I,* and in the 1960s two new tug tenders were built by J.I. Thornycroft, first the *Gatcombe II* and then a new *Calshot II.*

Also by 1962 the Alexandra Towing Company replaced the tug tender *Romsey* with the *Flying Breeze,* which only continued in service for a short time until 1967. This was because the passenger trade was diminishing through more passengers using the jet airliner than the ocean liners. With fewer ocean liners visiting Southampton there was less need for tug tenders, but the old tug tender *Calshot* continued in service until 1986.

Coaling the Tugs

Ron Williams started working in the docks in the early 1950s as a coal porter for two years. He would fill the Red Funnel tugs up once a day by shovelling coal into chutes at 20 Berth in the Old Docks. The other major towing company, the Alexandra Towing Company, had their tugs filled up mechanically by a grab at Northam on the River Itchen.

Within their tug fleet Red Funnel had the tug tender *Calshot* and the Alexandra Towing Company had the tug tender *Romsey.* Ron Williams: 'The *Calshot* and *Romsey* were the two biggest tenders in the world and were the two leading tugs for all the famous liners. You can see them in all the photos.'

Different manning levels would be used, depending on which tug was being worked on. On the Red Funnel tugs the coal would be shovelled into a chute especially made for the job. Ron Williams: 'On the *Calshot* you had to have an extra man when the coal went down the chute into the sliding door because the bunker was about 4ft away and the coal had to be shovelled from the platform to the hole and down the hole into the bunker. It was hard work, and we used to get 27s 6d (£1.37) a day. We got to know the crew very well, and the deck boy would make the tea for the coal porters. If he ran out of milk it meant he would have to run all the way down the quayside to get more milk – so our tea had very little milk in it. It was so strong you could stand a spoon up in it!'

A railway wagon with 20 to 30 tons of coal would be brought up and a chute would be tied on, and another chute went to the hatch for the bunker. Once the chutes were in place the coal porters would let the coal run. Ron Williams: 'You needn't do anything for about 10 minutes because the coal would continue running, but that was when it got so dusty. They supplied you with a bucket of water, a bar of soap and some rags to wipe yourself. No wash basins or showers in those days, and you had to supply your own overalls.'

In earlier days the coal was loaded onto ships by hand. Ron Williams: 'My dad was a coal porter, but in those days two men would have to run up a plank, on in front, one behind, carrying the coal, in what I think was called an "Irish cart". They would tip the coal into the door and run back down with it and keep that up for hours. In those days there was no such thing as a pension, and many of the men working were well into their 80s.'

Ron talks about the man who was in charge of his gang: 'He was very experienced in coaling the ships, and before the war he used to do it when they moored the ships off Netley and coal barges would pull alongside. The coal was loaded into baskets or buckets that were winched up to the coal ports and then shovelled down into the coal bunkers. It was dangerous work, there was no such thing as health and safety in those days. All you had to do was dodge it!'

Learning the job was gained through watching and listening. Ron Williams: 'They had all learned the job by experience, and there was only two ways to do the job, the right way and the wrong way.' When Ron started work he willingly took the advice of his father: 'Just keep quiet, listen and watch and you'll be alright.'

The tug tender *Calshot,* with open sides. (Courtesy of ABP)

The tug tender *Calshot,* with covered sides passing Netley. (Courtesy of Mick Lindsay Collection)

The Tug *Paladin*

The tug *Paladin* had four bunkers on either side and used to take between 20 and 25 tons of coal each time. There was one time when they were filling the tug *Paladin* with coal that a very funny event took place with the actor Peter Sellars. Ron Williams explains: 'We had a tug called the *Paladin*, and she was in the film called *The Mouse that Roared* with Peter Sellars. One morning it was frosty and freezing cold, and we were shovelling the coal down the chute. Then somebody said, "What the hell is that?" It was a hearse that pulled up alongside, and Peter Sellars got out with a pith helmet on. He went on the *Paladin* and all the crew, we knew all the crew because we saw them every day, all had these French jumpers on with the name of the ship on them.'

The filming turned out to be quite rewarding for the coal porters filling the *Paladin* with coal. 'We did very well out of that because in those days when you filled the tug up with coal you got 27s 6d. If she went off and came back you got another 27s 6d. Every time the tug came back we would fill her up. Well, what happened was that she would go down steaming and filming and she'd come back to top up. Nine times out of 10 the skipper, who was a really nice guy, would say "Top up the galley", so we would go in and top up the galley with 4cwt of coal and get another 27s 6d. She did it five times in one day, and we earned more money in that week than half the blokes did on piecework! It was only an afternoon's work.'

The Mouse That Roared (1959) was a comedy whose plot is based on the idea of how a country can prosper by losing a war to the United States. The Duchy of Grand Fenwick, located in the French Alps and founded by an English nobleman, the only European country where English is spoken, is going bankrupt. This is due to losing its only export of wine to a Californian company who has a cheaper imitation and had stolen its American market. They declare war on the United States and quickly surrender in order to receive aid under the Marshall Plan. In it Peter Sellers plays three roles and the tug *Paladin*, originally built in 1913 for Clyde tender duties, featured in the film.

Ron Williams: 'They used the *Paladin* to capture the *United States* Liner, coming into Southampton, with bows and arrows!'

Working on the Coal-burning Tug *Vulcan* in the 1950s

Wally Williams has family maritime links with the sea: 'My old grandad was the one. He was on the square riggers. There was a write-up about him in the *Daily Echo* because he was the oldest naval pensioner in Britain when he died in 1997. There was a story in there about an admiral who used to come and talk to grandad. Although he wasn't on his boat, he was in his fleet. The story was about when they went to China to get a peace treaty signed. They had to row ashore and travel seven miles inland to meet this Mandarin, but when they got there they only had quills and paint. Grandad had to run seven miles back to the boat, row out and get some pen and ink, row back and run another seven miles so they could sign the treaty!'

Sadly, during World War Two Wally lost one of his brothers at sea: 'I had Maurice and Fred, my two oldest brothers who were just old enough to join up in the war. Maury went down to Plymouth, did six weeks' training and his first job was escorting a Russian convoy and they got blown out of the water in the North Atlantic. That was Maury gone at just 18.'

Wally started working as a deck hand on the coal-burning tug *Vulcan* in the 1950s: 'When I started on the tugs you either had to have a relative working on the tugs or, like in my case, my best mate's dad did. He got me the job on there as the deck boy. I think it was about the end of 1949–50, and that was when all the big liners called at the port.'

Working as a deck boy in the 1950s was hard, and you had to be ready to go to work at any time of the day or night. Even so, there were some humorous moments, as possibly experienced by many in their early days at work, when little tricks were played on the new boy! Wally Williams: 'I always think now, the deck boy was the hardest job on the tug. As deck boy you couldn't stay aboard if the tug was tied up alongside. If you all went home for a night off you might be on at one or two o'clock the next morning. Apart from having to help out on deck day and night, we used to work right through. Apart from that, if you did have a break, whereas the rest of the lads could get their heads down, you had to scrub out, clean the brass work, make tea for the skipper, the mate and the engineer and you then had to feed yourself. You had to take your own food, and sometimes there were three or four days without hitting home. I lived in Sholing then with my mum and dad. I used to have a bicycle, and they used to give you a few hours' liberty. You used to jump on your bike and cycle home to ask mum for food because you had to go straight back.'

'If you had any time off, like the Christmas period, you had to write on a piece of paper where you were likely to be any of the days you were off, whether you were going to the pictures or going to a party somewhere. On one occasion I was at my sister's for a Christmas party when they upset mum because they came to the door and said "Is Williams there?" They said I had to report back to work immediately. You had to go otherwise you were out of a job. You were never off one full day. You were either coming on in the morning or going off. I hated that. You never had a full day.'

In the morning the deck boy would break up the big lumps of coal. He would get the paper and sticks and get all the fires going in the galley and get the kettles on. Then he would go into the accommodation area and get the tortoiseshell stoves going. While that was going on the deck boy would check all the navigation lights and lamps and top them up with paraffin. One day of the week they used to get a handcart to go up to the store to get paraffin and any rope and stores required for the tug. Wally Williams: 'They used to have fun with the deck boys, especially when they were told to go to the store and get 5 gallons

(22.7litres) of red paraffin for the port light, 5 gallons of green paraffin for the starboard light and 5 gallons of white paraffin for the other lights. When I asked the storeman for the different coloured paraffin they used to play along with the joke.

'As deck boy you had to get there an hour before, without pay, to get the fires going and the kettle on. We had tortoiseshell stoves in the accommodation. That was on the *Vulcan*, the one I was on. She had no electrics and that was another job for the deck boy, clean the glasses, top up with paraffin for the port, starboard and mast lights, accommodation lamps and then trim the wicks.'

Then there were the twice weekly scrub-outs and cleaning the brass. 'With the deck boy the job you had to do was the twice weekly scrub-outs. That's in the officer's accommodation on your own and then two days of brass cleaning. In those days lots of ships had brass telegraphs and capstans, everything was brass in those days. That was four days of the week. In between all that you were helping on deck all the time, pulling the wires in and letting them out. That is, if we were on the liners with the 45 and gog as we would call them [length of wire was 45 fathoms which went to the stern end of the liner]. On the *Vulcan*, she was built as a tug tender originally, but when I was on the *Canute* you had a huge shackle on the afterdeck. The gog was a rope that was 8–9in round. It used to go through this big shackle in the deck, and you shackled it onto the wire, right on the after end of the tug if he was on a 45 gog. On one of the Queen liners the captain used to run up alongside of the mast and get the wire up. The pilot, as he came up to the docks, would give instructions to the skipper. I don't know what the instructions were, but the skipper would say "Gog down", and while the wire was slack we would pull it right down to the deck with this big rope, which was casted, and lean back and hold it and the skipper would peel off. The idea of that was while the tow was on the stern of the tug it used to pull the tug back straight. Whereas, if it was straight off the towing hook, which was amidships on the old tugs, the tug could have turned sideways and turned over. That was because they would have been towing from amidships and the old tugs weren't as manoeuvrable as the tugs today. There is no comparison today.'

Wally Williams remembers the names of captains on the tugs at the time: 'Captain Pascoe was on the *Clausentum*. He was always on the "45 and gogs" with the liners because the pilots liked him. He used to anticipate where they would want him before they actually told him. Harold Hurst was the skipper on the *Canute*. He was a gent and always had a cigar in his mouth, a nice bloke. Capt Curley was on the *Calshot*. Jagger Noyce was on the *Hector* and Capt Follet was on the *Neptune*.'

When Wally started working on the tug *Vulcan* the crew consisted of skipper, mate, chief engineer, second engineer, two firemen and a greaser, able seaman, ordinary seaman and a deckboy. A crew of 10 and only one toilet: 'When I first went on the *Vulcan* the captain was Captain Little, but he wasn't there long. He came from the Middle East. He was English but had been out there on tugs, and they used to treat the crews out there like dogs. He used to think he could do the same here, especially the way he used to talk to us. He wasn't a very good skipper. He had false teeth and was always chewing gum, and if he got in a bit of a panic his teeth use to stick together! He always said to me "Never wash my dishes in soda water", which was all we used to wash up with. His had to be washed in plain hot water because he had a dodgy stomach. I was washing up one day, and one of the firemen said, "Is that the skipper's?" I said "Yeah". He dipped it in the soda water and I dried it. The captain went off sick for three weeks! The captain must have been right about the soda water.'

Compared to tugs of today the conditions on board the tug *Vulcan* were much more basic: 'The *Vulcan* was absolutely infested with cockroaches. We used to have condensed milk which we used to take in for our tea, and you used to make tiny little holes in the top and blow in one hole. The reason for that was so that the cockroaches couldn't get in your milk. I woke up one morning and had my packet of woodbines squashed in my pocket, and the cockroaches had been in the packet and taken every shred of 'baccy. There were just the perfect papers with no 'baccy in them!' The crew would cook their own breakfast, and cooking in the galley with the cockroaches was an experience: 'If you went up in the galley in the morning to cook your breakfast, bacon if you were lucky because there was still a lot on rationing then, you put the food on the plate and put the pan on the coal bunker and then go down below to eat your breakfast. When you came back up the frying pan would be absolutely full of cockroaches that had got in the fat as it cooled. You'd pick the pan up and put it back on the stove, and those that didn't jump out a frizzled on the top of the stove, fried in the pan.'

The *Vulcan* was the same tug that pulled the ship away from the *Titanic* as she was leaving Southampton on her fateful voyage, and the conditions for the those on the bridge were the same as in 1912: 'When I first went on the *Vulcan* there was no wheelhouse, and on the bridge there was just a canvas dodger around. We never even had bunks, it was the passenger accommodation, slatted seats was what we used to sleep on with just a blanket. There were no such things as a shower. If at the end of the day you wanted a wash you put a bucket on the galley stove to warm it up, and then we would go down in the rope locker, strip off and have a wash before you went home. We didn't do that much because it was the fireman really who needed the hot water as they used to get so black from the coal. That was one of the jobs when you finished and had tied up. It was pretty basic. They did put her in lay up, but it was after I went on one of the other tugs. It was 24-hour shifts on the better tugs. The *Vulcan* was a one-off. You had the *Canute, Hector, Clausentum, Neptune, Paladin* and the *Calshot*.'

Wally Williams spent some time on the tug tender *Calshot* and remembers an incident while the tug was in the Inner Dock: 'I did go on the *Calshot* for a little while my tug was in lay up. The AB on there was notorious, Harry Holland, they used to call him "Dutch" because of his name. I always remember Capt Curley, he was very fussy and he was on the wheelhouse watching Harry who was working on the deck. It was the lay up time. Harry suffered terribly with varicose veins, and he knocked his leg on one of the floats for passengers that we would take down to Cowes Roads to meet the liners. He threw two or three of them over the side. That was in the old Railway Dock, the Inner Dock. It has been filled in now. Capt looked down and calmly said, "OK Harry, get them back."'

It was often very dangerous working on the tugs, and Wally talks of some of the incidents he had witnessed: 'I have seen some real disasters, the old *Paladin*, she was the tug in the film *The Mouse that Roared* with Peter Sellars. We were on the same job when I saw an AB go up in the air. I think they were pulling the wire in, and what you used to do is stand astride of the wire as you pulled it in and they didn't let go of it on the ship, but suddenly the wire came up tight as he had his legs astride!'

'When I was on the *Canute* and we were pulling the wire in we used to wrap it around the capstan, but the ship was late. We had a slack wire, and with the wash of the ship (we were going to come round and push up as they call it) it took the tug away and it took the capstan in the air. The capstan on those tugs was about 4ft (1.2m) across. It was like a spinning top and then fell down in the water. On another occasion there were lips to guide the wire off the capstan aft, and we or the ship went away because of the wash. We managed to get it off the capstan that time, but didn't have time to get it off the lip on the for'ard. They were about 3ft (1m) high, real big ones like, probably weighing about 7 hundredweight (355kg), cast. It snapped that straight off the deck and we could see what was happening and dived down under the bulwarks. It missed the deck boy by inches! The bulwarks were the only safe place to be when that happened.'

Coming in to tie up was a very dangerous time, especially for the deck hand: 'It was a dangerous job. We used to come into the docks, and there was no one ever to take the ropes. If it were low tide the skipper would come in and on one particular occasion there were the fenders, the floats that the ships used to lay alongside, and the ropes used to hang down from the quay. The skipper would go in, put his bow in and it was up to the deck boy to shin up the rope to get up on the quay to take lines for the tug. On this occasion the skipper went in a bit hard and they had the big rope fenders on the bow. Nicky Pelmer, the deck boy, grabbed the rope. The tug bounced off, but was still going slow ahead on the engines. The rope from the quay had slack on it and the tug was going to crush the deck boy. The AB jumped up on the rope fender on the bow, hit Nicky on the neck (that was all he could do) to make him drop into the water. If he hadn't acted so quickly Nicky would have been crushed.'

Getting toggled was something the crew feared, and from one incident the firemen took special precaution in case it happened again: 'As a crew we got toggled. With the *Vulcan* we pulled a tanker off the Hamble Jetty with a westerly gale blowing, but the skipper couldn't get her round quick enough and was running with the ship to get the slack to take the wires off. The ship went away from us because of the gale blowing and the *Vulcan* went around broadside. We were at a good old angle, and we were up for'ard at the bow fender ready to jump. The tanker towed us down around Calshot until we got into the Thorn Channel, into the wind, when the captain was able to slow down to let us get the wires off. It was panic stations.'

The firemen from then on were worried that it could happen again and made sure they were considered by the captain. Wally Williams: 'This worried the crew a bit, and after that time we went down around Calshot on another job and the two fireman were making a lot of clattering noise with their shovels. We could hear all this clatter down the stokehole, which was just behind the bridge where you could look right down to the stoke room. There they were, rattling their shovels on the old iron rack to attract the skipper's attention. The captain called out "What's going on there Wally?" I said, "There's the fireman down there skip, come and have a look, they're down there with their life jackets on!"

'After that we did have a wire spring, but the trouble was that the axe was kept down below. They shouted for me to go down below to get it. The ship was learning right over, and we thought she was going to go over, and I wasn't going to go below if she went over because I would have been trapped.'

Wally tells of the dangers of the wires breaking on the old steam tugs: 'The old steam tugs are not like the ones now where the skipper has control of the engines on the bridge. Then the skipper had to use the telegraph and had to rely on the engineer down in the engine room to react quickly to what he asked for. Back in them days it was nothing for the wires to snap if the engineer was a bit slow to what the skipper wanted. It was dangerous because the wires, when they snapped, could cut you in half. You always knew if they were going to break because if he came up too fast on the wire it used to go round on a loop and you used to dive in the bulwarks. You knew it was going because it used to come back like a piece of elastic. I think the wires measured about 4in (10cm) thick.'

Wally also comments on how he looked forward to going to work in the 1950s, especially with the fact that you were earning a wage: 'We used to look forward to going to work in them days! You were earning money. Poor old dad was a chippy. Even with overtime, and especially when I was made up to ordinary seaman, I was taking home more money than dad was earning, and I thought things were going to get easier for dad, but then he died at the age of 57. I don't know, but he was in World War One when the Germans used mustard gas, and I think that was one of the things that killed him in the end. There were nine of us children.'

Getting Promotion

Although you could get promotion from the tugs on to the big liners, there were some seamen who transferred from the big liners to the tugs. It took time before a deck boy on a tug could normally get promoted to ordinary seaman, but Wally Williams was promoted early in his career: 'I caused quite a stir really because the normal time for a deck boy was 12 months and then you were in line for promotion to ordinary seaman. But the old skipper I was with on the *Vulcan*, Captain Little, recommended me for the ordinary seaman's job because he was going deep sea. That was what used to happen, because from the tugs you could get on the *Queen Mary*, *"Lizzie"* or any of them. He told the office he wanted me as his ordinary seaman, which caused a stir because I was the newest deck boy.' It was the arrival of an able seaman who transferred from the *Queen Mary* that caused Wally to leave the tugs, because the AB was less experienced than him, and he found he could not work safely with someone who was less experienced but also more senior in rank: 'I was on the tugs for three years, but left because the AB came off the *Queen Mary* where he was a steward. He knew very little about tug work, but he was the boss and was difficult to work with.'

It was fortunate for Wally that his mother had heard there was a mate's job going on one of the Williams Shipping barges. Wally Williams: 'My mum said, "if you are interested there's a mate's job going on one of the barges over at Williams." I just jumped on my bike and went straight over there and saw Mr Williams. It was on a Thursday, and he said, "When can you start?" I said, "Well, I'll start Monday." He said, "You're still on a tug." I said, "Yeah, but they could give me a minute's notice for dismissal, so I can give them a day."'

The company did not take it too well, however, and he found out that they had already had him in mind as a future tug master: 'Anyway, when I said I was leaving they called me up the office and told me they were really upset as they had me pencilled in as one of their future masters. The condition of tugs in them days is not like now, so I jumped at the chance of the other job. In fact some of the deck boys who I knew who are now retired, did end up as skippers. There was Jock who was AB on my tug. He ended up as skipper. He was always interested in what I was going to do and said, "You don't always want to spend the rest of your life being told what to do, you want to get up there [indicating the bridge where the skipper was] and tell them what to do."'

Williams Shipping

Williams Shipping was founded by George Williams in 1894 and he started trading from his base at Ashlett Creek, Fawley, with his first sailing barge called the *Spec* that he had bought in Portsmouth. Jimmy Williams took over the business from his father, and the business was later based at Town Quay, Southampton, where they were involved in the movement, arrangement and delivery of cargo. After the last war the firm was based at Town Quay and, as well as dealing with cargo, moved into provisioning the vessels in the docks and the Fawley Oil Terminal. Today, Williams Shipping have a wide range of marine services from their base in the Empress Dock, Southampton, including bunkering, hire and charter of tugs and launches, as well as operating one of the country's largest fleets of flat-top barges and pontoons.

Working for Williams Shipping

When Wally Williams left the tugs and joined Williams Shipping he was working with old wooden barges, and the main job of the smaller barges was storing the tankers at Fawley. Wally Williams: 'But the better job was going up to Newport for cattle feed, slag, fertilizers, and in the summer they used to serve up Double Diamond over there.'

Wally compares the work they had to do in loading the barges with that of the dock worker: 'Everything in those days had to be manhandled. If you were on cattle food we used to carry 100 tons, which is nothing these days, but then the railway used to push 10 trucks up the Town Quay, and when the first truck was in position we used to load the barge with the derrick. On occasions just one of us was up in the trucks with 1¼ hundredweight bags of cattle nuts, and one bloke on the quay would have a rope strop laid out and pull the bags over onto it. Six bags in a strop and lift it up by the derrick, swing out and one bloke below to stow the bags. On occasions just three of us would be doing that, but when you had done one truck you unshackled it, put your shoulder to it and pushed it on up the line and then unshackled the next one. For that we had a long pole with a steel wedge on the bottom, to wedge in to get the wheels moving because it was loaded with bags, and we would push that into position and unload that one. We would be there all day until we had done the 10 trucks. You would hear the "dockies" say how

hard they had to work, but they didn't have to do that job! We were there doing our cattle feed loading and the "dockies" came down to load a boat that came into Town Quay and used to run to Ireland. I think there was about eight in the gang to do just about 10 lifts of cattle hides, that was already stropped up in the hold of the coaster, and all they had to do was to hook it on the crane on the quay. There were three of us, or four, rather, because one was driving the windlass. He was only lifting the strops and lowering the load down.'

The *Wilanne*, Williams Shipping, 2008

Once the loading had been completed they used to sail over to the Isle of Wight: 'When we went to the Isle of Wight there were only two of us on the boat, the skipper and the mate. We used to go over to Newport, and they had a derrick on the quay. There was two of us hooking on which was quite an easy job.'

One of the ships that Wally Williams was on would take 1½ hours to sail from Dock Head to the Fawley Oil Terminal, and comparing that with the short time it takes today indicates the amount of extra time taken to complete the jobs in those days: 'I was on a ship called the *Exchange* where she had a rudder that was on her from when she was a sailing boat. It was a huge wooden rudder. The engine was a 33-horse-power piston, and half of the power from the engine, where this rudder was so wide, was lost. It used to take us an hour and a half to get from Dock Head to Fawley! So when they said we have a little job for you in the evening there was three hours running time apart from the time we spent alongside the vessel at Fawley! We used to do the Isle of Wight with her as well!'

In the early days of Williams Shipping the speed of the *Exchange* enabled her to beat the time of the other barges to and from the Isle of Wight because she had an engine! 'Apparently Jimmy Williams started from Ashlett Creek with the *Exchange*, and he was one of the first to have an engine put in, and all the other barges (this is what I was told) used to sail to the Isle of Wight with coke or whatever. The crew used to have to pole them up the Medina. With adverse weather some of the sailing barges used to take two or three days from Newport up to the berth in Northam where they used to load the coke. But Jimmy had this little engine and used to come up "pop, pop, pop!" and get to the berth first! They used to hate him!'

Stopping over in Newport in rainy weather was not always very comfortable for the crew with the leaking decks: 'If you were over Newport when there was hot weather the wood on the boat would dry out, and if you are in your little bunk and it starts raining during the night you had to put a bit of canvas up to deflect the water to the floor, where the water had come through the gaps in the wood. It was alright after a few hours because the water made the wood swell and closed it up again.'

Wally Williams looks back at some of the work undertaken at the time and compares health and safety matters in the 1950s to that of today: 'Amazing to think of it now, but we used to go down to Fawley Oil Terminal and used to have the galley stove blazing away and tie up alongside the tankers, waiting for them to finish loading before they sailed. Now they wouldn't allow you within half a mile! When I was on the tankers we were loading at No. 6 Berth down there and had a bit of canvas over the headers and there were the welders working on the top. One of the headers, which was petrol, was dripping and caught fire. Someone from the jetty came rushing out with his dry powder extinguisher. We all ran in the accommodation because we didn't want to breathe it in. Anyway, he put it out. That was the way they used to operate back in them days!'

Wally did eventually become a skipper, getting his masters certificate in 1981. In the 1980s it was easier to get a masters certificate than it is today: 'In 1981 I became a skipper. In those days you had to have done the master's job two years out of the previous five and then they would give you a ticket. I don't suppose there are many of us left who got those certificates. As a skipper I believe that a happy crew was an efficient crew, and if anything went wrong it was down to me, but other than that I was just one of the boys.'

Tug Tender *Calshot* from 1929

In 1929 the tug tender *Calshot* was built and engined by John I. Thornycroft & Co. Ltd for the then Southampton, Isle of Wight and South of England Royal Mail Steam Packet Company. She was launched by Mrs P.E. White from the builder's yard at Woolston, Southampton, on Monday 4 November 1929. The launch was followed by a luncheon at 12 noon, at the South Western Hotel. The *Calshot* was the largest tug tender in the Red Funnel fleet and was to replace the *Albert Edward*, built in 1886 by Day, Summers & Company at Northam, Southampton, for the Southampton, Isle of Wight & South of England R.M.S.P. Company.

The *Calshot* is a twin-screw tug, 600 tons, with a length of 157ft (47.85m), a 33ft 1in (10.08m) beam and a 14ft (4.26m) draught. She was designed and built specifically for two purposes, hence the title 'tug tender', and would carry out tug duties, mainly in a pushing role to manoeuvre the liners to their berths and as a passenger tender for conveying passengers, their baggage, mail, provisions and even cars out to the large ocean liners moored in the Solent, usually in Cowes Roads, off Cowes, Isle of Wight. She was licensed to carry up to 566 passengers and the accommodation for first class passengers was on the forward main deck with cushioned seats fitted around the sides and in bays. A staircase led down to the first-class refreshment room, with cushioned seats with upholstered backs, and the tables with revolving chairs were made of oak. The second-class accommodation was arranged on the main deck aft with wooden bench seats along the sides and an area for baggage.

In the 1930s the *Calshot* was also used as a relief ferry on the Southampton to Ryde service during the busy summer months. Also in the 1930s and 1940s the *Calshot* often transported world-famous celebrities, including film stars and politicians, to and from liners anchored in the Solent. These trips involved the *Calshot* sailing to and from Cowes Roads to service the liners.

Bert Moody: 'I remember the *Calshot*, she was always there. It is amazing if you look at shipping photographs the number of times that the *Calshot* appears. It is an indication that the *Calshot* had a very, very full life.'

Kenneth Fielder also remembers the tug tenders *Calshot* and *Romsey*: 'The *Normandie* was served by tug tenders, the *Calshot* and the *Romsey*. They used to bring in film stars such as Robert Taylor, Laurel and Hardy etc. My friend and I used to send off for the autographed photographs of the film stars, and whenever something like the *Queen Mary* arrived we had something in the post. I remember I got one from what was called "The Dead End Kids", and before the war they were in the original film called *Dead End* [1937] in which they were a gang in New York, with James Cagney as a gangster.'

During World War Two the tug tender *Calshot* was requisitioned by the Admiralty for service in Scapa Flow. Later, in 1942, she returned to the Red Ensign and was engaged in transatlantic trooping duties on the Clyde, ferrying as many as 500 American troops to and from the *Queen Mary* and *Queen Elizabeth* liners.

In May 1944 the tug tender *Calshot* had returned to Southampton in the build up for the D-Day invasion of occupied Europe. The docks were particularly involved in the D-Day (Operation Overlord) preparations, and the port was one of the principal embarkation points. After the end of the war, in June 1946, the tug tender *Calshot* had a major refit and returned to the Red Funnel fleet and worked for a further 18 years as a tug sailing up and down Southampton Water and the Solent.

On 14 October 1953 the *Empire Orwell* arrived in Southampton Water with the second group of ex-prisoners of war from the Korean War, the first group having arrived back the previous month on the *Asturias*. The tug tender *Calshot* transferred 150 ex-prisoners of war belonging to the Gloucestershire Regiment from the *Empire Orwell* to 107 Berth to be met by the official reception party and their families.

In 1964 the tug tender *Calshot* was replaced by *Calshot 2* and sold to Holland America Line. It was used to ferry passengers from the liners *Maasdam* and *Ryndam* anchored in Galway Bay to the harbour pier. The *Calshot* was renamed *Galway Bay* and later acted as an island ferry between Galway and the Aran Islands. She had diesel engines fitted, and her funnel was cut down, but when the *Galway Bay* finished with the ferry service she was taken to Kelly's shipyard in Cork.

It was in 1986 that the *Galway Bay* (previously the tug tender *Calshot*) was bought by Southampton City Council from Kelly's shipyard in Cork. It was the intention to display the *Galway Bay* afloat outside the planned Maritime Museum, as part of the redevelopment of the Princess Alexandra Dock that commenced in 1984. This was not to come to fruition, as the proposed Maritime Museum project was abandoned, and in 1990 the *Galway Bay* was renamed *Calshot* and in 1991 was opened to the public at a permanent berth at the Town Quay. Later she was moved to a berth at City Council Wharf.

Work was started on restoring the tug tender *Calshot* from April 1997 by volunteers of the Tug Tender Calshot Trust. In the *Daily Echo* on Thursday 27 March Terry Yarwood, a director of the trust, said, 'There is a lot to do on board *Calshot* and therefore a lot we can achieve. The bridge, chart room, radio room, agents office and galley all require attention. Later in the year we hope to be able to remove the cabins built in 1954, ready for the restoration of the second class cabin.' In January 1999 the *Calshot* was moved to Berth 42 by the kind permission of ABP. In November 1999, the 70th anniversary of the launching of the tug tender *Calshot*, however, there was exciting news for the trust when the tug tender was officially recognised by the National Historic Ships Committee who declared the *Calshot* a national treasure and an important part of the UK's maritime heritage. The *Daily Echo* reported on 3 November 1999 that 'unbeknown to the restoration group, experts from the National Historic Ships Committee came to see the former Red Funnel vessel and considered her so important that the tug is now listed alongside Nelson's HMS *Victory*, World War Two cruiser HMS *Belfast* and Brunel's *Great Britain*.'

The *Galway Bay*. (Courtesy of Calshot Trust)

The *Calshot* at 42 Berth in 2008.

On 4 November 2004 it was the 75th Anniversary of *Calshot's* launch in 1929, which was celebrated in the Queen Elizabeth II Terminal, by kind permission of Associated British Ports. The guest of honour was the Lord Lieutenant of Hampshire, Mrs Mary Fagan, and other guests included the Mayor of Southampton and Admiral of the Port, Councillor Dennis Harryman and the Sheriff of Southampton, Councillor Edwina Cooke.

On 10 May 2005 the ownership of the tug tender *Calshot* was transferred from Southampton City Council to the Tug Tender Calshot Trust.

The Restoration of the 1929 Tug Tender *Calshot*

The restoration work undertaken on the tug tender *Calshot* came under serious threat when there was a fire on-board. The *Daily Echo* reported on 28 July 2006 that the fire had started on the wooden fender at the bow of the ship. Ten firefighters from Redbridge Fire Station attended the fire, which started at about 10pm and was believed to have been started by some welding work that was being carried out. The watch officer said that, although the fire had been put out within an hour, it was very close to a paint store which was nearby to where the fire had started. Following a £50,000 grant from the Heritage Lottery Fund in 2006, the next stage of the tug tender *Calshot's* restoration was undertaken. This was a detailed survey of the hull, carried out by a company from Portland, Dorset, who were specialists in the field of underwater repairs and surveys. The outcome of the survey of the hull was very positive, with just some small sections that needed attention.

Visit to see the Restoration Work on the Tug Tender *Calshot*

In October 2006 Peter Godwin, a boiler maker and welder by trade and one of the volunteers, talked about the restoration work that is being undertaken to the tug tender *Calshot*. At that time there were the five volunteers working on the restoration, with Peter Godwin committing every Saturday from 6am to 6pm. The tug is moored on 42 Berth by the kind permission of ABP.

Calshot and *Titanic* Boilers

Peter Godwin: 'She still has one of her three original boilers, the same type of boiler that they had on the *Titanic*. The boilers on the *Titanic* were double engine boilers, and the one here on the *Calshot* is a single engine boiler. The size and everything about the boiler is the same as those on the *Titanic*.'

The *Titanic* had 29 boilers, and each boiler had a diameter of nearly 16ft (4.8m) and consumed massive amounts of coal to power the ship's steam engines. Of the 29 coal-fired boilers, 24 were double-ended and five were single-ended boilers, similar to the boiler on the *Calshot*.

The crew cabin.

Peter Godwin: 'We fixed the windows on the side and put back two original ones that had been taken out by the Holland America Line when they put the diesel engines in. They had filled in the two windows, and we cut all the windows out and put them back to its original plan. We also put back the stairway to the engine room and second-class area back. When she was first built the side areas were open, but the passengers complained and they were then covered in.'

In the second-class accommodation there would have originally been benches for the passengers to sit on, but when she worked as the *Galway Bay* in Ireland the benches were taken out

Original panelling.

The staircase down to the first-class bar.

and cabins put in. One of the jobs in the future is to take out the cabins and return the accommodation to its original state. From the second-class accommodation there are stairs down to the crew accommodation.

The gangway between second class and the boiler room is where there is the remaining single engine boiler. In the No. 2 engine room there are two diesel engines that were put in by the Holland American company. When the diesel engines were put in the original funnel was shortened; however, an extension to the funnel had been built and was at the time of the visit on the quayside waiting to be fitted to restore the ship's original appearance.

The first-class accommodation is in two sections. Peter Godwin: 'The upper section is for first-class passengers to sit and the lower section is for them to sit and have drinks. It still has the original panelling and the furniture is the original 1929. The bar is only for the first-class passengers. There is a pantry on the other side and two wine cellars in-between the bar and the pantry. The bar still has its original till, which has been taken away for safekeeping.'

The group now have both engines running and all the machinery and electrics are working. Two new water tanks have been made by Thornycrofts for replacement.

Original 1929 furniture.

CHAPTER 12

INTRODUCTION OF CONTAINER SERVICES

Preparing for the Introduction of Container Services

The introduction of containers services was beginning to impact upon the work of the docks, with ships carrying a mixture of cargo. Ron Williams talks about the Lykes Lines: 'We had all kinds of shipping lines in Southampton. The Americans had the Lykes Line, and they carried military equipment and also containers. They were the first ships I can remember to be stretched. They cut them in half and put sections in the middle so you had general cargo and containers fore and aft in the 1950s and 1960s.'

BRITISH TRANSPORT DOCKS BOARD 1963–1982

In 1963, the year that the British Transport Docks Board took over the management of the docks, work was started on the next stage of the reclamation of land for port expansion. This was from the King George V Dry Dock to the Redbridge causeway where the container terminals were to be eventually sited.

Dockers' Strike in 1967

Following on from the last years of the British Transport Commission and the early days of the British Transport Docks Board running the ports, there was a series of strikes that finally led to the dock workers' strike of 1967. This led to the introduction of the National Docks Labour Scheme, which guaranteed lifelong employment for dock workers; however, the new NDLS was not to prove very helpful for the employers in the future development of the container trade.

When the first quay for containers was opened on 28 October 1968 the first ship to arrive at Berth 201 was the *Teniers*. After unloading 30 containers and loading a further 30 containers, she sailed to New York.

Further reclamation work at Millbrook began in October 1968 to develop a new container terminal. Berth 202 became operational on 29 January 1972 with the arrival of the first TRIO Lines Far Eastern service vessel, NYK's *Kamakura Maru*.

Don Archbold: 'In 1969, up on 201 Berth, they started the container ships, and we also had cargo ships dealt with by Cunard, and a Ro-Ro terminal was provided at 201 Berth in the same year.'

Ray Strange: 'When the Dart ships started running you had a foot either side to get the container in. With an IMV (internal movement vehicle) it was difficult, but a tug was much easier. There were also ships that were Ro-Ro, and you could get containers on because then you had a 40-ton fork truck, and then you got ships that came in with bulk cargo like rocks and they would take about 20 containers back, but they weren't really container ships.'

The Development of Solent Container Services

When Solent Container Services started Berth 204 was still being constructed and Berth 201 had already been built in 1967 and was being used by the British Transport Docks Board and manned by docks staff as a common-user berth for any line to use. Solent Containers, however, were coming in with a new Far East and Continental trade.

Jim Brown had joined the Southampton County Borough Police in 1952, but in 1967 they amalgamated with the Hampshire County Police Force. He was not as happy in the police force anymore, and one of the problems as a member of the Hampshire Constabulary was that to gain any further promotion he would possibly have to move to another area of Hampshire, but he did

not want to leave Southampton. Although he was protected by regulation 20, which meant he could not be transferred against his will, he decided to explore the opportunities for other work. Jim Brown: 'In 1970, even though I had been promoted in the amalgamated force, I was then 38 and made the decision to leave the force, which I had loved and enjoyed. I was looking around and John Hovey, a lovely man, a real gentleman, had his own business in London. He'd been taken on as managing director for a new company to be formed called Solent Container Services. I heard about this from a contact

Reclamation from No. 7 Dry Dock to Redbridge Causeway. (Courtesy of Jim Brown Collection)

Cranes on Berths 201 to 202. (Courtesy of Jim Brown Collection)

I had in Dock House and met John Hovey. Lucky for me he took me on as chief security officer. Many of the Solent Container Services staff came from London initially, from Tilbury and the Port of London. I was the only local man in the company and was very useful to them by my local knowledge, helping with accommodation and other matters.'

Jim Brown had a family history of working in the docks. 'My grandfather was a coal porter, my father was a merchant seaman, I had a father-in- law who was a docker and I have lived in Southampton all my life, so I have a good detailed knowledge of the docks. I think that was one of the reasons that John Hovey took me on because I had a good working knowledge of dockers and it was obviously a bad time, especially for security.'

The British shipping lines, Ben Line, Union Castle, Furness Withy and P&O, formed a container consortium called OCL (Overseas Container Line). Similar major shipping lines in Germany formed a container consortium called Hapag-Lloyd and Japanese lines formed NYK (Nippon Yusan Kaisha) and Mitsui OSK. These three national consortia together formed the organization called TRIO. The intention was to set up a new container terminal in Southampton to deal primarily with the Far East, trade but also the Continent.

Jim Brown: 'So in July 1971 we kicked-off, and there were about half a dozen of us, including an engineering manager, operations manager, planning manager, computer manager, John Hovey of course, a secretary and myself as chief security officer. We were based in Imperial House on 109 Berth, a building with a history itself as a base for Imperial Airways.'

In the initial stages the group were doing all the planning and background, and interviewing all the staff to be taken on. Jim Brown was interviewing for security officers. He recalls: 'I had my own security staff and was also deeply involved with the administration manager and directly working alongside him, in effect as his deputy. I was also involved in the construction of the administration and canteen buildings and the layout of the terminal.'

Jim Brown: 'We initially used 202 Berth, and I remember the first ship

Reclamation for new container berths. (Courtesy of Jim Brown Collection)

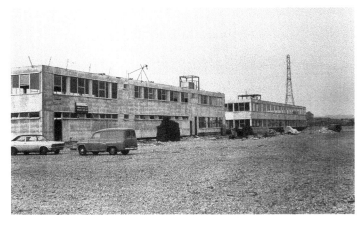

The new administrative and canteen buildings.
(Courtesy of Jim Brown Collection)

that came in was the *Kamakura Maru* in January 1972 from the Japanese Line. We had a temporary gatehouse to deal with the lorries coming in, temporary offices and buildings and still worked from Imperial House. When the administration and canteen buildings were completed we moved into them. I took photographs to record all the construction stages.'

At this time the employers were trying to end the restrictive practices and outdated systems of work and to cut the manning levels. As container ports are able to operate for 24 hours a day the employers wanted the dockers to work more flexible working hours and undertake shift work to gain the full benefit from the mechanisation and containerisation. Also in the 1970s the docks came under pressure from the competition of the more modern, government-subsidised ports in Europe, especially ports such as Rotterdam and Hamburg. These were more equipped to handle the new generation of container ships, and this began to take business away from the UK ports.

Jim Brown: 'It is a different ball game to today. You have to remember that the British Transport Docks Board ran the docks, and the dock labour force had two distinct groups. You had the crane drivers and the checkers that were in the National Union of Railwaymen (NUR), but the dockers were in the Transport and General Workers Union (TGWU). Job protection was very fierce. You couldn't do anyone else's job at all, and the dock workers were very deeply entrenched. They had a shameful history against them and had been treated badly in the past. In the old days, I know well from my family background that dockers would turn up for work and if there was one ship in they would be picked out, whoever the foreman fancied and who would reward him a share afterwards. If there was no work you were bumped, and if you were bumped you had half a crown, certainly a very small amount. They had a small token payment. The shippers were merciless really because if they had two ships in at once they wanted everybody they could get to work because they wanted their ships turned around as quickly as possible and would be happy to pay well to get the ship turned round. They weren't interested in giving people permanent employment. That was the past, and the dockers were treated shamefully. They have every sympathy from me.'

In the very early years, and for many years, the dock workers were still British Transport Dock Board staff and were allocated to Solent Container Services, who had to pay the Docks Board for the labour. Solent Container Services had no direct control, only through the dockers' foreman and shift superintendent. This was not an easy time for the SCS duty shift manager. If he wanted a job done, he would have to ask the foreman if he could arrange for the work to be done. Any effort to give direct instruction was met with a negative comment from the dockers, who would then tell the foreman what had happened and the ship manager would have to back off. They would only take instructions from their own foreman. It was seen as the dockers' job, under the direction of their foreman and superintendent. Jim Brown: 'The dockers, at the time Solent Container Services started, had the protection of the Docks Labour Board Scheme, brought in by the Labour government. They had a job for life, and they had job protection. They were employed as a permanent labour force, which was fair enough – the majority of dockers wanted nothing more than a good day's pay, with the job satisfaction of doing a good days work and going home again. You had a small minority who exploited this "job for life" situation, however, and again there was trade union power.'

Gradually over time, as people knew each other better, things were not quite so sensitive and more direct instructions could be given.

When Solent Container Services started it was the dockers who tended to have the power, and they used it very effectively. Jim Brown: 'When we started in the early 1970s the dockers "ruled the roost". They made demands which had to be met, and you really did have a weak dock management who would tend to give in to them. I also know that when talking to Docks Board supervisors and foremen about the old days they would tell me that they would blame the shippers rather than the Docks Board

Imperial House, photographed with more cars this time!
(Courtesy of Jim Brown Collection)

A straddle carrier. (Courtesy of Jim Brown Collection)

management because you would have a ship in, and the dockers would say, "Right we want an extra £5 for this ship", more than they were entitled to, and lay down rules. The shipper would say that they had to get the ships away and tell the board to give the dockers what they asked for to keep them happy. Once you had done that you made a precedent and didn't care about the ship coming in next week, they just wanted their ship away that day. They used to give in to unreasonable demands and, of course, human nature being what it is, you'll ask for something, not expecting to get it. For the dock worker the attitude was, "if we can get away for it we'll ask for even more."'

In his book *A Tale of Two Ports* John Hovey gives an example of the difficulties for port management at the time. If a crane driver tried to blackmail employers by working slowly on loading baggage the day before the *Queen Mary* departed, and his employer declined to submit to the blackmail, then the chairman of Cunard would be swiftly on the telephone to the port manager saying, 'How dare you hold my ship up. Pay the man at once!'

A number of the people who talked about their experiences working in the docks had referred to weak management. Ray Strange: 'There was a straddle driver and to get into the straddle carrier you had to climb a ladder, but there was oil on it. He refused to climb the ladder, and I said, "Why don't you get some rag and wipe it?" He replied, "No I'm not doing that – that's an engineer's job." There was a

Driving a straddle carrier could be dangerous. (Courtesy of Jim Brown Collection)

three or four days' stoppage over that. I used to sit round the table with the management and wait for them to say, "You're not doing that" – but they wouldn't! The management were scared of us! People might have enjoyed that position, but I didn't. We had a closed shop in Southampton. We negotiated that with the employer. He really shouldn't have done that, but he did. If you weren't in the trade union or in arrears you had it, you got sacked or didn't get a job. It was useful to have that because you had control over your lads.'

John Hovey also related a story to Jim Brown about when he was in the London Docks when containers first started coming in. There was a meeting, and he was asked by one of the dockers' trade union representatives if they were going to get any extra for losing their 'perks' He was concerned that they couldn't get anything from breakages if they were inside a container and asked if the dockers would be compensated for that? Jim Brown explains: 'He was quite serious about losing his "perks" and as everybody knew, they would deliberately break a carton to get the spoils. There is no one more wily or clever than a docker for making a small hole in a barrel of brandy or whisky and blocking it again so that no one would ever know. They were past masters at things like that. He was genuinely concerned because with containerisation everything was more secure, which was one of the reasons for it, apart from the ease of transport.'

With the container ship carrying already packed containers there was less need for gangs of dock labourers, who would have in the past manually stacked the cargo in the holds. Jim Brown: 'There weren't many real stevedores in Southampton, only a tiny number. A stevedore was a senior man who knew how to stow and pack cargo in the hold, and it was a skilled art to see that cargo didn't move when at sea. Dockers tended to call themselves stevedores, but they weren't, they were dock labourers, although very experienced.'

Jim Brown relates the first battle which John Hovey had with the dockers: 'When we first started we were working 202 Berth, and when we opened 204 that was OK, but then we had the question of a ship was being berthed at 204 and another ship that was working through the night. Bear in mind that container ships were turned around very quickly compared with the conventional cargo ship. You didn't have loads of people going backwards and forwards with hand trucks and electric trucks manhandling cargo. You had one man, the crane driver, picking the container up and putting it in the hold in one move. The contents of the box would, the old way, take hours to load. We had 24-hour working, not so much in the early days because we didn't have many ships coming in, but the situation first arose when a ship had completed loading and had left the berth early in the morning with another ship coming in on 204 Berth a few hours later to be unloaded. The first time that happened the dockers who were working on the ship that was due to sail said, "We've finished the ship we are going off now." We told them that there was another ship coming in, but

The later gatehouse on 204 Berth. (Courtesy of Jim Brown Collection)

they were not happy with this and said that another gang would be needed for that ship as they had finished their ship and were going home. They were told that the job had not finished and they were expected to work on the ship coming in. They were used to working quickly because the quicker they got the ship loaded the quicker they would go home, and they did not have two ships on a shift. Of course, in our system they would be required to work on the next ship. They didn't like that, and we had to make a stand. There was a stoppage for a few days, but they also realised that their future lay in the container terminal. They couldn't be too "bolshy" because they could lose their jobs altogether. The shippers could move their work to Felixstowe or other ports. But the threat was always there, throughout the whole time I was with the company, that the shippers could move somewhere else.'

Jim Brown describes other problems that occurred during the early days: 'Another demarcation line cropped up when 205 Berth was built and we had 204–205 Berths. Again, the same situation arose when we had a ship on 204 and a ship coming in on 205. They were saying that they were the "204 gang" and they were finished. We said that this was all Solent Container Services. This is our quayside and whether we have one ship, two ships 10 ten ships they are all here to be worked on the one quayside. There was a big stoppage for a week or so, and eventually we dug our heels in and won the day.'

Ray Strange, who was a shop steward, talks about the attitude of the dockers at the time: 'Once a job was finished we would go. Even if it was 2pm, that was it, we would go. The employer didn't like that as he wanted us to go somewhere else because he was paying you for the day. Not a lot of money in those days of course. It was partly them and us, and we wanted to get stuck into it and we really did. We negotiated a 40hr, £38.50 week in 1971. That was more than a teacher or the police were getting.' This was, of course, the blue book.

Ray Strange: 'I've been on various committees, and the one I enjoyed the most was when we were doing the deal for the blue book. We started about 1968–69 and finished in 1971. I was representing the shipside workers in the New Docks. There was a New Docks quayside shop steward, Old Docks shipside and quayside shop stewards and a trade union officer, and that was our committee. We sat down and worked out what we thought we were entitled to have and then took that into meetings with the employer.' When the employers negotiated for the blue book they put the dockers in for a night shift, 8pm–6am, which was a 10-hour shift on piecework. Ray Strange: 'Even Pirelli's worked 10pm to 6am, and I used to try to negotiate by suggesting we left out the morning coffee break in the morning and go home a bit earlier and come in a bit later.' The negotiations were successful and the dockers' committee got the money they asked for, but part of that deal was that if they finished at 2pm in the New Docks they might be required to go from there down to the Old Docks. 'We only had bikes in those days!'

Ray Strange: 'It took us 20 years to get rid of 24-hour working, but its all gone back now to 12-hour shifts. We broke it right down to eight to four, four to 11 and 11 to six. That was our three shifts and intermediate five to 12 voluntary. Everything has now gone to pot.'

The other demarcation line was manning levels. Jim Brown: 'We inherited the Docks Board system that they had on 201. The unions were very strong, they always were. The manning levels were because of the nature of the work, the noise, the stress levels. If my memory serves me right, there had to be two straddle drivers per straddle and three crane drivers per crane. You had to have one spare straddle driver and two crane drivers on reserve to turn about. Again, this was because of the pressure of working hard and fast, getting the containers lined up properly and the picking them up. The experience had to be built up, but we knew that in practice, in real life, half the straddle drivers were home and only half worked the shift. Also there was often only one crane driver, two at the most, not three.'

Ray Strange talks about double manning: 'Once the container ships came in we thought we were going to lose a lot of men from what was used on the conventional ships, such as the Union Castle, in particular. Yes we did overman, but we had to. I wouldn't admit that when we were negotiating!'

Negotiations for manning levels at the start of the containers found the shop stewards asking for far more men than they needed. Ray Strange: 'We asked for 12 men on a hatch at the start, and we went on a long time with that one, but they said no.' The employers' attitude was, 'A couple of men here and a couple of men there.'

The negotiations were successful for the union because they managed to get eight men per hatch, and this led to a restrictive practice called 'spelling.' This was the practice that Solent Container Services found themselves having to accept, albeit unwillingly. When Solent Container Services started, the labour force was provided by the British Transport Docks Board, and SCS paid the men through the BTDB; however, because they were the employees of the BTDB they had no direct control of the men. Ray Strange explains: 'The manning scales were so good when Solent Containers Services started that you could "spell". If

A crane collapses. (Courtesy of Jim Brown Collection)

you had eight men on a job you could do it with four and you could decide that, say, four could have the night off and the other four the next night. "spelling" was what they called it.

'We maintained those manning scales and stayed on that particular job, and then when that job finished some people trained on straddle carriers. I trained on IMV's (internal movement vehicles) and they were bone shakers. They must have bought them cheap because what they were really used for was towing aircraft around and there were no springs at all. We used to pick up the container from the quayside after it had been unloaded by the crane driver and take it up to the freightliner terminal, where they would pick up the box and put it on the train. Eventually they brought in the tugs which were sprung. Any cargo you were taking-off was called "striking". Driving a straddle carrier could be dangerous if the straddle drivers was not careful when turning: 'One came round too fast and went over into the water. He got out alright, but that wasn't the first one and you had to go pretty easy with those things.'

As a shop steward Ray considered himself moderate and had concern for the way this practice would, over time, seriously effect the amount of labour needed in the container port and the effect it would have on the livelihood of the union members. He also found it very frustrating trying to get the message through to the men that 'spelling' would not go unnoticed by the employers and used to tell them, 'One of these days, you don't think the employer doesn't know what you are doing. He's going to note it and put it down that you are double manned, and we are trying to keep as many men here as we can.'

Try as he and other moderate shop stewards might to convince the men of the danger of spelling, especially the young dockers, the practice continued and not only with the dockers, but also with the checkers, lashers and crane drivers. 'They would probably have 50 checkers on a night and within about 10 minutes there would be only 10 left.'

Ray Strange gives an example where there was some flatbed cargo with steel on that needed to be lashed by experienced lashers: 'One night two came up and asked for a hand to lash some cargo. We refused because there was supposed to be eight lashers on and they had already split by half and then half again. You just couldn't get it through to them. It was noticed by the employers!'

The Lashers

There was another job that was undertaken on board the ship once the containers had been loaded. It was the responsibility of the 'lashers', who secured the containers above the deck with lashing bars. The containers were stacked two or three high on board and had big lashing bars to keep the containers secure in bad weather. This was not a good job for the lashing gang to have when it was bad weather.

Ray Strange had vivid memories of lashing the containers and how it was generally the older dockers who took the risks: 'The first thing we didn't like when you lashed the containers was that from the deck to the top container was 45 to 50ft. In the early days you had to haul hawsers up and shackle them to the top container. In the winter we used to tell the checkers not to give us the last one with frost all over it. You had a ladder and had to climb up and onto the container. The young dockers wouldn't do it because they were frightened, and it was us 50-year-olds who had to do it. We had to make sure the last one was clear on the top because you had to crawl across to put shackles in on four corners. Another system they had was hawsers again and washers and then twist locks. Twist locks went on first and second containers and on the third you used crossbars. That was better because you could do that job on a ladder without getting on the top of the top container.'

Resignation of Experienced Shop Stewards

The moderate shop stewards became frustrated over time and resigned, but this was not a good move because it allowed in the more militant dockers to become shop stewards. Ray Strange: 'The trouble really started when the 20 of us shop stewards resigned én-bloc and the "not so moderate" shop stewards took over. They put everything in the way of the employer to mess up the whole system. They were the younger element and they wanted to get rid of us, the biggest mistake we made was to go. We eventually got back in again, but the port director at the time, who will be nameless, made quite a few of them up to foremen to keep them quiet. The port director was a reasonable guy, but he let us get away with murder at times! I think he regretted it.'

At the start and in the early days of Solent Container Services if the ship was finished early and there was no ship in for a few days the dockers would finish earlier and go home. That was apart from stacking, tidying up or dealing with incoming lorries. Jim Brown: 'As we built up and got busier and busier we still had the same manning levels and yet the dockers would work their own system, and two of them would decide what days they would work, "You have Monday, Tuesday and Wednesday and I'll come in Thursday, Friday and Saturday."' They would have another job, such as a painter and decorator, lorry driver or whatever on their days off, even though they were quite well paid. 'The crane drivers were the same, they would work one third of the time. The crane drivers were the cream. They were in the NUR. Historically, I think, when it was the Railway Board run by Southern Railways.'

Some dockers were required to go to the Port Health and Customs inspection. Jim Brown: 'The Port Health and Customs could, and did, demand boxes be opened up for the contents to be inspected. No way could a Customs officer or Port Health official start lifting boxes out of the container, it was the dockers job. We had an area set aside that was fenced off and Customs or Port Health, who had the authority to demand to see the contents of a box, instructed the box to be brought by straddle carrier and put on the ground. Dock workers would then break the seals and open it. The shipping agent would be there, and a foreman to supervise, but the actual opening of the doors, picking up of the cartons as directed by the Port Health or Customs officer to be put into the shed to be opened up, that was the dockers' function. They would put the goods back in the container to be resealed. They had strict demarcation lines.'

There Have Been Great Strides in Computerisation Since the Systems Used in the 1970s.

In the administration building on 205 Berth there was a computer room, 40ft x 20ft, that was air conditioned and had humidifiers. Jim Brown: 'It was a big room and when we first started, before the computer cabinets were put in, we had our first Christmas dance in that room. The computer cabinets were massive, and the hard disks were about a couple of feet across and several inches thick. I think the whole thing had about 5mb and calculators have got more than that now. Today my own PC is about 120gb. They had big security on the room and fire protection with Halon gas.'

Solent Containers IT staff initiated a computer system that was eventually to be used throughout the country. Jim Brown: 'As I understand it today the computer control systems are very sophisticated and most areas are now computer controlled; however, it was our computer staff, led by the IT manager, who devised the system that was used throughout the country. They, in fact, became so successful and got Customs clearance to form their own company called CNS. CNS was a subsidiary company of Solent Container Services and was a separate company that sold their services to other shipping lines and airports. It became a nationalised system that grew and grew. It was quite a big thing. That was a very desirable part of Solent Container Services when it was taken over.'

'In the 1970s we had a control room manned by SCS staff, not dockworkers at all. We were a private company running the terminal with our own staff, our own security, own control staff and our own ship planners who would plan the ship. From the control room we would allocate the straddle carriers, but the dock worker had to come from the Docks Board.'

In the early years of Solent Container Services the straddle drivers were controlled by radio. Jim Brown: 'They were directed by our control room to go to a position in the stack, marked in a grid pattern, to take a box to a ship or to a particular crane and would do the same with the incoming boxes. In those days it was a noisy environment and especially inside the straddle carrier's cab. We couldn't give the drivers ear protection, otherwise they wouldn't hear the radio control. The engines were down low on the ground, so I was responsible for having noise tests done as safety officer along with the Docks Board safety officer. I became responsible for safety a couple of years after the 1974 Health and Safety at Work Act.'

A manual T-card system was initially devised for recording the arrival of containers with slot boards, representing the ship or the stack. As a container arrived the number of the container would be written on the T-card and the card placed in a numbered position to indicate where the container was to be placed. For example, the numbered representation of the stack on the board and the card could be Alpha 41. The T-card would then be placed in slot Alpha 41 so that when the ship arrived the card would be taken out and details given over the radio to a straddle carrier driver of the hold the container had to go on the ship. Jim Brown: 'As the containers came in, they would know in advance that, say they were going to go to Tokyo or Rotterdam for example. There would be a section of board with slots in for the Tokyo or Rotterdam ship. That would be planned in advance with the shippers and our planners. Quite a complex operation, but now it is completely computerised.'

In 1979 Royal Consent was granted to name the container site the Prince Charles Container Port.

The Checkers, a Class Above the Rest!

Before container terminals were set up, the job of the checker was dealing with conventional cargo, checking the number of cartons going on and signing that it was correct. They would sign a document similar to a delivery document, confirming that the goods were delivered correctly and loaded on the ship. The checker had to gain experience in reading the various cargo markings on packing cases and boxes. On the introduction of containers the job changed quite considerably because basically all they were required to do was check the number of the container and that it was sealed. The contents were of no concern to them, unless of course Customs and Excise required a box to be opened to check a sample of the contents. Jim Brown: 'They had a simple function, but were still better paid than the dock workers, because historically it was a skilled job and again they had to be that much more intelligent than the dock workers. The dock labourer had to be strong for picking up and carrying things around, but the checker previously had to go through bills of lading, checking cartons and signing that all was correct.'

In 1964 Maurice Allen was transferred to outside operations in the cargo sheds at Berth 105. At first he worked on the cross-channel cargo ships which dealt with imports and Cape transhipment cargo. This was an ideal place to introduce young staff to the outside working of the docks because it was not too busy and the trade was regular, mainly very small cargo ships (coasters) serving Europe. They bought a small amount of import cargo from Germany, France and Holland, and other cargo for transhipment onto the Cape vessels at the adjacent Berths (103–104) for South Africa. The vessels would call at the berth at the beginning of the week and discharge, and then they would load a small amount of export cargo. Usually the discharge and shipping of the cargo would be finished by the end of the day. The cargo would be taken to the next shed by fork truck for transhipment. All the cargo had to be checked against the ships manifest. When a ship arrived the job of the clerical staff was to find out the hatches that were working and any gangs that would be loading or receiving cargo. The foreman would organise the labour and they would deal with the clerical side. There would be a checker with each gang and the checker was one position senior to a clerk.

Checkers in the Container Terminal

The job was a lot simpler for the checker in the container terminal. They were in the gatehouse and would check the ingoing goods arriving by lorry, check that the container was intact and sealed, and that the driver's documentation matched the number of the container. Import boxes in the stack would be checked at the exit lanes as and when they were collected by IMVs (internal movement vehicles). The same procedure of checking that the container matched the number and the documentation was correct was carried out. Jim Brown: 'They were rather more elite and their manning levels were quite high as well.'

Checkers' New Role

From 1974 Maurice Allen worked at various berths, including 204 Berth on nights. Solent Containers ran the berths and used the dockers, clerks and checkers. The work of the clerical staff was similar when the containers arrived. They would receive the paperwork for the container that was to be released by the shipping company and then cleared and released by the customs. If the container was opened in the container depot, the principle was still the same and sorted and taken to be stacked for delivery. Most of the clerical staff liked working in a container depot, but when another company took over they were moved to a different part of the port. Maurice Allen: 'On one Tuesday they told us that as from today work will be taken over by another company and we were "chucked out". We went to other berths. That meant that they were then overmanned. That gave them an excuse to say "we've got too many people" and they started making people redundant.'

Dockers Sue the BTDB

The British Transport Docks Board was privatised in 1980, and in 1982 Associated British Ports (ABP) took over the running of 19 ports, including Southampton. March 1981 had been a serious time for industrial relations in the docks when the British Transport Docks Board was sued by the dockers. At the time headlines in the press highlighted the dispute, saying: 'Union Backs Dockers' Action', 'Dockers dispute costs the city a fortune', 'Docks dispute in deadlock' and 'Dockers to seek pay for lock-out'. The dispute was in response to a lock-out by the port employers, after a ruling by the National Docks Labour Board that the dock employers were in breach of the National Docks Labour Scheme. Dock workers intended to seek compensation for the lost money due to the lock-out.

Ray Strange, who was a shop steward at the time, talks about the concerns at the time: 'The chairman at the time, although one of the young element, but good at his job, decided we were going to sue the Docks Board. We went to the trade union meeting with the area secretary and the docks officer who said, "We're not taking on the Docks Board, we'll never win this one. You are not going to do it." We told him we were going to do it and told him he could do what he liked. We saw an industrial solicitor and took them to court and won. It cost the employers about £678,000 as they had to back pay all the shifts and we hadn't even done them! That was one of the port director's mistakes. The port director before him was Mr Stringer, and he was a gentleman. His father was a railwayman and we used to get on with him alright. Three High Court appeal judges unanimously backed the National Docks Labour Board who had said that the action of the port employers was in breach of the 1967 National Docks Labour Scheme.'

The young chairman of the dockers mentioned above was Ritchie Pearce. John Hovey saw Ritchie Pearce as an extremely able shop steward, who had personal control of the Southampton dockers, and writes, 'They had good reason to respect and follow him, because he had presided over the years when the removal of the wage restraint had enabled some improvement.' He also mentions Dennis Harryman, an ex-senior shop steward who became the docks officer and helped create a 'workable link between the employers and the moderate part of the union.'

Associated British Ports

Bob Guille took over as managing director of SCS (Solent Container Services) from John Hovey on 1 November 1985 and then became involved in the preparation for the absorption of SCS into the new independent container operation to be known as the Southampton Container Terminal (SCT), which came into being in July 1988. This was to be a joint venture between P&O Containers Limited and Associated British Ports (ABP), with P&O Ports Group owning 51 per cent and ABP owning 49 per cent.

This effectively established the Port of Southampton, with SCT running the container terminal and ABP operating the rest of the port. It was also same year as the 150th anniversary of the founding of the Port of Southampton.

The National Dock Labour Scheme was Abolished in 1989

Jim Brown remembers when the National Dock Labour Scheme was abolished in 1989: 'Maggie Thatcher broke it in my time. I was on a cruise when I read in the ship's newspaper that the labour act had been repealed, and I couldn't believe it. I thought I would come back and find the terminal at a standstill. I still find it hard to believe now, what is now called multi-tasking. Dock workers are now known as port operatives. There are no longer any checkers, there are no van drivers, no crane drivers, no straddle drivers, no lashers, they are all port operatives.'

Strike Action

Peter Wareham: 'When the NDLB ended there was strike action. They announced it on the television, and we all came out on strike. Then we all had to go back to work and have a three-month cooling-off period. We had to have a ballot while they all got organised. We really lost the battle on the first day really. What happened was, when the ballot ended at 2pm on the Tuesday, by 3pm there was a notice on the board that anyone who wanted a severance of £35,000 could go on Friday. Of course, half of them went. We were defeated before we started really. We were out for three weeks.'

There was concern among some of the dockers that there had been a campaign against them, and many of the disputes were the result of this. Peter Wareham: 'I found out afterwards that when the Docks Labour Board went a lot of things came out. I think the National Port Employers had decided to get rid of the scheme and when they had their meetings they agreed to have a campaign. I put down that a lot of the disputes in Southampton Docks were attributed to their campaign, which took 10 years. They would do little things, and at least twice we were locked out for three weeks; however, we went to the High Court, and it was found to be against the law, and they had to pay us three weeks' money and average overtime money. There were all these little niggles and that contributed to the downfall of the port.'

The danger at the time for the container trade was the numbers of major customers, especially the Japanese and the Germans, leaving Southampton for good. The encouraging sign was the increasing numbers of dockers who were leaving the port by accepting ABPs severance terms, and for ABP this meant a substantial reduction in workforce costs.

This period for Solent Container Services was seen by John Hovey as crunch time, and he writes: 'We were in it with ABP up to the hilt, and it was kill or cure time.' John saw the breakthrough when there was a change in the chair of the union stewards: 'The stalemate continued and ACAS became involved and Ritchie Pearce, seeing that the employers were not going to budge, decided to take the severance pay and leave to allow an agreement to be made possible.'

From then on the employers found the negotiations more positive because the new chairman of the stewards and his deputy were more moderate and easier for them to deal with.

Terry Adams was one of those who decided to leave when the dockers were offered severance money: 'I finished in 1989. That was the day of the "evacuation", as we called it. I took £35,000 severance money and left. I got out on a Friday, and I think there were about 500 that went on that day. That was a lot of the experienced men and that left a lot of the rubbish. I'm sorry, but we did have a lot of inexperienced men because when we went on to day work they came to work in the docks because we were earning far more than other workers. You couldn't have inexperienced workers in the docks, especially when you were on piecework, you would never have a job.'

Chief Safety Officer for Solent Container Services

Jim Brown: 'As a company we were in the vanguard of lots of things really. When I became chief safety officer, before the Docks Regulations came out, I would have draft EEC directives about safe dock working conditions to comment on and many of the systems brought in by Solent Container Services were incorporated into the Docks Regulations.'

As time went on less and less workers were needed and voluntary severance was

Berths 204 to 207 fully operational. (Courtesy of Jim Brown Collection)

Grimaldi Siosa Line *Adige* being towed by the tug *Flying Osprey*. (Courtesy of Maurice Allen Collection)

offered to reduce the numbers of staff employed by SCT. Jim Brown: 'I applied but was refused voluntary severance because I was considered too valuable, especially on the health and safety side, and because I had developed the company's safety policy. Luckily for me they cut down the shifts, and there were five managers to four shifts, leaving the eight-hour working and bringing in 12-hour working, reducing the number of shifts. We then had surplus ship managers and assistant ship managers. I got in contact with one of them who was facing redundancy and asked if he wanted to take over the health and safety side. It was agreed that I could leave if I took six months to train the new man in health and safety matters. I was also required to update the health and safety policy before I left, which I did.'

Jim left Solent Container Services in 1990 at the age of 58 and became a health and safety consultant for a few years and is well-known as an author of books on Southampton's History.

ROLL-ON, ROLL-OFF: THE FIRST RO-RO SHIPS

Don Archbold remembers the when the first Ro-Ro ships came into Southampton: 'It was in 1963 when the first Ro-Ro ships, *Traviata* and *Rigoletto* came in to Southampton and docked at 110 Berth in the Western Docks. Cars were taken into the Renault factory. They had ramps from the side of the ship, and you had to time to the tides to land the cars. I dealt with the first one and it was a little ship called the *Traviata*, carrying 369 Renault cars. She was followed by her sister ship, the *Rigoletto*. Gradually the Ro-Ro ships got bigger and we got big cargo ships to take cars, which we lifted on by crane. We started loading 3,000 to 4,000 MGs and Triumphs.' Don finished working with Keller Bryant & Co. Ltd in December 1963 and in 1964 joined the agents Mann and Son (which was later taken over by the Wallenius Line).

In August 1990 the Southampton Cargo Handling's newsletter, *Cargo News,* reported an export success in the transportation of Rover minis to Japan. The Rover group was planning to ship 10,000 minis in the year and ship them from Southampton through Wallenius and other leading shipping lines. This was to be a large increase on 1982 when just 1,000 minis were sold to Japan. It was planned for one shipment a month being loaded at the Eastern Docks.

One year later in August 1991 the *Cargo News* reported that Wallenius Line intended to boost transhipment of vehicles through the port to the Canaries, South Africa and the Mediterranean, including developing Southampton to the status alongside Antwerp as a transhipment centre between Northern Europe and North America. Captain Mark Bookham, operations manager for the Wallenius UK agents, commented: 'We feel Southampton has as much to offer as Antwerp on the transhipment side. The change since Southampton Cargo Handling took over has been remarkable. Wallenius are very happy with the labour relations in Southampton and the flexibility of the labour.' At the time Wallenius and Japan's NYK line operated a regular four-ship shuttle service between Northern Europe and North America, using Southampton as the UK port. *Cargo News* also reported that the traffic eastbound had been helped by the addition of Honda Accord vehicles, with 3,000 a year being shipped from Jacksonville to Southampton.

Ray Strange remembers quite a humorous situation with regard to the Ro-Ro ships, although it proved quite expensive for the employers. This was an example of when there was a disagreement as to 'who was to do what!' 'I remember one time going on Ro-Ro and we said we were going to drive the container loading vehicles, called "tugs", on to the ship, but the crew said it was their job. The driver was not happy with this and left the tug vehicle on the ramp and took away the keys. The ship wanted to sail, so they sailed and dumped the tug vehicle down the river! This was a £10,000 loss to the employers!'

PART 3

CHAPTER 13

SOUTHAMPTON DOCKS IN THE 21ST CENTURY

Cable Laying

It was in 1954 that Standard Telephone built a factory at Southampton Docks to manufacture British designed lightweight submarine telephone cable. By 1962 another factory had opened on the same site, this time to manufacture the US lightweight cable.

When British Telecom was privatised in 1984, BT (Marine) Ltd was set up to operate a fleet of cable ships. These ships were named, *CS Alert*, *CS Iris*, *CS Monarch*, *CS Sovereign* and *CS Nexus*. In 1994 these vessels were transferred to Cable & Wireless (Marine) Ltd when they acquired BT Marine.

The Pirelli works, covering 35 acres on reclaimed land, was built in 1914 and in its time employed over 4,500 in Southampton. After the company built two new factories in Eastleigh and Bishopstoke in the 1960s, it was gradually run down and finally closed in 1990. The site has been used for retail outlets such as Toys 'R' Us and Furniture Village, and with the development of the West Quay shopping area the Pirelli works that was built in 1981 to construct submarine cable was closed in 2003. The site was cleared and in April 2009 a new IKEA store is due to open on the site.

Kenneth Fielder still maintained contact with Southampton Docks and up until his retirement in 1988 worked for a cable-laying company: 'I was with a company known as Stubbs Welding Ltd, a Warrington (Lancs) company, and it used to take me into the docks to do quite a lot for work on the ploughs used for cable laying. I found the work of the telephone engineers responsible for cable laying absolutely fascinating. What they would do is plot the course and lay the cable. It was preceded by a plough which would plough into the ocean bed, and then the cable would be laid into it. We were responsible for hard facing and helping to keep the plough in working order.'

'From the afterdeck of the ship they would have this large spool of telephone cable and as the plough was put over the side, over the stern of the ship, so the cable would be laid. Pirelli manufactured the cable, but it was laid by the branch of the telephone cable companies. Cable and Wireless took it over, but I remember it before it became Cable and Wireless. You can imagine the plough would become abrazed due to the ocean floor, and we had a system where it could be hard faced. They used to have booster on the cables to boost the signals which, as I remember, were about £1,000,000 each. What they must not do is kink the cable, and so it all had to be done very carefully.'

Cable and Wireless CS *Mercury*. (Courtesy of Bert Moody Collection)

Banana Trade

The banana trade had a short revival in the 1990s when Associated British Ports opened the Windward Terminal at Berth 101 in the Western Docks in 1992 for Geest bananas. By 1999, however, ABP had upgraded the facilities in the docks for importing bananas, and the Fyffes banana traffic was transferred from Portsmouth and combined with Geest at Berth 101 in Southampton. The first ship to arrive was the 10,291-ton *Canterbury Star* discharging a cargo of bananas from Belize and Honduras. This arrangement did not last long because in 2002 both Geest's and Fyffes's banana traffic was transferred to Portsmouth, with a loss of work for 70 Southampton dockers who were made redundant by Southampton Cargo Handling Company. This is the same company that was formed after ABP gave up their cargo handling in the port in 1989–90 and made their 189 employees redundant; however, this was the first dockers' co-operative that was formed when APB allowed 125 of the workers who had been made redundant to contribute £10,000 of their redundancy money towards the formation of the Southampton Cargo Handling Company.

PORT FACILITIES IN SOUTHAMPTON:

Container Terminal

This is a four-berth container terminal enabling four deep-sea vessels to be handled at the same time, and it incorporates 1,360m of continuous quay. The berths are numbered 204, 205, 206 and 207 with Berth 207 being able to handle the deepest

Southampton Container Terminal. (Courtesy of ABP)

draught container ships. The terminal has room for 13,673 TEU (20ft equivalent units) containers and 404 mechanical handling equipment and cranes to move them. There is a railfreight terminal located alongside the Container Terminal to move the containers to destinations around the country by rail.

Dry Bulks

The Port of Southampton exports cereals and imports various bulk cargoes. The Bulk Terminal is in the port's Western Docks on Berths 107, 108 and 109. These berths handle bulk cargoes and minerals, such as sand, aggregates, gypsum and marble chippings. There is a rail link to enable bulk to be distributed around the UK. There is also a purpose-built glass facility which recingles glass and then ships the refined glass around the UK coastal ports for use in the bottle-making industry. Also in the Western Docks there are flour mills that imports and processes wheat for use in the food industry. In the Eastern Docks a 16-silo grain terminal was opened on 47 Berth in 1982, and a year later the second grain terminal was opened on 36 Berth with capacity for approximately 30,000 tons for the export trade. The grain terminal on 47 Berth was closed in 2004 and taken down, leaving only the grain terminal on 36 Berth operational.

Dry bulk cargo.

Fresh produce.

MV *Lion* at the Esso Terminal.

The car carrier *Global Spirit*. (Courtesy of Richard de Jong Collection)

Fresh Produce
In 1991 a new temperature-controlled Canary Islands Fruit Terminal opened on 104 Berth. Southampton is the sole UK import port for Canary Islands produce that includes tomatoes, peppers, avocados and cucumbers. To help keep the produce fresh, the fruit terminal has cool and cold storage and two deep-water berths, 103 and 104 Berths, that are capable of berthing two ships at a time. The produce is then transported across the country to shops and supermarkets.

Liquid Bulks
The main liquid bulks consist of oil and alcohol. Bacardi-Martini had their sole bottling and distribution centre based in the Western Docks, but the last shipment came on the *Jo Spirit* in April 2007. The plant and the operation have since been closed down and the buildings demolished. Both the Esso and BP oil refineries have their berthing arrangements in Southampton Water to handle crude and refined petroleum products.

Ro-Ro (Roll-on, Roll-off)
Over 700,000 vehicles are handled by the port each year, including heavy wheeled vehicles. Car manufacturers use the port for exporting and importing new cars. These include: Ford, Renault, Land Rover, Toyota, BMW, Peugeot, Jaguar and Honda. Honda has its own wash-house and inspection facilities in the port to prepare their cars for the UK market after their overseas voyage. There is a rail link to the port quays for car trains to discharge the cars near the car carriers. To overcome the problem of space for storing cars in the port area, Wallenius Wilhelmsen Logistics UK has constructed a multi-deck storage facility for 3,120 cars. This method of car storage avoids using a large area because the cars are parked on decks above each other. A second multi-deck car terminal, the Empress Terminal, has been built and has a storage capacity for 5,200 vehicles. A third multi-deck terminal has since been constructed for Honda cars and is also in the Eastern Docks.

Passengers and Cruises
Southampton is the centre for the cruise industry, with both P&O and the Cunard Line, now part of the Carnival Group, maintaining their UK fleets at the port. Other holiday companies that use the port include the Fred Olsen Cruise Line, Saga Holidays and Royal Caribbean. The three existing cruise terminals are Queen Elizabeth II Ocean Terminal on Berths 38 and 39 in the Eastern Docks, the Mayflower Terminal on Berth 105 and 106, and the City Cruise Terminal on Berths 101 and 102 in the Western Docks.

The Queen Elizabeth II Passenger Terminal is now the home base for the *Queen Mary 2* who has taken over the transatlantic route from the *Queen Elizabeth 2.*

The New Holland America Eurodam passing the P&O *Oceana* berthed at the QEII Ocean Terminal. (Courtesy of Richard de Jong Collection)

Red Funnel Ferries to Cowes, Isle of Wight, passing the BP Oil Terminal.

Ferry Links

People also travel on ferries to connect with the Isle of Wight from Southampton. Red Funnel ferries are important because they also carry cars, delivery transport and buses to convey people and goods to and from the island. Red Funnel also provides a high-speed link for passengers, which cuts down the sailing time considerably.

There is also the Hythe ferry that takes people from the Hythe Pier across to the Town Quay, Southampton. This is a very important ferry for shoppers, workers and supporters of the 'Saints' football team and only takes 15 minutes. This saves a journey of 16 miles from the Waterside around to the Southampton shopping centre.

Hythe Pier

The history of the Hythe Pier goes back to the 19th century when the building of pier on the opposite side of Southampton Water started in 1879 and was completed in 1881. The ferry transported passengers the shorter distance across Southampton Water to and from Hythe to the Town Quay. At the time of building a hand-operated narrow gauge railway was constructed for transporting goods. Hythe Pier is 700 yards long (640m) from Hythe to the deep-water channel of Southampton Water.

In 1922 the Hythe Pier single-track railway was electrified and used electric locomotives that originated from a World War One mustard gas factory at Avonmouth. The locomotive was employed to pull a small number of wooden passenger cars and today is often seen pulling the same carriages and a four-wheel fuel tank to transport fuel to the ferries at the end of the pier. The train is recognised in the *Guinness World Records* as the world's oldest pier train. The ferries were, and still are, important for transporting passengers across Southampton Water instead of having to take the long route via Totton and Redbridge into Southampton.

Hythe ferry.

Hythe Pier.

Hythe Pier train.

Hovercraft

It was in 1960 when Southampton became linked with the development of the Hovercraft. The Hovercraft Development Company, founded by Sir Christopher Cockerel, moved to Hythe, on the opposite side of Southampton Water to the Old Docks. Sir Christopher Cockerell had invited Dr E.W.H. Gifford to help him set up the first commercial Hovercraft Development Company in the world.

In 1955, while living in East Anglia, Christopher Cockerel had the idea of a vehicle that would move over the water's surface floating on a layer of air, thus reducing friction between the water and vehicle. To test his theory Christopher Cockerel put a smaller cat food tin inside a coffee tin, and by blowing air with an air dryer into them the downward thrust, pushing down on a set of kitchen scales, was measured as greater than when air was blown into one can. The original test equipment can be seen in the Hovercraft Museum at Lee-on-Solent. It was Sir Christopher that first used the term 'Hovercraft', which has remained ever since.

The first prototype hovercraft, the SRN1, was 30ft in length with a 24ft beam and weighed 3½ tons. The first test flight was from Calais to Dover on 25 July 1959 and took two hours. There was no 'skirt' on the prototype, and the jets were turned inward around the edge to create a wall to hold the cushion of air beneath the craft. When a skirt was fitted later it resulted in less power being needed to 'lift' the craft, as less air leaked away at the sides. After more experiments the SRN4 cross-channel ferry commenced in 1968 carrying 254 passengers and 30 cars. Later versions could carry 396 passengers and 53 cars.

Hovercrafts are still built in Southampton by the Griffon Hovercraft Company. The Griffon Hovercraft Company was formed in 1976 by Dr E.W.H. Gifford because he believed that the hovercraft would be better built like a boat rather than an aircraft. The company is based in Woolston on the River Itchen.

Griffon hovercraft.

Developing the Ferry Terminal, 29 March 1969. (Courtesy of ABP)

Ocean Village

It was in the 1960s that changes began to take place in the Old Docks. BTDB (British Transport Docks Board) started redevelopment of the Inner and Outer Docks in 1963 and decided to fill in the Inner Dock for car storage. The entrance to the Outer Dock was increased to 325ft (99m). The Outer Dock had opened in 1842 but was later renamed the Princess Alexandra Dock, when Her Royal Highness Princess Alexandra opened the new ferry complex on 3 July 1967.

Normandy, P&O Ferry Services, Townsend Thoresen and Swedish Lloyd services started from there; however, by the early 1980s the ferry service from Southampton was transferred to Portsmouth. Townsend-Thoresen Ferry Services transferred there in 1983 and P&O Ferries in 1984, the year that work started on redeveloping the Princess Alexandra Dock into the present Ocean Village complex.

Ocean Village is a marina, residential and leisure development in the Old Docks area on the River Itchen. There is a 375-berth marina and overlooking the marina is the Royal Southampton Yacht Club. The residential development is known as Admirals Quay, and leisure facilities include two cinemas (Harbour Lights picture house and Cineworld Cinemas), restaurants and wine bars where the Old Dock warehouses once stood.

A postcard of Princess Alexandra Dock, showing, from left: *Patricia/Hispania*, *Dragon/Leopold* and *Viking 1, II* or *IV*. (Courtesy of Bert Moody Collection)

Calshot Spit lightship, taken from the boat deck of the RMS *Queen Mary* in June 1963. (Courtesy of Bert Moody Collection)

The *Calshot Spit* Lightship

The *Calshot Spit* lightship (LV 78) was a Trinity House navigation aid and was used to guide ships entering Southampton Water from the western end of the Solent, coming around the sand and shingle of Calshot Spit. It was built in 1914 by J.I. Thornycroft shipyard in Southampton and was decommissioned in 1978. Since 1988, the lightship has been a static attraction at the entrance to the Ocean Village marina. It was reported in the *Daily Echo* on 12 March 2008, however, that ABP plan to move the *Calshot Spit* lightship to the site of the old Trafalgar Dock as part of it redevelopment of the dock area, in connection with the construction of the fourth cruise terminal nearby. It is hoped that the area will become a visitor attraction in the Eastern Docks.

SOUTHAMPTON CONTAINER TERMINAL IN 2004

With the larger ships being built it was necessary to deepen the main channel, and in 1996 it was dredged to allow the increasingly deeper draught vessels to enter the port. The following year the fourth deep-sea berth (Berth 207) was completed at Southampton Container Terminal. This berth was built specifically to take the deepest draught container ships arriving in the docks.

It was just two years after Jim Brown left Solent Containers that Derek Smith, business development manager for Southampton Container Terminals (SCT) arrived at the Port of Southampton to work in the Southampton Container Terminal. Jim Brown remembers Derek Smith from the previous time he worked at Southampton as a ship planner, planning the loading and discharging of container ships for seven years before he moved to Felixstowe in 1985, a rapidly expanding port. He worked initially as planning manager at the newly constructed Trinity Terminal, and within three years he was promoted to port logistics planning manager. He returned to Southampton in 1992 as business development manager.

Derek Smith explains what it was like at the terminal when he arrived and how it has since developed: 'When I arrived here in about 1992, driving down the road it was very quiet and appeared rather neglected. At that time we were moving about 450,000 TEU (20ft equivalent units) per year, compared with this year, 1984, when we expect to handle close to 1.5 million TEU. This is a huge growth, and my current role covers the strategic, commercial and customer/public relations requirements of the company. So in my strategic role I am involved in developing the optimum use of space and the equipment involved in the logistical process of making the "boxes" move faster and more efficiently. As well as that, I am looking at the medium-term and longer-term planning for how we might produce higher outputs, reduce costs and increase revenue in years to come.'

The business development manager is responsible for dealing with contracts with the companies that are part of major 'alliances' such as the Grand Alliance of Hapag Lloyd, German, Nippon Yusen Kaisha, Japanese (NYK), Orient Overseas Container Line, Chinese (OOCL) and the Malaysian International Shipping Corporation (MISC), known collectively as the Grand Alliance. The Grand Alliance is by far the largest consortia or 'alliance' in the world and have 11 calls each week at Southampton to all ports in the Far East, from Northern China to Thailand. The Grand Alliance also has two calls each week with CP Ships (Canadian Pacific) to and from the US, covering New York in the North to Houston in the South.

The second largest alliance is the New World Alliance with American President Lines, (owned by Neptune Orient Lines of Singapore), Japanese Mitsui (OSK), S. Korean Hyundai Merchant Marine and the French CMA-CGM. The New World Alliance has two calls each week to the Far East and is expanding quite rapidly. SCT also handles eight weekly feeder services. Feeder vessels take cargo from the larger ships to other ports in the UK.

China is emerging as the highest trading nation in the world, and significant numbers of imports coming in via Southampton far outweigh the exports going back to Asia, with almost 30 per cent of containers going back empty to be refilled again.

The aim of SCT is to get the containers in and out of the terminal by road and rail much quicker, especially in the peak periods. Every year there is the 'pre-Christmas rush.' With the shops filling their shelves from October, the warehouses have to be able to meet the demand for goods. SCT has to ensure that their manning levels and equipment meet the demands of the increased and seasonal trade through the terminal. To do this SCT now have 'Sprinter' straddle carriers to move containers to Freightliner's Maritime Rail Terminal to be loaded onto the trains. The up-to-date data system passes information from the shipping lines computers to the terminals computer, and with the faster 'Sprinter' straddle carriers SCT can now move 1,000 boxes or more each day, much faster than their previous tractor and trailer operation.

An aerial view of Southampton Container Port. (Courtesy of ABP)

Container cranes.

The size and capacity of the ships are getting larger, and this is a huge challenge for SCT. The business development manager explains: 'The draught (depth) of some ships is generally between 12.5 to 14.0 metres and sometimes can be as much as 14.5 metres. This can be a problem at times for the shipping line. For example, in Southampton there is a tidal window of about two or three hours to get a vessel in and out at 14.5m metres draft and this will become a bigger problem in the future. At the present time the terminal only has three of the 13 deep-sea calls in a week that are in this deeper range. This is a challenge for the future and will become a strategic problem in the channel and also the depth alongside as well. The berth has to be deep enough to meet the required 60cm underkeel clearance at all times as a safety margin.'

SCT are at present dealing with challenges for the future as they occur. The business development manager explains: 'There may be problems to overcome with berthing and turning these huge ships in the future, as well as the need to have larger cranes and deeper channels to match their height, width and draft. [The largest ship today is around 340m long (1,115ft) and 45m beam (150ft)]. This means cranes will need wider booms, and the increased weight will make the cranes heavier and will ultimately require more piling so the berth can support the weight of the crane and boxes.'

Not only are the ships getting bigger but so is the container size. Eight-foot high was the standard, but then it grew to 8.6ft high, and now some containers are 9.6ft high. With six or seven piles of containers on deck (as well as the nine layers below deck) the height is increased by 6ft (2m).

SCT has already responded to the challenge of the increasing height of the containers. The business development manager explains: 'We have heightened five of our cranes by 5m. Time is money and lines are looking at port times at no more than 36 hours for up to 4,000 moves. That is why we need to have five cranes, and sometimes six, for each ship to boost the numbers of containers being unloaded at the beginning of its stay. When other ships come alongside some cranes will be moved to unload them. Therefore we have to work faster. At the moment we are about average in Europe, but probably the best in the UK, moving about 21 to 22 moves per crane per hour, and with four cranes on average you get 88 moves per hour, and in a 24-hour period you are going to get something like 2,100 moves. This year our target is 2,400 moves per vessel per 24 hours, and we will endeavour to increase this year on year.'

Advance Preparation for the Arrival of a Ship is a Key to Efficiency

The advance information from shipping lines and forwarding agents (who control the inland movement of containers), enables the terminal to preposition containers to where they are needed and get the boxes delivered quickly to road, rail or smaller feeder vessels.

The business development manager explains the process: 'Before the ship arrives we start to receive containers by road and rail up to seven days before and we know which berth the ship will come in on. We can, therefore, instruct all our equipment drivers via our computer system to take all the containers as they come in and put them in their locations, either in temporary high-density areas or directly to their location close to the berth. We have straddle carriers for delivering imports to road trailers, reach stackers receiving full export containers into high density stacks and empty container handlers (ECH) picking containers from lorries and sprinters for taking containers to the Maritime Rail Terminal. All our yard equipment is equipped with radio data control to communicate through the central control system and differential global satellite systems (DGPS) to make sure we place the containers in the correct location. When a vehicle arrives at the transfer areas the reach stacker, ECH or

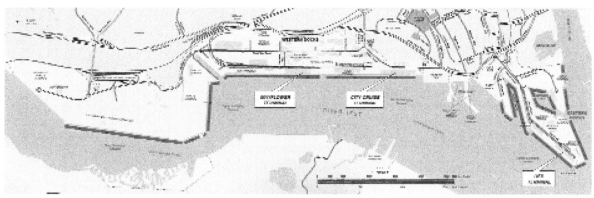

(Courtesy of ABP)

straddle carrier driver inputs the last four digits of an 11-figure container number into the on-board computer. The system then places the full details of that container on the screen so that he can confirm he has the right container, and then it will tell him where to take it in the yard. If the driver attempts to stack the container in the wrong location he will get a warning on the screen.'

The movement of all containers is tracked electronically and this is then used by the terminal staff to ensure that all containers are in the right place at the right time. Over 2 million moves each year are tracked by the DGPS system, which updates the graphical screens used by the terminal staff to allow accurate planning of the loading and discharging of ships as well as tracking the movement of containers to different areas of the terminal for checking by HM Revenue & Customs, Port Health or the shipping lines.

Proposed Dibden Bay Development

In 1997 Associated British Ports (ABP) announced their intention to build a new container terminal on land they owned at Dibden Bay. There was immediate concern and campaign groups for local residents, RSPB, Friends of the Earth and Hampshire Wildlife Trust started to make their objections to the proposal.

The actual formal application by Associated British Ports to build a 1.85km long, six berth, deep-water quay at Dibden Bay occurred in October 2000. Due to the record number of objections the government announced there would be a public inquiry. The public inquiry was held from November 2001 to December 2002, with the planning inspector's report being submitted to the government in October 2003.

On 20 April 2004 the transport minister, Tony McNulty, accepted the recommendation of the Dibden Bay inquiry inspector to turn down proposals for a new container terminal on Southampton Water. The transport minister said that one factor in the making of the decision was the environmental impact on internationally protected sites. This was a disappointment to ABP and their plans for the future development of the port. The port director gave a warning that as a result of the government's refusal to give the go-ahead for a container terminal at Dibden Bay that 'tough choices' will have to be made.

CHAPTER 14

ABP MARINE DEPARTMENT IN 2004

Deputy Harbour Master in the Port of Southampton

The management and safety of 18 miles of waterway and 45 miles of foreshore is the responsibility of the Associated British Ports (ABP) who acts as the Statutory Harbour Authority. The co-ordination of the work of the Marine Department is the responsibility of the deputy harbour master, based in the VTS (Vessel Traffic Services) Centre at Dock Head on the Eastern Dock.

On 26 April 2004 Capt Mike Evans talked about his work as deputy harbour master for the Port of Southampton. Capt Mike Evans had spent 18 years at sea for British Petroleum, where he qualified as a master mariner before coming into the ports industry. He became harbour master in Falmouth for five years and was then ferry port operations manager in Portsmouth for a few years. Capt Evans was the harbour master in Portsmouth before becoming deputy harbour master in Southampton.

Capt Evans: 'My own role as deputy harbour master is to oversee the ongoing operation and ensure the safe arrival and departure of ships in and out of the port. That means pulling together all the necessary important information to be communicated. Good communication is important and the feature of our work here. I look after the welfare side of the staff as well, for 125 people, which is a significant part of my work. I am also responsible as harbour master for all aspects of the safe

Vessel Traffic Services (VTS), Dock Head. (Courtesy of ABP)

A pilot launch. (Courtesy of ABP)

A patrol launch. (Courtesy of ABP)

delivery of pilotage services and for the conduct of all the ships using the harbour area, not just the piloted ships. I have to keep an eye on the behaviour of all the ships, including the recreational craft that use the water to ensure they are not obstructing other vessels in any way. If necessary we have port bylaws. We have, at times, had cause to use the bylaws to either issue warnings or ultimately prosecute people who are breaking the bylaws.'

The department is large because it works 24 hours a day, 365 days a year. Most of the people in the department are on shift work as there is a need to cover day and night, due to the varying tide arrivals of the vessels that enter and leave the port. It is not always the vessels that demand time, it is making sure the berth is ready for its arrival. There are people moving fenders around the docks to make sure the berth is properly 'prepared and dressed', as it is called.

The deputy harbour master works closely with other relevant local authorities that are connected or affected by the operation as a port. This includes all the local authorities such as Southampton City Council and the District Councils that front on to the Solent. The Marine Department liaise closely with them for environmental matters.

'In the case of a port such as ours, with a large oil refinery and large oil delivery installation on either side of Southampton Water, oil pollution is always a risk and a threat. We work very hard to make sure that, A, it doesn't happen and, B, if it did it would be quickly contained and cleaned up. We have had one or two spills over the years, and I am pleased to say there are not too many and none of major significance. This is where my role comes in, not only to make sure that our oil spill contingency plans are right up to date, but that they are also regularly exercised for instant readiness'.

The Marine Department operates eight small boats, with three manned and operational 24 hours a day. Two pilot boats are located at the eastern approaches to the port and operate the approaches to the Solent around the Nab tower from their

Gosport base. The pilot boats and crews wait for the vessel's arrival to board and take-off the pilot, whose responsibility is to navigate the vessels in and out of the port area.

A patrol boat is manned 24 hours a day and is used to escort the larger ships through the harbour waters and off Cowes and Calshot. This is to ensure that the channels in and out of the port are clear of smaller craft that may not be aware that the larger craft can only use the channel because of the depth of their draught.

There is a day-working hydrographic team, based in the VTS building, which is continually engaged in surveying the channels and the margins of the channels to see that the depths used are maintained. The hydrographic surveyor will, on a daily basis, go around and check various areas of the whole port to see that the required depth of the water needed for each area is correct. This is a vitally important task because vessels berthed in the dock will need to be able to float with a safe clearance of water underneath the keel at all states of tide.

At the top of the VTS centre is a control room, which looks very similar to what you would expect to see in an airport traffic control tower. There are five staff on duty, 24 hours a day, keeping watch on radar all through the Solent and the approaches to Southampton, Portsmouth, Cowes and Langstone harbours. This is to ensure that all vessels are safely moving through the deep-water channels and know exactly what is going on throughout their passage, which can last up to four or five hours in the case of the larger ships.

The VTS officer is effectively the duty harbour master for the duration of his watch and will make sure that tugs, and any other assistance that the pilot and ship need, are in position to give that assistance. His job is to liaise closely with the towage contractors and berth operators involved with the ships.

If there are large tankers going to Esso Fawley refinery, or the BP (British Petroleum) Hamble jetty, the VTS needs to liaise with the shore staff to make sure everything is ready for the ship. It is important that everything is planned well in advance so that the larger ships can take advantage of a high tide when entering or leaving the port. It has to be pre-calculated by liaison with the pilot, VTS officer and the terminal itself to make sure the tugs are ready and the tide is doing what it is predicted to do. This information is shared with the marine pilot, VTS officer and the container terminal. There are electronic tide gauges in various points around the harbour, where read-outs are displayed on a computer screen, to make sure the tide is behaving itself and the vessels arrive and depart safely and to plan. There is also a small team of clerical workers who provide administrative back-up to ensure that the operations run smoothly and arrange cover for anyone who is sick.

Capt Evans: 'Another of my responsibilities is to liaise with adjacent harbour authorities and work closely with other harbour masters to make sure that anything we are doing does not have an adverse impact on them or vice versa. It is quite interesting to work alongside the Royal Navy, as Portsmouth is a Royal Navy dockyard port. A Royal Navy serving officer is in charge, and he will change every couple of years. They have different objectives to us. We run a commercial business and facilitate trade, while their objective is the protection of the crown and crown property and to ensure that their warships are ready for warfare. If required we will, of course, do our best to support them in this important role without detracting from our own core business.

'That's one aspect of the job, and the last bit is dealing with local yachtsman and local yacht clubs to make sure we liaise closely with them when they are having major or minor yacht races. They need to know what we are doing shipping-wise so that they can plan their day's racing or events around that programme. If they have a special event they will see me in advance, and we will issue a local notice to mariners from this office.

'It is a very dynamic situation working alongside other harbour authorities who have different objectives. We are unique in the mix of commercial and recreational craft. This is probably the most densely used area in the country, if not the world, for recreational craft in a major commercial and naval port. Managing it on a daily basis is never dull. It is a very interesting place to work, and no two days are ever the same.'

Background to the Present VTS (Vessel Traffic Services)
In the 1920s and 1930s communication between ship and shore was through visual signalling, involving light and flag signals. There was a signal station at Calshot Jetty and also the main signal station at Dockhead that controlled the movement of all vessels inbound, within the docks and when outward bound. As a vessel approached the docks the main dockyard signal station took control and the duty signalman informed the dockmaster that the ship had been sighted. Instructions for berthing were signalled to the vessel by means of flags and numbered boards by day and coloured lights by night. The arrival of the ship and weather conditions at the time were then noted in a log book. The signal station also had a powerful foghorn to use when necessary. Other pierhead signal stations were situated within the docks, and all came under the direct control of the dockmaster.

By the early 1950s Calshot Castle was used for a Harbour Board lookout. A year later the planning and construction of a new signal station began, and in January 1958 the world's first port VHF radio and radar station was opened by the minister of transport on top of Calshot Castle on Southampton Water. The Port Operation and Information Service then included a system of ship-to-shore radio that linked the harbour master, dockmaster, Calshot, both the Fawley Marine Terminal and the BP Jetty and two radio-equipped launches that patrolled on Southampton Water.

Calshot Spit.

The New Port VTS (Vessel Traffic Services) facility was officially opened on 7 July 1972 on 37 Berth, Dock Head in the Eastern Docks. This facility was to replace the one at Calshot. Until then all vessel movements were monitored from a blacked-out room specially designed for the use of radar equipment. The call sign of the new station was SPR (Southampton Port Radio), and the patrol launches duties were continued checking navigational aids, looking for oil spills or other forms pollution and providing escorts to large vessels.

Changes were being implemented within the IOW pilotage district, with the Trinity House vessels being phased out of service and replaced with faster launches. The Pilotage Act 1987 replaced Trinity House as the pilotage authority and ABP became the Statutory Harbour Authority. The VTS building became the base for the pilotage service, with the Trinity House staff being absorbed into ABP. The station callsign 'SPR' (Southampton Port Radio) eventually changed to 'Southampton VTS.'

The VTS (Vessel Traffic Services): The responsibility of the VTS Officer

The VTS Centre is manned 24 hours a day, seven days a week, by five personnel, one of which is the VTS officer. Under him are four other assistants, one of whom allocates pilots to their ships and the other assistants work at the two radar desks monitoring the vessels within the VTS district. This is from the Nab Tower, past the entrance to Portsmouth and Cowes right up Southampton Water and as far west as the Needles. To cover the area there are four radar sites. All vessels, including yachts, recreational and commercial craft over 20m in length, are required to call in on VHF channel 12 when they enter the VTS district. There are certain reporting points throughout the district in which they are again required to report passing and at these points. The VTS will then update them on any relevant traffic information.

Safety of navigation is the primary role of VTS, and it is the duty VTS officer who is responsible for carrying out this task. He is also responsible for the allocation of pilots and the monitoring of the pilot launches at Gosport whose role is to transport pilots to and from the ships. There are nine pilots on 24-hour shifts each day and accommodation is available in the VTS building and at Gosport if needed.

Also under the control of the VTS officer is the patrol launch stationed in the Port of Southampton, which is not only the 'eyes and ears' of the VTS but also assists on pilot operations. Some ships, especially the container ships that have a deep draft, can only navigate the deep-water channels at certain times. It is the responsibility of the VTS officer to manage the traffic movements. He will do this by working out a programme or 'slot' times for ships in and out of the port. Also under the guidance of the duty VTS officer is the berthing officer who attends the berth to see the ships safely on and off.

The Port and Vessel Information System (PAVIS) contains all ships' details, times of arrivals & departures, and it is from here that the VTS officer will be able to plan and coordinate ship movements.

The VTS tend only to work 36 hours in advance because details often change. Ships are getting bigger, which makes careful planning even more important. This is because cranes could break down, and just half an hour delay can cause quite a problem to the traffic movements.

One of the passing points for large ships is at Fawley, and it requires accurate timing from the pilots to get that right. The pilots have large responsibility to get the timing right, and for one ship to drop back half an hour all the shipping movement plans can be disrupted. Any ships coming into the port will only be allowed so far without its berth being free, and that is very important for the deep-draft ships. The VTS officer will be making those decisions in conjunction with the master of the ship and the pilot. If the pilot or master of the ship were not happy with the conditions then the ship would not come in.

The cruise liners like to be in port during the day, rather than at night, arriving about 6-7am and sailing again at 5-6 in the evening. That is to get passengers on and off and to airports. Sometimes there are organised sight-seeing coach trips which can be done during the day. The large car carriers also do not like spending nights in port. In general the only vessels that are going to be committed to tidal conditions are the very large container ships and also the large oil tankers. Tankers can be seen coming in at the Fawley refinery about 30 minutes to 45 minutes before high water. That allows the tanker a slack water passage as it comes past Cowes, making the turn to enter Southampton Water. The slack water period is between the flood tide and ebb tide, which means the waters are not flowing east or west. The biggest tides are when the high water is at midday or midnight. So if the high water is at midday 12 o'clock it will be called Spring Tide and has the largest rise and fall, and if at 6 o'clock in the morning or 6 o'clock in the evening it will be known as Neap tide, where the rise and fall is very small. These times advance about an hour each day.

The VTS control centre, with the VTS officer in the foreground. (Courtesy of ABP)

The VTS Control Room

VTS assistants are under the direction of the VTS officer. The importance of the VTS control centre is summed up by Martin Thomas, one of the VTS assistants: 'Our main aim is the safety of the port and the environment. The environment in this day and age is very important, not only to the local community around here but to the port itself. We pride ourselves on maintaining this through operating live radar systems and a port management system which we call PAVIS. We monitor shipping movements from the time they enter our area to the time they berth and the pilot disembarks'.

This is done by maintaining two desks with identical computer systems operating at the same time, with each operator working for two hours on each desk so that they have a break every two hours. This is to ensure that operators get adequate rest to maintain their concentration and not get overtired.

There is another operator who works on the pilot desk, and his main task is to manage the pilots. Ships will give three hours' notice of arrival at the Nab tower, and the operator has to assign a pilot, arrange transport and ensure that the pilot is on station, ready for work. His next job is to make sure the arrangements on the ship are correct. This will mean checking what side the pilot ladder is on the ship and ensuring the ship will be in position at the right time. Once the pilot is on board the operator has to make sure the pilot has no problems. Finally, when the ship has berthed and the pilot has disembarked, the operator will make sure that transport is available to get the pilot back to the pilot station.

The assistants on the two desks monitor the movement of each vessel by radar to make

Inside the Coastguard Tower. (Courtesy of ABP)

Yacht racing. (Courtesy of ABP)

sure it is safe, that there is ample water depth and that it is not going to conflict with other traffic. If two vessels are too large to pass it has to be arranged for them to pass at a certain place, and in these instances timing is critical. The passing point in Southampton Water is between the Esso Marine Terminal and the BP Oil Jetty. The vessels are monitored by the VTS centre all the way to their berth in the docks.

A traffic separation scheme has been set up because the English Channel is one of the busiest stretches of water in the world and ships travelling east up the channel towards the North Sea, or west to the North Atlantic, are not allowed to enter the area. The only ships allowed are those whose course is 90° to the flow of traffic, and these are usually the ferries between the UK and France.

One of the main concerns in the VTS area is the number of yachtsmen using Southampton water. This can be as many as 1,600 to 2,000 yachts on one day for the 'Around the Isle of Wight' race. At that time the operators in the VTS centre have to monitor vessels moving through the yachts safely, which can mean monitoring as many as 20 to 30 ships.

Automatic Identification System (AIS)

There is an AIS (Automatic Identification System) system where VTS can monitor ships up to 250 miles away and can follow them down the English Channel. The AIS is a transponder which has all the ships' details and the unique number given to each ship for identification. It has details such as the ships' draught, length, destination, ETA (Estimated Time of Arrival) and cargo. All that information is transmitted as a VHF signal, and most modern radars can now receive AIS information. Before the use of AIS, ships would maintain their own observations and communicate information to the VTS centre by radio. This could be information such as, 'a ship is 20 miles off my port bow'. Nowadays this information and interaction between two ships is done automatically. There is an AIS website that covers the whole of the North Sea and English Channel up to the Isle of Wight.

The Precautionary Area

The area from the Hook Buoy to Prince Consort Buoy is an area of concern and is designated the Precautionary Area. A large

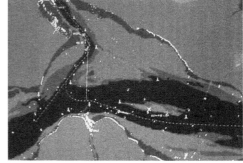

turn is quite crucial and critical. The pilot will liaise with the master of the ship and the VTS control room. The operators will then know exactly what the ship will be doing, and the master is aware of what the pilot is attempting to do, so the whole voyage from the Nab tower to the berth is monitored.

The Needles channel (western approaches) is restricted by what is known as the 'shingle bank,' a sandbank that moves constantly. Some smaller vessels still come down the western approaches, and these include smaller UECC car carriers. The *QE2* used to come in the Needles channel, but for safety reasons Cunard decided to bring the *QE2* around the Isle of Wight into the Solent.

Screen view of the Precautionary Area.

Marine Officer on the Patrol Launch

John Hardwick talks about his work as a marine officer. He started on the patrol boats as a coxswain in 1977, and he was later promoted to marine officer. 'When on duty my job is to represent the harbour master, and we are his eyes and ears for all that happens inside the port limits. Although we are the voice of authority on the water, we do not go around waving a big stick but try instead to persuade people into our way of thinking. The harbour master produces "Notices to Mariners" to inform all who use the water about designated areas for water skiers, points for crossing the main deep-water channel for small craft, speed limits and information about navigation safety. These are all governed by the notices, and we generally try to persuade people to abide by our rules; however, there are occasions when we will prosecute for things like dangerous navigation or being unfit to navigate the vessel through drinking.

'The port by-laws are for all mariners to pay attention to. Avoiding oil spills, chemical spills, discharge of waste, fishing and speeding are just some of the by-laws. I have the right to stop vessels, question people, take samples and prepare a case for prosecution. Also at night we go right around the port checking that every light and marker buoy is working correctly. They are checked once every 24 hours by the patrol boat crew. Because of our concern for the environment we are constantly monitoring shipping for any oil spills or any discharge of waste. In some cases it is illegal to discharge bilge water or ballast water taken on in certain ports because it has been discovered that you can transport foreign species of weed that can damage the local water and shore life.

'My direct line manager is the VTS officer in the control room, and I liase with him on what work we have to do during the course of the day. For instance, today we are going down to do a patrol for a VLCC, which is a "Very Large Crude Carrier", and then after that I will be picking up an electrician to take him out to two of our buoys that are malfunctioning.

'One of our main problems is the number of yachts there are in and around Southampton Water, and on a Sunday everybody will be out on their boats. So what we do is liase with the pilot of the ship and enforce what is known as the "Moving Prohibited Zone", which is the area around the ship of 50m to the side and 150m ahead. Nothing is allowed in that area as the ship moves along the Thorn Channel.

'We generally have a benchmark of ships over 180m, although if perhaps there is a ship under tow and we need to keep people away from it then I will take up a position for that. Some ships are constrained by their draft of over 10.5m where they can take very little avoiding action whatsoever if a craft gets in the way, other than stop the ship. It is like navigating a little boat up a muddy creek where there is very little room for error. With some of the tankers they have an escort tug, and that escort tug has the capability of stopping or controlling the ship, especially if there is a loss of power into or out of port. With the container ships, with a draft of 14m, they are restricted to the main channel, and they have to stick rigidly to that as there is no scope for error. She will fly three red lights at night or a black cylinder during the day, and that will denote that she is restricted by her draft. We will position ourselves 150m in front and move all the yachts out of the way because there is no way she can actually manoeuvre around them. Although I must say I have seen some pilots who have managed this in an emergency.

'Many of the yachtsmen are not sure of the channels, and some are very surprised when they go aground on the Brambles bank because they are right in the middle of the Solent and don't expect that. On one of the big tides in August people come out from Cowes and play cricket on the bank.

'When you get down to the West Brambles buoy you have to be very aware of the tides. You get a strong tide on a flood tide which will come up from the West Solent. The ship will be on the reference line, and when he gets to the Brambles he will veer off to starboard and then he will kick her round, because with 240m (800ft of ship) with 25ft of it under water it is a large mass. If you imagine putting your hand in a small running stream and the pressure of water on your hand, just imagine what the tidal pressure would be on the side of the ship?

'It is all these things that make the job so interesting for me and is one of the reasons I have stayed here so long. There are constant changes such as the weather, which can change every hour, and when the weather changes the job changes also.'

Marine Pilots: Brief History of Pilots and Pilotage
Pilotage is one of the oldest professions, and reference to pilots can be found in the Bible and are mentioned as being in charge of craft on the River Nile 3,000 years ago.

It was possible that the work of the pilot began through mariners using the knowledge, experience and assistance of local boatmen and fishermen when approaching unfamiliar coastal waters or estuaries. This would no doubt have eventually led to a charge being levied to the mariner and the development of pilotage as a profession began. The estuary or outer pilots were probably fishermen, who while working off their own ports were able to assist approaching vessels into those ports, while the docking or inner pilots conducted vessels into unmarked creeks or minor ports.

They became independent entrepreneurs employed as pilots on a casual basis and continued so until the appearance of merchant guilds, which made authorities aware that a well-organised and efficient pilot service was a very necessary feature of a port. The term pilot stems from the Greek *plous* or *pelous*. A *periplous*, in ancient times, was a form of sailing direction (*peri* = around a circle, *plous* = navigation: thus *periplous* = circumnavigation). *Plous* or *pelous* was modified to pilot.

A Lodestar is a star used as a guide in navigation, a prime example being the Pole Star. In the early Middle Ages the general term used for a pilot was lodesman. This originated from the Anglo Saxon *lad*, meaning lead or guide. The terms *lods*, *lotse* and *loods* are still used today in Scandinavia, Germany and the Netherlands.

In its application for a charter in 1513, the Trinity House of Deptford, a brotherhood of mariners who were called the Guild of the Holy Trinity, used the terms lodesmen, pilot and pilot-lodesman. Henry VIII granted the Guild a Royal Charter in 1514, 'so that they might regulate the pilotage of ships in the King's streams.' It was about the same time that pilots in the Cinque Ports were hired to take ships through the dangerous Dover Straits to the ports on the Continent and also to the mouths of the Rivers Thames and Medway. The Dover pilots were supervised by the Court of Lodemanage and would remain at sea ready to pilot inbound and outward ships that required their service.

In 1717 an Act of Parliament was obtained to strengthen the Court of Lodemanage at Dover, and in 1732 Trinity House of Deptford Strond obtained a similar Act, which also recognised the existence, rights and obligations of other Trinity Houses around the coasts. From 1733 model Acts of Parliament were produced for other ports around the UK.

In 1808 compulsory pilotage was introduced, and Trinity House took over the examination and licensing of pilots. In the 40 outport districts, sub-commissioners of pilotage, appointed by the corporation, examined pilots and recommended them for licences.

The new local pilotage district for Southampton was called the Isle of Wight outport district. The Isle of Wight pilots and the Southampton pilots all became the Isle of Wight pilots. As the port developed the work of the Southampton pilots increased and the sea pilots were divided into two services, the inward service and outward service. When a pilot first applied to be licensed, he had to have British nationality, have five years experience as a watch-keeping officer of a ship, hold a foreign-going master mariner's certificate and be less than 35 years of age.

Once the trainee pilot was taken on, he had to spend at least three months accompanying a licensed pilot in the district. He was not paid and had to fund himself. The trainee pilot was required to learn how to recognise all aids to navigation in the district. He was required to know the depth of water under and around the buoys, the depth of the water in the channels and alongside the berths and understand the tides specific to the district. After his trips with the licensed pilot he was then given an oral examination in front of a group of examiners, two of which were licensed pilots. If successful the trainee was granted a third-class licence, but if not successful the first time he was told to undertake further trips for another month.

During the 1920s there were five large sea-going sailing cutters in which pilots would cruise the western and eastern approaches to the Solent, waiting to pilot ships into Southampton. These cutters were named *Totland, Southsea, St Helen's, Culver* and *Bembridge.* The pilots worked a rota system, with as many as 12 pilots cruising on each cutter for a week at a time; however, at that time there was no VTS (Vessel Traffic Services) to monitor the arrivals is ship as there are today, and pilots would rely on the experience and knowledge of shipping lines that regularly used Southampton. This is clearly expressed by one pilot working at the time: 'In those days the ships arrived at regular times. You could sit down on a Monday morning and I reckon, give 90 per cent of the arrivals within an hour. And you got no confirmation whatsoever, you just relied on, "Well, this is the time he came last month or last week". There was the Union Castle, one o'clock at the Needles, Royal Mail, a quarter past 12 at the Needles from Cherbourg. The Cunard and the White Star had their regular times.' (*Oral History Unit, Southampton.*)

Pilots working on the cutters tended to have plenty of spare time waiting for the vessels to pilot and would use the time on hobbies and fishing. This is an account giving by a pilot of the life on board one of the cutters: 'Life was pretty good. You cruised for a week, then you went on reserve for a week, then you went the other end lot the Isle of Wight for a week, then you were reserve for a week. When you were on reserve to the Eastern Station invariably you were out every night.

'We had one Launchman and a cook, George Scribbins, who was a past master at plum duff. Accommodation was pretty primitive. There were four bunks and a small table in between, so you sort of fell out of your bunk into your porridge. There was a bit more comfort on the steam cutters. The accommodation was down below. You had a lounge up top. It was somewhat different, but funnily enough you didn't seem to get the fun that you got out of the old sailing cutters.

'The vessel used to make as much of a lee as it could, and you came alongside in the small motor-boat and a ladder was put over the side for you to climb on board. After you'd boarded, the pilot launch went back to the pilot cutter and you proceeded on your way either to the Needles or through the Spithead up to Southampton, or to Portsmouth or wherever the vessel wished to go to.

'We had no such thing as radar. You had to know where you were going and you had to know all your buoys and how much water there was on either side and just proceed with caution, and if the weather was that thick-set you couldn't proceed with caution, well then, you just anchored as convenient and waited until the weather cleared and then proceeded on.

'There was something very attractive in the way it was operated. And the funny part about it was you would think, with the information you had, it would be an awful lot of hit and miss, but it wasn't.

'Five o'clock in the morning, get the spinners out, trawl up and down the Old Bridge there. Mackerel for breakfast, right out of the pan! Oh boy, it was good living then. You had all sorts of hobbies. People used to do painting and drawing and mat-making, playing bridge and poker.

'Anyway, it's changed. It had to come, but I don't think you get to know each other as well as in the days when we cruised, and we sometimes think that the characters have gone that were around, but I think probably it's because we don't know people so well.' (*Oral History Unit, Southampton.*)

By 1932 the sailing cutters were replaced by three new steam cutters, the *Brook*, the *Gurnard* and the *Penda*. The 1983 Pilotage Act consolidated the Merchant Shipping Act 1979 and the Pilotage Authorities Act of 1936.

The Isle of Wight Pilotage District, provided by the Trinity House, extended from Selsey Bill to Peverel Point and organised by a body of sub-commissioners whose headquarters were in Southampton.

There were two services, the Southampton Pilots, working from Southampton and known as the Isle of Wight Outward Service, and the Inward Sea Pilots, who lived and worked from the island. It was the responsibility of the Southampton Pilots to pilot the ships to either the west or east ends of the Isle of Wight and for berthing the inward-bound ships that they met at Netley. When a ship approaches the Isle of Wight Pilotage District, she would be met by the pilot cutter. The inward sea pilot would then board the ship and bring her through the Solent and Southampton Water where she would be met by the Southampton pilot who would then take over. As the ship approached the dock she would be met by tugs that would then assist by manoeuvring her into her berth under the instructions of the pilot.

One pilot who joined the service in 1931 describes the work of the inward and outward service: 'There were 23 pilots on the inward service from the Needles and the Nab up to Netley, who were then relieved by the outward pilot who docked the ship.

Marine pilot Gareth Mead calls the VTS.

There were 18 pilots on the outward service. The inward service had to work in groups with three groups of six pilots and one group of five pilots, working a week on and a week off.' (*Oral History Unit, Southampton.*)

It was on 1 October 1988 that the Pilotage Act 1987 came into force. This act abolished all pilotage authorities creating new Competent Harbour Authorities or CHA's. After almost 500 years of Southampton's pilotage history with Trinity House as the Pilotage Authority, it was abolished and replaced by CHA-ABP.

Although this ended a tradition that stretched back to the 16th century, and although no longer responsible for local pilotage, Trinity House is still authorised to license deep-sea pilots. Deep-sea pilotage is not compulsory, but if a ship's master is new to European waters he has the option of taking on board a deep-sea pilot to navigate his vessel through the unfamiliar waters.

The Work of the Marine Pilot in 2004

This account of the work of a Marine Pilot gives an insight into the similarities and differences between the times that Trinity House organised the Isle of Wight Pilotage District, with the inward and outward pilots' responsibilities working from Southampton and the Isle of Wight, and today.

Training to Become a Marine Pilot

To become a pilot in England the basic requirement is for a master's certificate, and it takes five years to be able to pilot the large ships that come into the port. The work of the pilot is interesting and varied, and once fully qualified the day may start with a small 70m (229ft) grain boat, and the next ship could be a 300m (984ft) container ship or a cruise ship such as the *Oriana* or *Aurora*, and the final job of his watch may be a small tanker going into the oil terminal of the Esso Oil Refinery.

This is an account of his training, given by Gareth Mead, a Southampton marine pilot. 'I am presently employed in Southampton as a marine pilot, bringing the ships in and out of the docks. When I first joined ABP I spent two years on the pilot boat before starting my pilot training. To become a pilot in England the basic requirement is for a master's ticket before you can even start to think about it. Certainly in the Port of Southampton that is our base level. Once you've been interviewed and accepted for the post you have a three month training period. Within that three months you have to do 100 trips with qualified pilots in and out of port. These trips have to be split between day and night and in that time you have to visit as many berths in the port as possible. You have to do about 12 trips on tugs when they are working ships, where you get to know how the tugs work. You spend time at VTS (Vessel Traffic Services), on the patrol launch and on simulators at Warsash doing radar training and practising coming in and out of the channels in fog and various emergency situations.

'In that time you have spent 13 weeks learning what we call 'the district,' which is the area we work in. You then have an examination, which is an internal exam carried out by the harbour master and two pilots. It's an "all and all" exam, meaning that if you don't pass you cannot continue with your training. They give you various situations that you may come across and ask you to work out some calculations for tides and spend up to two hours making sure you know the area. You will have to have completed a number of assessment trips with assessing pilots, so they have actually spent time on board the ship with you. If you pass that exam you then spend six months or 100 trips on ships up to 110m in length. After that you spend a further six months or 100 trips on ships up to 140m long. At the end of that time you do what I think is possibly the best course I have ever done, the "man model" course. You sit in models on lakes at Marchwood and drive the models around for four days, which is absolutely brilliant, a really good course because they act like proper ships. You also then do two more assessment trips, one in and one out with pilots and then more time on tugs. Then you are allowed to go onto ships up to 170m and stay at that level for two years, where you are expected to do 400 trips. After that you start doing trips on the large cargo and some of the smaller container ships and then you sit what we call our Class 1 Exam. This is another examination in front of the harbour master and two pilots. On this occasion there is quite a bit more written work involving passage plans and tidal calculations. After that it is a case of a year on ships up to 220m long and then another year on ships up to 60,000 gross tons, which means you are almost going on to the big container ships. In that period you are doing extra trips with qualified pilots on large container ships. So it takes five years to be able to pilot the large ships that come into Southampton. It takes a long time to qualify because I was 17 when I started at sea and 32 when I took my final exam.'

The Job of a Marine Pilot

A normal working day for the pilot starts at 8.30am, the earliest time they can board a ship at the Nab Tower, at the east side of the Isle of Wight. The pilots are taken by taxi from Southampton to the pilot station at Gosport. They are then taken by pilot boat to the other side of the Nab Tower, a journey of about 30 to 40 minutes.

The pilot will have been informed of the name of the ship and which berth it's going to, where they are boarding the ship, or if it is leaving the port, which berth it is leaving from. The most important information is the draft of the ship, so they can work out if there is enough depth of water to bring the ship in at that time.

When on the pilot launch the pilot radios the ship and informs the master what position they want the ship for boarding. Boarding the ship can be quite hazardous because the pilot still has to climb a rope ladder and in rough weather accidents can still happen. The height for the pilot to climb can be anything up to over 9m, but if more than 9m, half will be climbed by rope ladder and the rest on a gangway. All the time the pilot is boarding the ship and pilot boat are still moving.

Once on board, the pilot is taken to the bridge by one of the crew and will introduce himself to the master and discuss how they will take the ship in. There is a 'passage plan' that has been prepared by the pilot and this will be discussed. The pilot will then call VTS to inform them that they are safely on board. As the pilot will have already decided which channel to use on the way into port he will give the course directions and wheel orders to the helmsman.

Once on board, the pilot assumes full legal responsibility for the safe navigation of the vessel. He sets the vessel's course and speed, can order the letting-go or weighing of anchors, and he can order the letting-go or sending ashore of mooring ropes. He can also order the making-fast or letting-go of tugs. In the event of an accident, the pilot is held responsible. The master remains in command of all other aspects of the vessel's operation (other than the navigation), but in extreme circumstances he may take control of the navigation away from the pilot if he thinks the pilot's conduct of the vessel is dangerous. But if he does, the master will then be held responsible for anything that happens subsequently. The above only applies in compulsory pilotage districts, of which the Port of Southampton and its approaches is one.

Depending on the size of ship, the time the pilot spends on board can be 3.5 hours on a large container ship and 5 hours on a tanker. He keeps the master informed of the course of the ship and explains how they want the ship to tie up. He explains the berthing plan, the ropes to be run out, where the tugs will meet the ship and will discuss any berthing manoeuvres, such as turning the ship around. The relationship between the master and the pilot is very special because he has to trust the pilot with his ship when coming in or leaving the dock.

Once the ship is entering the docks the pilot uses a handheld radio to make direct contact with the tugs to tell them when to push or when to pull. The pilot is also in contact with the berthing officer on the quay, who will tell the pilot when he is happy with the ship's position.

Bringing Tankers in

Gareth Mead explains the process of bringing the large tankers into the oil terminals: 'The large tankers for the Esso Oil Terminal are boarded four miles south of the Nab Tower. They are boarded then so that they arrive at slack water on the tide when there isn't a great current flowing. There is a big turn that the vessels have to complete off Cowes before going into the Thorn Channel and then turn at Calshot which they have to arrive at a certain time. If they are going too fast it will take far

Oil tanker *Targale*.

A plan of mooring a ship at the berth.

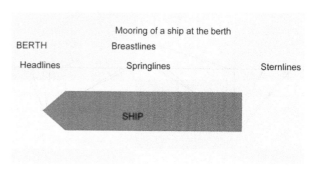

more effort to stop the ship and that is why the tug at the stern is so important, it helps the ship to slow down. Once the tanker is off the berth it is then turned and the tugs push the ship alongside the berth so that the bows are facing the way they will sail when leaving the terminal. The actual tying up takes longer because the pipelines on the ship have to line up with the pipelines ashore. The ships are a lot heavier so it is far more critical that the ship is in exactly the right position, and this takes more time because everything must be done much slower.

'On the big tankers for the Esso and BP terminals, the two big oil berths, there are always two pilots on board. This helps the main pilot to concentrate on the navigation while the second pilot does the radio work and also explains the passage plan inward bound to Esso and also the tie up plan at the berth. When the tankers are inward bound the escort tug is attached to the stern all the time the pilot is on board. The tankers outward bound from the terminal are empty and then the escort tug is only required as far as Cowes. Esso have their own tugs, but BP use the Southampton Dock tugs. There are four docks tugs capable of doing the escort work.

'The Esso Oil Terminal specifically requires their ropes run in a certain order. This are the breast lines, which go out at 90 degrees, the head lines, which come out from the front of the ship, and then the stern lines, which come out from the back of the ship at an angle – normally at about a 30 or 45 degree angle to help keep the ship alongside and not moving up and down.'

'Tying up' or Mooring the Vessels

ABP Pilot Gareth Mead explains the process of mooring the vessels: 'The terms for "tying up" are "running the ropes" or "running the lines". That is when the ropes are being given from the ship to the berth. Different ropes from a ship come out at all different angles and they do a certain job. Some ropes keep the ship alongside and some stop the ship moving up and down on the quay. Usually the spring lines are put out first, which stops the ship moving up and down the quay and helps with the final positioning. The normal tie up for a container ship is known as four and two, which means four headlines, four stern lines and two spring lines. If it is a very windy day the decision may be made put out breast lines first, which come out at 90 degrees.'

Hydrography: Early Methods of Hydrographic Surveying

Evidence of early methods of surveying the depth and character of the seafloor has been identified from Egyptian paintings, showing men on craft with sails using sounding poles and line and sinker sounding methods dating back to 1800 BC.

These tools and techniques did not appear to change much, and for centuries hydrographers would use chronometers, sextant fixes, sounding poles and lead lines to determine time, position, and depth. Early soundings were made from small boats, where the crew would have rowed to each position and maintained the position of the boat while stopped. The position of the boat was determined by three-point sextant fixes to mapped reference points ashore. To collect the depth data a leadsman would drop a hand-held lead line, weighted with a piece of lead, over the side of a ship. This was known as taking a sounding. The lead line had depth markings on the line, and it would be lowered until it touched the seabed. The leadsman would then read and record the depth manually. Despite gaining accurate data, only a limited number of soundings could be taken in the survey area and used to plot the nautical charts. One of the problems with this method compared to today was that the information between each soundings was missing. Safe navigation for the mariner would be compromised because they would not know if there were any hazards on the seabed between the sounding points.

By the early 1930s there was the development of single-beam echo sounders which enabled measurement of depth from the sonar 'ping.' This increased the speed and efficiency of producing a hydrographic surveys and allowed more data points to be

A survey launch. (Courtesy of ABP)

measured. The development of electronic navigation systems in the 1940s was further advancement in hydrographic survey. With the introduction of the modern multibeam swathe mapping systems, however, there was an increase in the amount of coverage by using multiple sounding sensors and improved quality in the data collected.

The Hydrography Department Based in the VTS Centre

In May 2004 William Heaps, senior hydrographer for the Port of Southampton, talked about the work of his department. It was through his interest in geography at school and in water and sailing that led William Heaps into this field. He took his first degree at university, studying maritime geography and then for a further year he studied hydrographic surveying and qualified as a hydrographic surveyor. After working off-shore undertaking survey work for oil companies he became a hydrographic surveyor for a dredging company, doing all the surveying before and after a dredger comes in. He has been a hydrographer at the Port of Southampton since 1997: 'Hello, I am William Heaps and I lead the team of port surveyors in the Port of Southampton. I work for the harbour master and his job is primarily safety of navigation and maintaining the depths of the channels into the port is an important part of that. Port surveying is very specialised and there are not a lot of openings. Traditionally, port surveyors come from the services, such as the army and navy, especially the navy, and I think I am the first civilian port surveyor in Southampton.'

William Heaps goes on to explain the work of his department: 'Hydrography is the science of measuring the sea and how deep it is. It is important to know that when there are a lot of large ships coming into the port. These ships will need enough deep water beneath them otherwise they will go aground.'

To check that there is enough deep water in the channels the senior hydrographer leads a team of port surveyors who go out most days, apart from in rough weather, to make sure there is enough water for these ships to float in. The reason is because mud and silt come in from the sea and down the rivers and builds up and the depth of the water gets less and less. When there is not enough deep water the dredgers are called in to restore the correct depth. After the dredgers have been in another survey is completed to see they have done their job properly. It is a very important and ongoing job for the surveyors and must be done regularly and very accurately.

'Some of the big ships that enter the port have less than a metre between the bottom of the ship and the seabed. For example, the draft of the container ships is often 14m deep, but the channel is only dredged to 12.6m at lowest water. So for a ship to come in safely he will need at least 2m of tide just to clear bottom and about another metre on top of that for safety. The ship will need a tide height of about 3.6m just to come in safely, so it is very important that the pilots know the tide times to bring the ships in safely. The master of the ship will plan their arrival as the tide is coming up. Southampton has a very unusual high water in that out of 24 hours there is 17 hours of either a rising or high tide before it falls away. What happens is that it rises quite fast and stays up for four hours, (where in a normal port it would be one hour) and when it falls the water rushes out very quickly.'

The *Queen Elizabeth 2* and *Queen Mary 2* (even with her exceptionally deep draft of about 10.5m) do not have to wait for high tide and can come up the channel at any time. It is mainly the container ships and oil tankers that are the ones that have to come in on a tide.

The siltation is critical in the main channel, which the large ships use, and a survey will need to be completed at least four times a year. In the other areas, such as the edges where the small sailing dinghies go, a survey will be undertaken about once every three years because it is not so important and doesn't change so fast. Some of the berths where the big ships go are just big holes in the seabed for the ships to sit in, and these are surveyed every six weeks.

'It is interesting to note that container berths are often situated well inland. This tends to be similar around the world where you will find that the deepest berths are generally the furthest inland, often in the most awkward places. That is because in the old days, when the ports were developed, they started near the sea and built the quays and dredged out berths that were deep enough for the ships of the time that might have been 4 or 5m deep. So they built all the quays for that sort of depth. When the ships got bigger and bigger they had to build new berths further up the river for the larger container ships. That is why in many European ports all the berths are further up the rivers. There is also a need for a huge amount of land behind the container terminals to store and move containers and for transport and trains. This sort of space is often not available in the older port areas.'

How the Survey Team Work

William Heaps explains, 'to make a chart there are two things you need to know: Where are you? How deep is the water? The survey launch has a GPS (Global Positioning System) to tell the surveyors where they are. This system is not the same as the one that can be bought in shops but a much more accurate system called the GPS differential system. A very accurate correction signal is sent out for the boat to pick up all the time they are working.

'To find out the depth of water the boat has an echo sounder which sends a pulse of sound down through the water, the sound bounces off the sea bed and because you know the speed of sound in water you can calculate the depth of the water.'

Hydrography surveyors at work.

Gathering the Data

Each day the survey team have an area they are going to survey. To do this a series of straight lines are planned across the area, spaced out every 12.5 or 25m apart, depending on the size of chart they are going to make. The coxswain will steer the boat backwards and forwards along the pre-planned lines displayed on a computer monitor. All the time the position from the GPS and the depth from the echo sounder are being recorded very rapidly onto a computer. For example, on a line about 300m long the position would be recorded every 0.6 of a second and 10 depths every second logged straight onto the computer. William describes the work before computers: 'In the early days, before the collection of data by computer, the hydrographer would have had to take much fewer positions and many fewer depths with a lead line and write it all down by hand. So the process of surveying nowadays is very fast by recording a lot of depths and positions swiftly on to the computer. That information is brought back to the office on a disk and processed.'

Processing the Data

The first thing the surveyor has to do to process a survey for a mariner to use is to convert all the depths to one level. This because the tide goes up and down, and surveying at low tide with a depth of 10m may become 15m at high tide. That is no use to a mariner who wants to reduce it all to the same datum, the same level. Therefore a sea chart is reduced to the lowest level the tide ever goes. When a mariner sails in and does not know what state the tide, he knows it cannot be less than the lowest tide. If he has a depth of 10m on the chart, he knows it can be no less than 10m, plus the height of the tide above that. That lowest level is called 'chart datum' and all the soundings on the chart are reduced to chart datum.

The surveyors will record the height of tide, and that is also recorded on to the computer. This will be checked from tide gauges with sensors which constantly record the tidal level and that is displayed electronically on the computer screen. Traditionally they were boards at the side of the jetty, and examples still can be seen at Calshot and Dock Head. When they return to the office they have a record of the position and time a sounding was taken and the height of tide. If the height of tide is taken off the depth that was measured it will bring it down to chart datum. This is all calculated in seconds by the computer.

At the same time the surveyors use their skills and experience to check all the measurements to see if there are any 'spikes.' This could be where the launch is sailing across a channel and the echo sounds bounce off fish or a piece of rubbish in the water and makes it look like there is a big 'spike' in the channel. This could be a rock or rubbish that has fallen off a ship and that will need checking. This is quite an easy decision for the surveyor to make between what is real and what is not by experience. Once the survey data has been reduced the surveyor can then plot the data.

A chart has to be drawn after taking thousands and thousands of sounding on a day survey. To do this another piece of computer software checks each line recorded on the survey. This is to find the shallowest depth on that line, because that is what the mariner is interested in. It is the shallow sections that the mariner is likely to hit and need to be avoided. The computer software will find the shallowest sounding or depth and draw that and continue either side of that to find space to record another number, all the time checking for the shallowest depth.

On a normal working day approximately 2km of channel will be surveyed and the data will be processed that day. The charts produced are given to the pilots on the same day. The surveys are also sent to the United Kingdom hydrographic office, the national centre for gathering marine charts. All the survey work undertaken at the port is available to any mariner in the world because you can buy UK charts at every port.

DREDGING:

Maintenance Dredging Campaigns in the Port of Southampton

The work of the hydrographic department includes preparing the pre-dredge survey in advance of the two maintenance dredging campaigns the port has each year, one in the spring and one in the autumn. The UKD *Bluefin* is used because it is the largest dredger and is more efficient for the dredging operations at Southampton because of the distance to the licensed deposit site, at the Nab Tower, off the Isle of Wight. Once a dredge is completed and the vessel's hopper is full, it then proceeds to the Nab Tower deposit area.

After the dredge is completed the bed levellers come in to level out the seabed and pull materials from the seawall or inaccessible areas. The plough will pull the material out and the dredger can then suck it up. The operation is becoming more and more technically advanced, with equipment such as sophisticated GPS positioning systems and up to date hydrographic surveys. The dredger cannot waste time dredging materials in the wrong position and so uses the GPS equipment and echo sounders to dredge to the correct location and correct depth, and it will then take the dredged materials out to the deposit site and return in the shortest time to save costs.

The UKD *Bluefin,* a Trailing Suction Hopper Dredger (TSHD).

A suction pipe being lowered into the water.

The crew consist of master, chief mate, second mate, chief engineer, second and third engineer, two dredge masters controlling the dredging equipment, a cook, an able seaman on deck for tying up and other deck duties and an able seaman assistant dredge master if there is need for cover on the bridge, otherwise he will work on deck.

The Trailing Suction Hopper Dredgers (TSHD) work for 24 hours and will have 11 crew on board at any one time. There are two crews for every vessel, so the *Bluefin* has 22 crew members with 11 crew working two weeks on and two weeks off. The company works for 362 days a year and only stops for three days at Christmas. The accommodation on board includes each crew member having their own cabin with showers. There is a cook on board, working in the galley, so during the two weeks the vessel is working it is completely self-contained and only needs to come alongside to take on enough fuel, water, food and provisions for a two-week period. The *Bluefin* will spend two months in Southampton and the rest of the time in South Wales, the Humber, Egypt, Portugal and Spain.

The vessel has to dredge forwards all the time, and that is why it is called a trailing section, because it is constantly trailing the suction pipe behind the vessel, just like a giant vacuum cleaner. There is a central console on the bridge, which is the general navigation point on the vessel when working in a wide channel, but when in a more confined area, such as a berth, the port and starboard wing controls are used for driving the ship.

The dredge master at the back of the bridge controls the dredge equipment, the dredge pump speed and depth of the drag head, dredge pipe angle and the pressure the drag head is putting on the seabed. Two computer screens show the depth from the sensors on the bottom of the pipe and the tide gauge input, so the operator knows the water level and the draught of the

Dredge master.

Filling the hopper.

ship. The electronic display shows a digital map of the seabed for the area being dredged. It is colour coded to indicate which areas need to be dredged and which areas are already deep enough or have already been dredged. The display updates the colour automatically as dredging progresses. When the post-survey is undertaken it should coincide with what is seen on the screens.

The process is therefore thus: The hydrographic surveyor does a pre-dredge survey, the dredger takes away the excess materials and the bed leveller follows to flatten anything out that is left behind. The hydrographic surveyor will then undertake a post-dredge survey to check that all is in order and the required water depths have been achieved. This is done before the dredger leaves so that any areas that the post-survey identifies as a high spot or a section missed can be rectified.

The depths are dictated by shipping requirements. In the main channel at Southampton the required depth is 12.6m and in Ocean Dock (the dock that the *Titanic* sailed from), the depth is 10.2m, with two deep berths either side down to 11.7m. The reason for the deeper berths is to allow for the larger ships that come in at high water to remain afloat at low tide. The berths have different maintained depths depending on traffic requirements. For example, the cruise ships need less depth than the container ships, which have maintained depths down to 15m. There could be 4m of tide which would make that 19m if the ship docked at high tide. The depths are at chart datum, which is the depth at low tide.

Dredging the Ocean Dock

Ocean Dock has a history in Southampton as it was the dock that the *Titanic* sailed from and where the *Queen Mary* and *Queen Elizabeth* liners docked. The task of the dredger was to take the depth to 10.2m and 11.7m at the berths. The master of the UKD *Bluefin*, who is also the senior master of the UKD fleet, explains the process: 'The *Bluefin* is a 3,900 cubic metres trailer hopper dredger, and we are currently dredging the Ocean Dock in the Port of Southampton with the aim of taking the depth of the dock back to its original level.

'At the moment we are dredging down the centre line and the materials are being sucked up and dropped into the hopper. These materials appear to be silt, which is what we would expect in the Port of Southampton. We are working one pipe only at the moment. We would normally be working two pipes, but as it is such a small area we are having one pipe down at the moment. We are trying to dredge a depth of 10.2m beneath the lowest water level of the tide.'

The ship was being driven by the chief officer as the master is not required to drive the ship all the time. The master explains: 'My main role is day work, and the mates on the ship who are expert ship handlers tend to drive the ship most of the time. Also on the bridge we have a dredge master.

'The dredge master is very particular rank not found in the rest of the merchant navy. He is of a petty officer level and is there to operate all the dredging equipment, which includes putting the dredge pipes on the bottom, operating the pumps, maintaining all that equipment and generally trying to maximise the production of the material we are picking up. It is very important we pick up the material as fast as we can then achieve maximum density in order to reduce the length of time of the cycle. The cycle involves taking the material from the dredge area, "steaming" to the licensed dump site south of the Nab Tower, returning and starting the cycle over again. On average that cycle takes about 6.5 hours which is fairly typical of a Southampton cycle. This is quite long in dredging terms and in Southampton we "steam" about 26 miles. When we are dredging on the Humber, which we do regularly, the site for dumping is only about 10 minutes away, so you can see the difference in the dredging cycles between the Humber and Southampton.

'The *Bluefin* is 100m in length by 18m beam and with a maximum draught of 6.5m. The ship can carry 3,900 cubic metres of materials and the weight of the material, depending on density, is about 6500 tonnes.'

The master explains the process: 'When we are using two dredge pipes and, dredging in one direction only, we can fill the hopper in about 25 minutes. In Ocean Dock we are using one pipe which involves "backing and filling". That means we have to lift the pipe off the bottom and back up to dredge by going forward again. It will take us about two hours to fill the hopper because the area we are dredging is only about 300m long by 20m wide. At the dump site it only takes about 20 seconds to get rid of all the material. The method we use to get rid of the material is by having hydraulically operated doors at the bottom of the ship. We know we are in the correct position over the dump site because we have a GPS which plots our exact position. It is part of the licence requirement that we have an accurate positioning system. We have six GPS on board, but they are designed to be able to position our drag and suction ends of our pipes to within 1.5m. It is important that we know exactly where the drag ends are so that we don't encroach on any other territory. We also know the depth of the drag ends to within 10cm because it is important that we do not take too much away from an area, and at the end of the dredge I would like to make sure I hand over to the hydrographer a dredged depth of 10.2 metres.

The UKD *Sealion,* a Bed Leveller.

'The standard methodology of a typical area like this is to involve a trailer hopper suction dredger where we vacuum the seabed and put the materials into a hopper. Inevitably, because we are trailing drag arms across the bottom of the seabed, there will be grooves to a certain extent, so it is far more efficient that we have a bed-levelling tug that will follow after we have finished and he will plough the bottom of the seabed and make it nice and flat. It is far more efficient for the trailer hopper to take the volume out and the bed-levelling tug to tidy the seabed up at the end of it.

'We have two bed-levelling tugs working in the port today doing exactly that job from work we had completed last week. The hydrographer will pass an echo sounder across the bed to see that it is nice and flat and level.'

Once the dredger is full it then takes the material out to the dumping site. As it leaves Dock Head to sail down Southampton Water the dredger is very low in the water because of the weight of the material it has dredged from Ocean Dock.

The *Bluefin* spends about 65 days a year in Southampton, and that is a typical length of time to get the Southampton areas down to the original design. There are two dredging campaigns, one in the spring and one in the autumn because it suits the port system. Some ports have to have particular times for dredging. This occurs in the Welsh ports where they have maximum siltation in the winter months as a result of the winter storms in the Atlantic. The storms stir up the seabed and it tends to fill up the channels in the winter. In the Humber the channels are traditionally dredged in the summer months because it is a fast flowing river and doesn't silt up so much in the winter, but in the summer when it is calmer and the particles that are held in suspension when the river is running fast will settle on the seabed, and then it is an ideal time to dredge the channels. This is helpful to the company for its planning because the port requirements are different for the times of the year. This helps the ship's programme because it can spend the winter in Wales and the summer on the Humber.

'The *Bluefin* does dredge European ports and other ports countries, including work in the port of Damietta, Egypt. In the last three years the *Bluefin* has worked in the Baltic, Portugal, Denmark and France. This means that about 50 per cent of the time is spent in dredging ABP ports and the other 50 per cent are outside contracts.

Finally, the master explains the working pattern of the two separate crews that work on the *Bluefin,* 'We work two weeks on and two weeks off. There is a crew at home at present enjoying leave and after two weeks there is a change over and we will go home.'

UKD *Bluefin* leaving Dock Head for the dumping site.

THE JOB OF THE TUGS TODAY

When Wally Williams started working on the tug *Vulcan* in the 1950s the crew consisted of master, mate, chief engineer, second engineer, two firemen and a greaser, an able seaman, ordinary seaman and a deckboy, a crew of 10. Today the total crew of the tugs consists of the master, mate, chief engineer and an able seaman.

The job of the tugs today is basically the same as in the 1950s in meeting a large ship that is moving below the steerage speed of 6 knots. They will take over and assist, guide, push and pull the ship into its berth. The same process applies when the ship leaves its berth outward bound, when the tugs will manoeuvre the ship until it gains the correct steerage speed.

Ships nowadays have all sorts of aids to assist with docking and these can consist of controllable bow, stern and side thrusters instead of the propeller and active rudder systems. The *Queen Mary 2* ocean liner is designed to dock itself without necessarily having tugboats. This is because some of the ports it visits will not have the same facilities as there are in larger ports. However, in winds in excess of 30 knots it may be necessary to ask for tugboat assistance to arrive at its berth safely.

The tugs are getting more powerful, more sophisticated and bigger. There is a perception that the tugs look very small. When you look at the bridge the amount of glass windows ensure that there is maximum visibility so the master can see what he is doing at any given time. The systems used replicate the major ship systems. For example, there will be the compass, radar, GPS and duplicated radio systems for communication between ship to ship and to shore. Everything down to the cell-phone is there.

The tug is fully supported for the crew to sleep and eat, and with whatever needs is necessary to sustain itself for a considerable time. Contrary to what many would think about cramped quarters, the accommodation consists of a galley for cooking, full mess room, day and night suites for the master and the chief engineer and cabins for the remainder of the crew. There is no concern over fresh water as the tug carries copious amounts, especially necessary for the ballast and stability of the tug.

The tug *Lady Madeleine.*

The limiting factor is that tugs are designed and built for power. They are not designed for economy, and sheer brute force is what is looked for. When you see the engine room of a modern tug it has at least four combustion engines on board and at times five engines to generate power. There is a need to generate a lot of power to work the hydraulic and electrical systems in order to do the job. There are very heavy loads to be moved and the power must be available to do so.

There are two main engines that are air started, so there is an important need to run compressors from the generators in order to power the tugs. If you were to look around a tug it is not a small ship, it is really a large ship but in a compact shape and size.

The tug company will provide a service for ships from 90m upwards (about three times the size of the tug). The largest ships they service are the container vessels and oil tankers.

CHAPTER 15
ROLL-ON, ROLL-OFF

There are frequent car carrier visits to and from the Port of Southampton. These include EUKOR Car Carriers, Höegh Autoliners, NYK (Nippon Yusen Kaisha), STX Pan Ocean, Grimaldi Lines, Wallenius Wilhelmsen Logistics, UECC and other feeder services. Wallenius Wilhelmsen Logistics has its UK base for its operations at Southampton.

Wallenius Wilhelmsen Logistics in the 21st Century

By 2005 the UK base for the Wallenius Wilhelmsen Logistics was Southampton and over the years they have developed the port for exporting cars from the UK. Captain Mark Bookham is now the UK port and terminal operations director for Wallenius Wilhelmsen Logistics and is based in Southampton. He has quite a diverse role, which encompasses the whole of the UK, including the ports in Dublin, Liverpool, Teesport, Sheerness and Bristol.

The service offered by Wallenius Wilhelmsen Logistics is the deep sea Ro-Ro (Roll-on, Roll-off) trade and they have services in many parts of the world. They ship cars, high and heavy machines and project cargoes to and from all destinations in the world and also have a high involvement in bringing factory new cars from Japan and Korea into Europe. They operate a fleet of 65 ships under Wallenius Wilhelmsen, but they also own 80 per cent of EUKOR, which used to be called Hyundai Merchant Marine, so the company have a total of about 135 ships. The head offices are in Stockholm and Oslo, and they have regional offices in New York, Tokyo and Sydney in Australia.

Geographically, Southampton is well positioned for access to and from the South Coast and the English Channel, so there is minimum deviation from the main shipping lanes inbound and outbound from Europe. Also there are no locks in Southampton so there is 24-hour berthing, which again allows for flexible operation and movement of the vessels within the port limits. The other advantage is that they have good links with the motorways and rail network, which is a key consideration for the major car customers.

Southampton is now the third largest port worldwide for Wallenius Wilhelmsen, behind Bremerhaven in Germany and Nagoya in Japan. The company identified the need to phase out some of the smaller ports for the deep-sea ships and operate a hub concept, which is the idea of placing all the trade into one large port, with cargoes delivered through the UECC feeder ships in and out of the Port of Southampton. To put a ship into port is expensive, and that is why all the imports are brought into the terminal and then shipped out on feeder vessels, which are more cost-effective than the large ships visiting all the ports.

The emphasis on the hub terminal means that Southampton has developed as a 'transit' port, where they undertake a lot of transhipment using feeder vessels and trucks to final destinations throughout the UK, Europe and the Mediterranean. An example is the link between Egypt and America, via Southampton. This means cars are brought from the US into Southampton, transferred to the UECC feeder vessels and then shipped out to Alexandria, Egypt. Other transhipments are cargoes brought in for export and shipped out on deep-sea vessels to Australia and North and South America.

In the past, terminal managers have been responsible for all the terminal development, but the difference now is that the emphasis is driven regionally or centrally. Wallenius has an owner and president, Lone Forss Schroeder, who has wide experience in running terminals for Maersk but now runs the Wallenius part of the company.

The company name was changed from Wallenius Wilhelmsen Lines to Wallenius Wilhelmsen Logistics because there was a realisation that as a company there is a need for more direct contact with customers regarding movement of cargo. Rather than the port-to-port scenario, where the customer has to arrange shipment from the port to the company, Wallenius Wilhelmsen Logistics aim is to give a door to door service. It has become clear that there is the customer and a ship and that the terminal sits right in the middle. That is the most effective place to be because then logistics will start from the terminal back to the customer. As a result, terminals are taking a much higher profile and this is one of the main reasons for the company name change.

There are approximately 65 Ro-Ro vessels that call at Southampton each month, including 30 deep-sea ships

An aerial view of the Wallenius Wilhelmsen Logistics Terminal Operations. (Courtesy of ABP)

UECC *Autoline.*

and about 40 UECC vessels. The UECC ships are the feeder vessels which are used to carry cars around the UK coast and into Continental and Mediterranean ports. Wallenius Wilhelmsen Logistics has new vessels coming out over the next two or three years that will carry up to 7,500 cars.

The first Wallenius Wilhelmsen vessel to be flagged under the Red Ensign and registered in Southampton was the *Torrens*, launched in December 2004, with a capacity of just over 7,000 cars. Other ships in the fleet are being modified by being cut in half and lengthened by 40m to enable the vessels to carry about another 1,000 cars. With the arrival of eight new vessels, as they are built and launched the older vessels will be withdrawn from the fleet for scrap.

The main problem in Southampton is space, and that is why in 2002 the company decided to build the Southampton International Vehicle Terminal, essentially a multi-story car park. To give an idea of the space cars take up, you can store seven containers in the space used for three cars, so if the port managers have to decide on priorities for efficient use of space, they are more likely to go for the storage of containers. That is why the company has identified the need to build up rather than out.

On 23 May 2006, His Royal Highness the Duke of York opened the Empress Terminal, the second multi-deck car terminal. With the addition this new terminal a storage capacity for 5,200 vehicles is available.

Some imported cars are brought into Southampton, but because they tend to take up space and time the company concentrates mostly on exports. The biggest trade for the company is the imports of Mitsubishi, Honda, Toyota, Daewoo and Suzuki cars for the European markets, brought into Bristol.

Bristol is the other big port in the UK used by the company, and they have about 120 ships a year calling into the port, mainly imports from Japan and Korea and forestry products coming in from the eastern seaboard of America. The company focuses on shipping out cars, trucks and tractors to America from Southampton and use Bristol mainly for imports and Southampton for exports. This is mainly due to the space constraints in Southampton. It is not unusual for cars to be stored at Bristol for up to 18 months waiting to go to dealers to be sold. A lot of second-hand cars are brought in from Japan because they use right-hand-drive vehicles in that country and there is a growing market in the UK, mainly going to car auctions.

The company has contracts with Jaguar, Land Rover and also handles large volumes of high heavy cargoes, such as tractors, Caterpillars and JCBs. All the Jaguar cars come in by train, but instead of three trains a day carrying 280 cars per train in 2004 there is one train a day in 2006 carrying approximately 250 cars. A lot of mobile homes are also taken abroad.

The movement towards PDI (Pre-Delivery Inspection) is highlighted in a company in the US called DAS. As an automobile specification company they undertake the PDI's and prepare all the vehicles before they are sent out by ship from the US. This further highlights the shift and support towards ocean terminals and PDI's. Wallenius Wilhelmsen Logistics has now moved away from the trucking side and is working towards Pre-Inspection Delivery. The high cost of fuel and large number of trucking companies makes it more cost effective for the company to book a trucking company as and when needed to move the cars around the UK.

Wallenius Wilhelmsen vessel *Torrens*. (Courtesy of Bruce Williams-pics)

The company is already linked to the CAT company that does the logistics for Renault. The Renault vehicles are built in France and Spain and then moved on through the CAT network. Southampton is a big CAT importer with all the Renault vehicles shipped in from Le Havre and Santander. The cars are landed, marshalled and are then driven to be stored or to the PDI (Pre-Delivery Inspection) centre. From there the cars are delivered to various dealers in the UK. It is a big operation with an approximate turnover of 90,000 to 100,000 cars a year. Wallenius has a 40 per cent stake, along with a company called Auto Logic and TNT, who own 20 per cent.

As well as vehicles, boats are now loaded on the top weather decks of the ships and taken all over the world. Some are taken to Australia and the Miami boat show. Because of the fragile nature of boats on the top decks in rough weather, the ships will make a direct route to Miami and not visit other ports.

Wallenius Wilhelmsen multi-storey car park in the foreground and the Empress Terminal further back. (Courtesy of ABP)

The floating crane begins to lift a boat.
(Courtesy of Bruce Williams-pics)

A floating crane is used to load the boats on the ships. It is mainly Sunseeker boats, which are sailed around the coast from Poole where they are built. The boats will come alongside the quay and are lifted by a mobile crane out of the water and placed on trailers on the quay. This part of the operation cannot be undertaken by the floating crane because stability is not good when the wash from passing ships causes turbulence. This could cause damage to the ship or the boat.

On the day the ship is due in port all the boats are lined up for when the floating crane arrives to lift the boats onto the ship. The process is for the floating crane to lift a boat from the quay and then sail to the outboard side of the ship and place the boat on the top weather deck. It then repeats the operation until all the boats are loaded. Two Itchen Marine tugs assists the floating crane in the operation.

The ships can take up to about eight boats, and when in position they are lashed down on the top deck. There is a check to ensure there are no loose fittings that could fly off in high winds at sea and damage important parts of the ship, such as the radar.

Other cargoes can include mobile homes or boxed cargoes and car clubs ship their vehicles across the world for rallies and shows. An example is the Alvis Owners Club, who shipped 40 cars to the US for a show.

There is also a realisation that there are a lot of markets opening up in the world. South Africa is an emerging market, as is China. Volkswagen, Toyota, Nissan and BMW all have large factories in China. This is an emerging market for cars, especially for their domestic market. The move towards more industrialised development in China has resulted in families becoming more affluent. They now want to move away from the bicycles culture to owning their own cars. At the present time China is only just coping with the domestic market, which leaves little opportunity for export. However, in 3 or 4 years, when everyone has a car, that will be when the market will open up and Wallenius Wilhelmsen Logistics wish to be in position to handle the cargoes.

The other big market is Russia and the company already has a terminal in Kotka, Finland. From there they transport a large number of Mitsubishi, Hyundai and privately owned cars to St Petersburg, where there is a huge market. There is no seaport, so ships go to Polish or Baltic Sea ports, but the company is developing a huge terminal in Kotka with cars being trucked down to St Petersburg.

SOUTHAMPTON CONTAINER TERMINAL DEVELOPMENT

In 2005, SCT started on a major redevelopment of its yard layout and gate processes with the aim to increase its capacity to almost 2 million TEU. It was found that from 2001–2004 the increase in the number of trucks arriving at the terminal to collect or drop off containers resulted in congestion at the dock. This increased the times that the trucks were in the terminal and not only was the congestion felt by the terminal itself but also by the local community through the increased congestion on local roads. Following the setting up of a new VBS (Vehicle Booking Scheme) in 2005 there was a significant improvement in the trucks' turn around time.

In 2005 571 deep-sea container ships visited SCT, but by 2006 there was a significant increase to 693 vessels calling at the container terminal and 49 feeder vessels at Berth 203.

SCT planned expansion is in three phases and the first phase, announced in August 2006 was to open Berth 203 as a fifth berth to handle feeder containers ship up to 150m at the Port of Southampton. A new 100-ton mobile harbour crane was purchased and soon the service was increased from four vessels

The pre-gate entrance area.
(Courtesy of STC)

A mobile harbour crane. (Courtesy of STC)

to eight vessels per week, and in November 2006 21 feeder vessels alone in were handled on Berth 203, including the mobile harbour crane moving 2,500 containers across the quay in the month.

The rejection by the government of the application by Associated British Ports (ABP) to construct a six-berth deepwater container terminal at Dibden Bay was a blow to ABP and a concern that the port will lose trade through container ships going to other ports; however, the second phase of development is to redevelop space used for car storage by converting Berths 201 and 202 into a deep-sea container terminal for the larger container ships. Southampton Container Terminal has increased its container yard by agreement with ABP to lease 10.5 acres of land, previously used as a vehicle terminal and for roll-on roll-off operations.

ABP will be deepening Berths 201 and 202 to accommodate the larger container ships that will be entering the port fully loaded with a deeper draught. Berths 201 and 202 were the first container berths in the port, and therefore the quay wall is capable of taking containers. What it is not capable of doing, however, is taking the deepest draft ships. The aim will be to re-pile along the existing wall the 550m of Berths 201 and 202 and then dredge down to 16m (52.46ft) below chart datum so it can take the 14.5 and 15m ships when they come in the future.

Some of the largest container ships today are 400m in length, and by completing the work at Berths 201 and 202,

A reach stacker. (Courtesy of STC)

Noel straddle carrier. (Courtesy of STC)

where the length of the quay is 550m, those ships will be able to dock in Southampton. The problem for the port is that if this work is not done then the shipping companies would go elsewhere. The third and final phase of development in the future is to create fully automated loading and unloading facilities at the terminal.

SCT operates 24 hours per day, 365 days per year with 11 ship-to-shore cranes, 90 straddle carriers, five sprinter carriers, six empty-container handlers, four reach stackers and a fleet of small vehicles.

The Closure of the King George V Graving Dock

By 2005 the port was handling 40 million tonnes of cargo annually and 700,000 cruise passengers passing through the port, but the facilities for dry docking was finally ended when the King George V Graving Dock (No. 7 Dry Dock), the last available dry dock in Southampton, was taken out of use. This was because the dock gate was in such poor condition that the cost of repair would be too great, also the dock had been losing money year on year. The cassion gate, which is 150ft wide and 60ft deep, has been removed, but the dock is still used by feeder vessels.

The MV *Monte Rosa*, an oil/chemical tanker, was one of the last ships to use the King George V Dry Dock when she came in for repairs because of major problems to the rudder. The problem was discovered in Karachi, and the vessel sailed to Rotterdam and Belfast to discharge cargo before arriving at to Southampton to dry dock for repairs.

The last cruise ships to undergo repairs in the dry dock were the P&O cruise ships *Oceana*, *Sea Princess* and *Adonia*. The King George V Dry dock was the last of seven dry docks in the port. It was the end of an era for ship repairing in Southampton and a sad day for the city.

The MV *Monte Rosa* in No. 7 Dry Dock. (Courtesy of Skip Handford)

An aerial view of the No. 7 Dry Dock after the cassion gate had been taken away. (Courtesy of ABP)

CHAPTER 16

SOUTHAMPTON DOCKS IN 2008

The Port of Southampton Looks to the Future

The future for the cruise industry in Southampton seems to be going from strength to strength, with a new fourth cruise terminal being built in Ocean Dock. The new terminal will be opposite the site of the old Ocean Terminal, where many of the famous transatlantic ocean liners berthed when the port was known as the 'Gateway to the World'.

Southampton was able to look forward to an exciting 2008, with an increase in the number of cruise ship visits to the port. In 2007 there were 245 cruise calls at the port, and it was expected that 2008 would increase to 290 cruise calls and up to a million passengers passing through the port. On 7 December 2007, the day the *Queen Victoria* sailed into the port for the first time, ABP signed a 20-year contract with Carnival UK. The *Queen Victoria* is 90,000 tons, 293m (964ft) in length, has a 37m (106ft) beam, has 12 decks and carries 2,014 passengers and 1,000 crew.

In April 2008 the new P&O Cruises *Ventura* arrived at the port and left on 18 April for her maiden voyage to Spain, Italy and France. The *Ventura* is 150,000 tons, 290m (950ft) in length, has a 36m (118ft) beam, has 15 passenger decks and carries up to 3,600 passengers and 1,200 crew. Also in April 2008, the largest cruise ship built to date, the Royal Caribbean International *Independence of the Seas*, arrived in Southampton. The ship statistics are as follows: 160,000 tons, 339m (1,112ft) length, 56m (118ft) beam, 8.5m (28ft) draught, has 15 decks, carries 3,634 passengers and 1,360 crew.

The *Independence of the Seas* spent her first six months cruising out of Southampton and left on 6 November 2008 on her last cruise for the season and then repositioned to Ft Lauderdale, Florida, for the winter in the Caribbean. Passengers who had left Southampton on the *Independence of the Seas* would end their cruise at Fort Lauderdale and fly back to the UK from Miami Airport.

Doug Morrison, Port Director for ABP Southampton

Doug Morrison, port director, talks about his vision for the future of the Port of Southampton: 'It is almost like crusade, but something I feel very strongly about, and I would like other people to understand exactly the implications of not doing something about it.

Progress of the new fourth terminal in November 2008.

The Cunard *Queen Victoria*. (Courtesy of Richard de Jong Collection)

'When you look at the wonderful Port of Southampton today and you think of the legacy that we've been left with. The people who have built this port over the last 150 years or so, and I look at that fabulous legacy that we are all benefiting from today. The many thousands of people who are relying every day on the success and growth for their work, and the revenue, which is about £2 billion a year that the port generates for Hampshire, not just Southampton.

'I ask myself, and I want other people to start thinking about it, how do we leave a legacy for future generations to benefit from? We cannot or must not think that we can rest on our laurels, we need more space and more land to continue to grow.

'Everything you see in Southampton has been, almost entirely, reclaimed from the sea. There comes a point when we need to build for the future, and the difficulty we will have is getting the necessary permissions. We know only too well how difficult that is from our Dibden Bay experience.

'We should think how seriously we want to grow this business, because one thing about global warming is that it would not make the UK any less of an island. Ships will always have to trade with the UK. At least 95 per cent of the goods that come into and leave the UK are seaborne, and Southampton's role through the centuries has been extremely important. We want that to remain so for centuries to come.

'So…we can build multi-decks for car storage. We can improve land utilisation with the latest technology, but there will come a time when you will need more land.'

The Three Cs

Doug Morrison: 'Southampton is a very consumer-led port and the main elements of our business are the three "C"s, Containers, Cruise and Cars. We do lots of other things, and sometimes when we talk about the port we forget about some of the other trades like fruit, wind blades and bulks. It is a very diverse port and that is part of the success story. More than 90 per cent of the containers that come in to Southampton are from the Far East and it is all the products that are purchased in the high street. The cars, very consumer led, but there is a credit crunch on and people are not buying new cars. This year new vehicle numbers are down on last year and likely to be so next year; however, the cruising industry recorded numbers up by 20 per cent this year, and that is on the basis of people booking their holidays in 2007. I worry slightly about next year and the numbers booking cruises, but this is a very successful and growing business and we are very confident in the long-term growth, hence the reason for the construction of the fourth terminal.'

The three 'C's.
(Courtesy of Richard
de Jong Collection)

The DP World logo. (Courtesy of DP World)

The Future of the Container Port

In March 2006, DP World took over P&O Ports, which therefore meant they took over 51 per cent share of Southampton Container Terminals. On 1 July 2008 the terminal began trading as DP World Southampton.

It is unlikely that the new container ships being built will get much deeper, because there would be so few ports that could take them, but they will certainly get longer and wider. To be able to meet the requirements of these new ships two new cranes were built for the container terminal at Southampton during 2008. They are higher than the cranes on site and have a longer reach. Each crane is 80m tall and 117m when the boom is up. The boom is 60m long and has an outreach of 22 containers in width. Each crane weighs in excess of 1,000 tons. To climb the cranes there are 366 steps to the top of the A-Frame.

WORKING IN THE DOCKS IN 2008

Derek Burke is well known as a Southampton city councillor who has been the Mayor of Southampton, as well as working in the docks when the National Docks Labour Board was abolished and the dockers made redundant. He became a shareholder in the new Southampton Cargo Handling when it became wholly owned by the employees, and he still works in the docks in 2008. Derek talks about the changes in the work of dockers in his time at the docks and the life working in the docks today:

'I've worked in the port for over 40 years having started when I was 21. At first I was working for Southampton Cargo Handling as a temporary employee, but after four years I was taken on by the British Transport Docks Board as a permanent employee.

'During the course of my career we have changed from the British Transport Docks Board to Associated British Ports, and I have now come back to working with Southampton Cargo Handling. I have worked on all types of cargo handling: from the Cape boats where we used manual handling of cargo, to moving cargo on pallets and using fork lift trucks today. Our main concern today is to get ships unloaded, loaded and away on time as efficiently as possible. It is a different time scale to the past when years ago ships were in the docks for four, five or even six days sometimes. These days a ship in dock is not making any money for the company and the need to get them back at sea is very important. Today with roll-on, roll-off the ship is loaded as quickly as possible, as tightly as possible and as safely as possible.

An aerial view of the new cranes in operation. The difference in height can seen by comparing it with one of the older cranes. (Courtesy of DP World)

The new crane displaying its height and reach.
(Courtesy of DP World)

'The reason I am working for Southampton Cargo Handling is because Associated British Ports, in their wisdom, when they abolished the National Docks Labour Board decided to make us all redundant. We had the choice of walking away with our cheque or do something with our money. We decided to form our own company with a managing director and a board of directors and away we went. We are all shareholders and have a stake in what happens. To that end we have a great motivation, not only to make money for the company but also because our reputation depends on making sure every ship gets away safely and on time. In Southampton Cargo Handling we have a one-stop shop approach. We receive the cargo, we tally the cargo, label the cargo, plan the cargo and load the cargo. Today we are the fastest turnaround port in the world for passenger and cargo ships.'

The Past Compared with Today

'My first day in the port was on a Cape boat, the Safmarine SA *Oranje*. I didn't work all day and went to work at 5pm, just one small job and then went home. I thought it was the best job in the world. The next day when the hatch was up the ship was packed with boxes of oranges on five decks, packed so tight you couldn't get a cigarette paper between them. We spent the next four days literally humping them out and onto a crane hoist to be lifted down to the quayside. It was exhausting work and I could hardly move after the four days because I was aching so much. Today, I could almost wear a suit under my overalls because I rarely get dirty. A totally different world.

'Most of the goods for loading are on pallets and moved by fork lift. It is easier work physically, but mentally it is a strain because you have to concentrate more in the use of the equipment to move the goods as it is all very expensive.

'One of the losses from the past dockers life is the gang system. Today we are multi-skilled and have to drive cars and other vehicles, fork lift trucks and undertake other port work, almost on an individual basis. With the gang system you would be together all the time and you could rely on people. We would get to know each other well and also our families, where we could go out together for meals in our leisure time. Now that camaraderie has gone, although we are still a good group of people who generally get on well together in work.'

Safmarine SA *Oranje*. (Courtesy of Mick Lindsay Collection)

Southampton City Councillor

Balancing the life as a Southampton city councillor and working in the docks relies on the need to leave work to attend a meeting or a function and being able to return to work and continue where you left off, and of course an understanding employer. Derek Burke: 'I was fortunate to be elected to the city council and have found my employers extremely helpful in assisting me in that. In 1999 I was elected Mayor of Southampton, and it was tremendous to represent the city for the year.

'The mayor is the highest ranking naval officer in the land, and when you go on board a ship you are an admiral and they have to salute you. We did the maiden voyage of the *Aurora*. When I boarded a naval vessel to be taken to the *Aurora* at Dock Head I got piped aboard. When on board the *Aurora* we went on the bridge with the captain to sail into the docks. After we had docked I told the captain that I had to leave to get the luggage off the ship. I went down and got changed into my working clothes and went on the quayside to work in my docker's role. In fact the captain came down to the quayside because he really didn't believe me and saw me at work.

'The company were very good to me while I was mayor and allowed me to leave work and change into mayor's regalia, and then I would go back to work when the function was over.'

When Derek undertakes city council work as a councillor or as a magistrate he doesn't get paid. 'I don't mind that because I am doing it in my time, not company time.'

Derek is always interested in the work of other docks around the world and will always visit one, even when on holiday, much to the consternation of his wife: 'I have travelled the world as a member of delegations and always spend sometime looking at other docks and see how they work. When in China I visited one dock and found it interesting to see the dockers marching to work, as they do in that country.' He could not, however, see his work colleagues doing that in Southampton Docks!

'We carry about 112 to 114 in the full-time work force and we are very efficient. As an agency we pay above the minimum wage and are good to work for. Even some of the old dockers still come in to work on a part-time basis because they still like to be part of the docks life.

'We still "bump" if there isn't a ship in, but today you probably still get 80 per cent of your wages, and some dockers are happy to be "bumped" because they may have to go somewhere on a particular day, and some even ask to be "bumped" at times. To encourage people not to want to "bump" we have agreed with the unions that they will lose a percentage of their wages. I would probably lose two hours' pay if I "bumped".

'You now book in for work, which is usually is done by telephone. Not like the past when you would assemble in the allocation hall in Canal Street to be given work by the port allocation officers.

'Today there are no ships in, and I have been to a shops steward meeting this morning. I could "bump" tomorrow and take my wife shopping. When things are a bit quiet you may decide to "bump" for various reasons. It's a very flexible system. I have loved every moment of it because no two days are the same; even no two hours are the same sometimes.

'Here we are in 2008, nearly 2009, and the port is expanding tremendously, attracting new work. Next year the port is going to be very busy with more passenger liners and a new fourth passenger terminal, and to be working in the docks now is a very exciting and a fulfilling time.'

SHIPPING AGENTS

The Ships Agency Department

Don Archbold had started work for a ships agency in the 1940s. 'I started work when I was 14 years and two weeks old, and that was in 1942. I was just an office boy to start with, and as it was wartime we had a lot of Dutch coasters into port that had got away before the Germans invaded and it was my job to look after them, seeing that they had their stores, food and supplies in good time.' Today, although the work remains similar in dealing with arrival and departure of the ships and looking after their requirements while in port, it is no longer necessary to go on the tug tenders out to Cowes Roads or to climb a ladder up a ship's side. Also, with modern technology, it is now much easier to keep in contact with ships anywhere around the world.

The main function of the ships agency department is to make the ship's call at port as smooth and trouble free as possible. Various shipping companies have their own agents for their shipping lines.

Shipping Agents for the Cruise Ships in 2008

Lynn Fox, shipping agent for Carnival UK, talks about the job of the cruise ship agent:

'We book the cruise ships in with ABP at least one year in advance. At the beginning of the year of the ship's call we confirm the booking and at that time the actual berth is allocated. In advance of the arrival of the cruise ship at the port the tugs and pilots are booked, and we then get involved in the quayside work by booking the mooring gang, labour for unloading and loading of baggage and loading of stores. Sometimes we have to get involved in stores coming from the Continent and arrange for the Customs formalities, breaking of the seals and presentation of documentation. This is not happening so much now as more and more stores are being supplied by British companies which, for the most part, are ordered by our Hotel Services Department in Southampton.

'On some ships, such as Princess Cruises', it may be necessary for us to arrange transport and hotels for crew that arrive at

Southampton. Carnival UK do have their own Fleet Personnel Department and they look after crew who arrive at London by air and book their hotels and transport to Southampton. The same applies for the crew being discharged from the ship and going on leave.

'My first job after the ship has tied up is to go on board and visit the captain to discuss any requests that he may have while the ship is in port. I then visit the purser to see if he/she has any concerns. Sometimes the chief engineer may require a sludge barge, refuelling barge or road tanker, but this is usually arranged well in advance of the vessel's call.

'As ships agents it is well known, regardless of whether it is a cargo ship or cruise ship, that we are the first in and the last out!'

Cruise Ship Visits: A Day in Port for the Royal Caribbean International *Independence of the Seas*

The cruise ships arrive in Southampton usually in the early morning, disembark the passengers and their luggage, restock the ship with stores and provisions, embark new passengers and their luggage and sail again in the early evening. It is a well planned operation where all working in the terminal know what is required of them and work to ensure that the ship gets away on time. There are times when the ships are later leaving the berth, but this is mainly due to external problems, such as coaches bringing passengers being late through vehicle accidents that may block the motorways. It is the captain's final decision, however, when the ship sails, and sometimes passengers do miss the ship and have to fly to join the ship at her next port of call.

Derek Burke: 'The day before the *Independence of the Seas* arrives, the duty men go to the City Terminal to prepare and clear up the quayside and put the all the machines and equipment ready for the ship. It is important that all machines have fuel and are ready to go so we do not get any hold-ups during discharge.'

It is in the early hours of the following morning when the terminal is secured in preparation for the arrival of the ship at the berth. All is prepared with the port operations, security staff, road traffic marshals and dockers ready and in place.

The Arrival

The *Independence of the Seas* arrives at approximately 4.30am, and when she is passing the terminal to the turning basin you hear music playing quite loudly across the water. An early call for the passengers!

The ship proceeds to the upper swinging ground basin to turn and arrives at Berth 101 on its port side. There are times when she turns at the lower swinging ground and backs up and docks and, using its starboard side thrusters, comes in sideways to the berth.

Quayside Operations

Once the ship has arrived and is moored alongside the berth the dockside operations begins. First the unloading of baggage begins from three positions where the shell doors are open. One near the bows, one in the middle of the ship and one near the

The *Independence of the Seas* arrives in the early hours of the morning.

An aerial photograph looking across at the Royal Caribbean International *Jewel of the Seas* berthed at the QEII Ocean Terminal Berth 38/39. The grain silos are on Berth 36 and the Wallenius Wilhelmsen Logistics Ro-Ro Terminal is on Berth 34/35. (Courtesy of ABP)

stern. Baggage on trolleys are loaded from the ship into the baggage cage and then unloaded on the quay. Fork lifts take the trolleys into the shed where the baggage layout teams put the baggage in the correct areas.

All the dockers working know exactly what is required of them and go confidently about their individual jobs. If it is unloading baggage they will take it by fork lift to the shed where it is laid out in deck positions, making it easier for the disembarking passengers to find when they leave the ship.

Derek Burke: 'All the luggage has colour tags so we know where to put it in the shed. When the passengers come off the bags are in order, for example: red, green, yellow and so on. The passengers find their bags from the correct section and go on their way.' This operation usually takes 2½ hours.

While the unloading of baggage is going on lorries carrying supplies and provisions are unloaded. The pallets from the lorries are then taken by fork lift and placed on the quayside ready for loading after all the baggage has been taken off.

Derek Burke describes the work of the dockers: 'I have the job of loading the luggage onto the ship. That's my job and I know exactly what I have to do. The baggage cages are divided up into various decks so when the baggage is loaded onto the ship it can be put to the cabins as soon as possible.

The luggage is taken off.

198

A teletruck loads supplies.

'We've got two of those at each end of the ship and one in the middle. There are probably eight or nine positions where people know what their particular job is and what they are doing. The stores dockers know exactly what they have to do when loading the stores. They know the ship's storeman who is on the quayside to direct the loading of stores. The lorries are unloaded and the stores placed on the quayside ready for loading. I know all the blokes on the ship now, laugh and joke with them and tell them what I want. It makes it all go much smoother.'

To an observer the amount of movement on the quayside with fork trucks 'whizzing around' and other quayside activities it is amazing that everyone knows exactly what to do and when to do it.

Derek Burke: 'Dedication to the job, professionalism, that's what it is. Let's be fair – I get paid from 5am to 5pm. That's my job and I get it done. Working with the ship's crew, and if you get a good ship's crew you really work well together, then the whole job is completed more smoothly and the ship gets away on time. We know the crew of the *Independence of the Seas* very well now and they always get away on time – 5pm on the dot!

'Most of our people are quite professional and want to get it done. It a 12-hour day and the stores people get about a half-hour break and we get about 45 minutes, but the ship usually gives us rolls and coffee while we are working. If you really want to be pedantic you could say, "I'm not eating like that, I want a sit down." But they don't.'

To get some idea of the amount of stores that is loaded for a weeks cruise:

Supplies and provisions for a cruise will include loading a large quantity of hotel provisions and ship stores; however, for the *Independence of the Seas* to provide 234,000 appetizers, 105,000 main meals and 300,680 desserts within a week's cruise, they will need to take on board: 20,000lbs of beef, including 69,000 steaks, 12,000lbs of chicken, 4,000lbs of seafood, 2,500lbs of salmon, 1,400lbs of lobster, 65,000lbs of fresh vegetables, 35,000lbs of fresh fruits, 5,800lbs of cheese, 28,000 fresh eggs, 18,000 slices of pizza, 8,000 gallons of ice cream, 1,500lbs of coffee, 1,500 gallons of milk, 11,500 cans of soda, 19,200 bottles and cans of beer and 2,900 bottles of wine.

The Passengers

After docking, the gantries and gangways are put in place and there is a phased disembarkation of passengers. Some crew will be joining the ship and some will leave to go shopping in Southampton and travel to and from the ship by a crew bus.

Escalators have been set to bring passengers down to the ground floor, where they collect their luggage and proceed through Customs. Some will travel by the coaches waiting outside the terminal building, some will collect their own cars and others will be met by friends or take a taxi to the railway station.

Once all passengers have left the ship, collected their baggage and left the terminal, usually by 10am, the escalators are reversed and the whole operation for the arrival of passengers and embarkation of passengers begins. This is where the importance of a smooth traffic control operation is important, and this is undertaken by experienced traffic marshals. The arrival of coaches, taxis and other traffic are filtered into the correct lanes. There can be as many as 800 passenger cars which

There are not many passengers on deck in this picture, taken as the vessel moves sideways away from the quayside, because it is very rough weather.

are to be parked in the port for the duration of the cruise. Their baggage is taken by the porters to go through x-ray screening and sorted into forward, amidships or aft before being loaded on the ship. Passengers carry their own hand luggage and enter the terminal. After they have passed through security checks and have checked in they embark onto the ship. A band will arrive to entertain the passengers prior to the ship sailing and while it leaves the berth.

It is a very busy time, and when you see the stores and baggage building up in the quay you think the dockers and the ship's loading crew will never get it done in time, but they do and the ship sails on time.

At approximately 4.45pm the dockers are in place to release the ropes. Gantries and gangways are pulled away from the ship and all is ready for the departure. At 5pm the ropes are released, and the ship gives three loud blasts on its siren, a big cheer erupts from the passengers on board and the ship moves away from the berth.

The *Independence of the Seas* passes the Royal Pier, QEII Ocean Terminal and down Southampton Water.

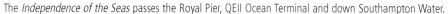

The *Independence of the Seas* uses her side thrusters and the ship moves sideways out into the channel. Once safely away from the berth the forward thrust of the propellers starts the cruise. Once in the channel the *Independence of the Seas* sails away past the Royal Pier, Dock Head and into Southampton Water and the Solent, past the Isle of Wight and into the English Channel.

On any day there can be as many a four cruise ships in port, and the details given above will be happening on each berth. With the addition of the fourth cruise terminal these numbers will no doubt increase.

It is great credit to the Port of Southampton that the whole port operation in turning the ships around in a day is conducted with such precision. It could be said that it is the precision of 'a well-oiled machine.'

Queen Elizabeth 2

Since the queen launched the *QE2* in September 1967, by September 2007 and after 40 years' service she became the Cunard's longest-serving ship and their longest-serving flagship. The *QE2* has crossed the Atlantic over 800 times and completed 25 world cruises. It was a sad day for Southampton on Tuesday 11 November 2008 when the *QE2* sailed out at 8pm for the last time on her final voyage to sail to Dubai, where she would become floating hotel.

Alan Passfield works as a security officer on the quayside and has fond memories of the *QE2* when she has been in port. He describes one such day: 'Three tugs depart down the river, a sure sign that she is on her way up, then after a few minutes she appears in all her majestic charm from the dank gloom of Southampton Water for another turnaround at the *QE2* terminal. She glides past, one tug at the bow, one on the stern and one amidships, she turns, always a great sight, and slowly returns to glide gently to her berth.

'The mooring gang do their job and then the hustle and bustle of another day begins. In goes the overhead gangway, the old wooden gangway for the crew, the old red baggage conveyors and finally the two car ramps. All of these will be a thing of the past once she sails for the final time.

'The baggage comes off first, most important, then waste and empty pallets, before the stores are loaded. The vegetables, chilled and frozen are all loaded via the forward car ramp. Beer, spirits and wine are craned into the forward hold, and the technical stores go via the stern car ramp. All are loaded to a strict schedule.

'The *QE2* is probably the most efficiently loaded ship ever with all stores and provisions taken straight on board by a forklift and then via a large lift taking the many pallets down to the respective decks. As the loading of the stores ease it is back to loading the next trip's baggage. By about 4pm the ramps and conveyors are gradually removed to once again reveal the graceful lines of the sleek hull sharply tapered at the bow to slice through the North Atlantic waves, swelling amidships to the full width and then gently tapering away to the beautiful round stern.

The swinging of the *QE2*.

'At 4pm on the dot there is the booming of the ship's siren. They say it is an old Cunard tradition to call the crew back from town with one hour to go. Although always expected, it still puts a chill through your body and gives you goose bumps.

'At 4.30pm the pilot is on board and by 4.50pm two tugs are reappearing ready for sailing at 5.00pm. The rope gang appear and right on 5pm the ropes go and she is gently eased sideways. As she goes forward the siren booms again, and she is on her way.'

Those days will never be repeated since the *QE2* sailed out of Southampton for the last time on 11 November 2008.

Tugs pull away.

THE FINAL DAY OF THE *QE2* IN SOUTHAMPTON DOCKS

As the *QE2* arrived at the entrance to Southampton Water at approximately 5.25am she ran aground on the Bramble Bank just off Calshot. She was returning from her last Mediterranean cruise with 2,700 passengers and crew when it is thought that she was blown off course by Force 7 winds. Most of the passengers were asleep at the time and no alarms were raised. The port authority and coastguards were alerted and five tugs were sent and pulled her off the bank as the tide rose. The *QE2* eventually arrived at the QEII Terminal under her own power.

The *QE2* is safely moored.

Many thousands of people were keen to see the *QE2* on her last day at Southampton, and that included many of the people who work at the docks. Here are a few personal recollections:

Alan Passfield was fortunate to be on duty on the quayside from 5am waiting for the arrival of the *QE2*. He describes the day: 'Everybody is in an hour early for she is due at 6am. The quayside at dockhead is covered with TV outside broadcast equipment, ready for the last joyous but sad day of the *QE2*. The tugs go down as usual but something is not quite right! A small crowd have already gathered outside the gates to witness her arrival. Time ticks on, then the rumour goes around "she has grounded off Calshot", confirmed finally by the TV crew. People say she is saying "she doesn't want to leave Southampton"!

'Finally, an hour or so late, the *QE2* hoves into view and the normal procedure begins as she finally docks at 7.40am. From then on it was one of the busiest days I have ever experienced.

'Throughout the day stevedores, security staff and ex-crew members all come to the bow of the *QE2* to reminisce and take photographs, all of them sad to see her go.

'At 10.45 the Duke of Edinburgh arrives to say his last farewell, and at 11am a Lysander and Auster scatter poppies for Remembrance Day. At 1.40pm the Harrier arrives at the bow of the *QE2* to bow in recognition of her role in the Falklands War. This is followed by a sail past of three Royal Navy ships.

'The loading and unloading of stores carried on until 6.30pm. Passengers have been arriving since midday, and the divers gradually work their way from stern to bow checking for damage caused by the early morning mishap.

'Gradually the dockside empties and the car ramps are hoisted up into the bow hold to go with the ship to her final berthing place in Dubai. This was another sad reminder of the days when she carried luxurious cars across the Atlantic, the only modern ship to do so.

'The TV crews are in full production now. Two tugs arrive at the bow and two at the stern. Then at 7.15pm the ropes go for the final time and she eases sideways

The *QE2*, photographed almost at the quayside. (Courtesy of Alan Passfield Collection)

A fly-past and one million poppies dropping on the *QE2*. (Courtesy of Richard de Jong Collection)

A Harrier jet bows before flying away! (Courtesy of Alan Passfield Collection)

and astern to back up to the Mayflower Park for a farewell firework display. At 8.00pm she returns, surrounded by a flotilla of small boats for a final small firework display on the quayside. The *QE2* gives a long blast for the final time of that famous siren and then she was on her way. A few of the old stevedores had a tear in their eyes. So ended a long, hard busy day, but a very nostalgic one. Not to be missed!'

Jeff Graham was a lad of 16 when he watched the *QE2* arrive at Southampton Docks for the first time in 1969. Little was he to know that almost 40 years later he would be working at the QEII Terminal on the very day the *QE2* would leave on her final voyage to Dubai:

'I was out front on traffic duty watching lots of English crew members removing their personal effects. One such lady officer was loading all her belongings into her parent's car. I said, "It looks as though you're moving home" and she replied, "Yes, it has indeed been my home for the last 16 years, and after this last trip to Dubai I will be retiring from the sea. There is no other ship would mean as much to me as the *QE2*."

'What a start to the *QE2*'s last day, I personally think that getting herself stuck on the Bramble Bank at 6am in the morning was her protest at being pensioned off (a little bit of attention seeking perhaps).

'Being a veteran of the Falklands War, I think it rather fitting that Cunard should say goodbye to her on the 11th day of the 11th month, and it was nice to see people honour the two minute silence.

'From taxi drivers to passengers, we all waited to see the fly-past when the aircraft dropped the poppies all over the *QE2*. The coastguard helicopter said goodbye as well as the naval vessels on the river, though the best part for me was the Harrier jet which hovered over her for a short while then took a bow before blasting off towards the New Forest.

'The evening went off without a hitch. It was nice to see so many people on the quayside, some happy, some sad, with a very large flotilla of little boats on the river. Everyone was enjoying themselves, and the firework display was not skimped on in any way. It was rather like being back in the '60s when people could walk along the quayside saying farewell to friends and relatives before the security had to be tightened up as it is today.'

Doreen Russell had feelings of nostalgia when she went to work at the QEII Terminal on the *QE2*'s final day in port: 'Working for G4S Marine you do get used to working with all the ships, but some ships are special and the *QE2* falls into that category.

Look at the craft on the water: the *QE2* berthed with the RFA Mounts Bay, passing yachts, a Red Funnel high-speed ferry, a tug and a hovercraft! (Courtesy of Richard de Jong Collection)

A Harrier jump jet hovers over the *QE2*. (Courtesy of Richard de Jong Collection)

She has not only played a major role in Southampton's marine history, but I can feel nostalgia too, as her birth coincided with the birth of my first daughter'

When it was announced that the *QE2* was to leave the port on 11 November 2008, many of the staff who had been working for years at the docks wanted to work on the day. Doreen Russell: 'I was one of the lucky ones, and I felt very privileged. There was a great deal of excitement and most of us turned up much earlier than our allotted shifts just to be part of it, as we felt sure it was going to be a carnival-like atmosphere. Passengers were arriving from all over the world there were even Japanese ladies dressed in traditional Kimono dresses. It was all very befitting the "Grand Old Lady", as the *QE2* is affectionately known. There was a Jazz Band playing as the passengers booked in, but surprisingly they were all very quiet and as they came into through the x-ray screening. Their mood seemed very sombre. Talking to many of them it was obvious they were all very fond of the ship, and for one lady she was embarking on her 104th, so I am guessing their mood was reflective of the occasion.

'As the ship was due to sail, with all the passengers safely on board we went onto the quayside. The atmosphere was fantastic. The Scots Guards Band was playing, passengers lining the decks with flags waving. Thousands of people lined the waterfront on both sides of Southampton Water. The river was full of small craft, everyone wanting to be part of this momentous day. She finally set sail on time to be towed up river to Mayflower Park where a firework display was a backdrop to the ship; finally she sailed back past her berth to more fireworks. The blasts on the horn could be heard for miles and all the small yachts and boats joined in. I saw many people wiping a tear or two away, including me. Southampton did her proud in her send off, but she has done us proud in being part of our city and our lives for almost 40 years.'

Geoffrey Le Marquand was working on the *QE2*'s last day helping passengers who needed special assistance, disembarking and embarking in wheelchairs. 'I did work on the last *QE2* sailing and it was a long day, from 7.00am–9.00pm; however, it was well worth it. She did arrive a little late (due to the collecting of some sand off Calshot to take out to Dubai). It was non-stop and the last passengers were off by 11.30am, but by that time I found that passengers were getting ready to board, so I moved from disembark straight into embark. At about 2.00pm I was boarding with a passenger, but just as I got aboard, who should be coming off but Prince Philip and his entourage. The security was not impressed, as no one should have been around. Never mind, I somehow messed up the system! My passenger, who was an American, was very impressed when I told him who it was.'

'By 4.30pm all passengers were aboard and I had a break. Then about 7.00pm I moved out onto the dock as I felt this was the best place to see her pull away for the last time. I got up onto one of the pillars, which put me way above the rest of the people who were also on the dock, and I had an excellent view of her when she pulled away. She went stern first up to the Mayflower Park and stayed for some time while the fireworks went off. Then she moved slowly down the river and passed Berths 38 and 39 for the last time with her whistle blowing. What a sight. Although I never sailed on the *QE2* it was sad to see her go, especially as over the last five years I have got to know her working shore side.'

The Duke of Edinburgh had been on board for lunch and to meet crew members that sailed on the *QE2* when she conveyed troops to the Falklands in 1982. He was introduced to the former captains of *HMS Ardent*, *Antelope* and *Coventry*, the ships lost in the Falklands War.

The author was on the quayside at Berths 38 and 39 from the early evening and the following describes the atmosphere at the QEII Terminal: When I arrived at Dock Head the radio, TV crews and presenters were in full action, and yet I felt a time of

The sky is lit up with fireworks. (Courtesy of Richard de Jong Collection)

sadness, especially at the memories that were being shared by the docks' staff and others on the quayside. I was able to walk along the quayside and look at the wonderful 'Grand Old Lady' at her moorings and seeing the moving patterns being projected along her side.

As the time ticked away more and more people began to arrive at Dock Head, and especially those who worked in the VTS centre. They were arriving with their families, carrying cold boxes and hampers into the building where they would have a good view as the *QE2* sailed up Southampton Water. It was very cold and most were sensibly wrapped up.

Earlier on in the evening the water was clear of other craft, but as the time passed more and more vessels of all sizes appeared, including the Red Funnel ferry vessels and passenger craft with their booming announcements from the crew to their passengers. Tugs were moored near the *QE2* and the excitement began to grow as the tugs started to move towards the ship, and you could see the crewmen on the *QE2* getting the ropes ready to throw to the tugs.

At 6.45pm Jerry Dibben, the pilot who was to take the *QE2* out of Southampton, left the VTS centre and boarded the vessel to prepare for leaving the quayside. All appeared still and quiet for a short for a time, as though all were waiting in anticipation. Suddenly there was the booming of the ship's horn that seemed to go on forever! I could only see the bow at the time but felt very sad when I saw the ropes go and the bow slowly back out of sight behind the QEII building as she moved stern first with the tugs to opposite the Mayflower Park.

Once she had stopped by the Mayflower Park there were the tremendous booms and whizzes of the firework display and the sky lit up. I decided to view the proceeding from the QEII Ocean Terminal balcony and what a wonderful sight it was. As the *QE2* was ready to start her final voyage to Dubai she gave three long blasts on the ship's horn, and this was followed by all the ships in the port answering. The atmosphere was electric and yet emotional. As the *QE2* slowly moved forward the flotilla of the craft around her went with her, and as she came alongside the QEII Terminal a salute of fireworks erupted from Berth 38–39. There was much cheering and waving and the passengers that were lining all the decks of the *QE2* were clearly heard singing the National Anthem as the ship passed the berths.

The *QE2* gradually disappeared from view as she went down Southampton Water, and it left a lump in your throat. There was little talking as people went to their cars to go home, and in the silence of the moment everyone was left with their own personal thoughts and feelings.

A pre-recorded message from her master, Captain Ian McNaught, was broadcast to the crowds on large screens in the Mayflower Park, and it is apt that this book concludes with Captain McNaught's address:

'For almost 40 years, *QE2* has been acclaimed all over the globe as a symbol of British excellence, and throughout her life, imprinted firmly on this symbol of excellence for all the world to see, has been one word: Southampton.

'*QE2* belongs to Southampton. This is her home, just as it is now for the home of *Queen Mary 2* and *Queen Victoria*.

'She has put into her home port more often than she has visited any other port in the world. Wherever she has been, she has always come back here, home to Southampton.

'But the day which had to come some day has come today, and when the *QE2* leaves home she will not be coming back. For this time, her 726th time, is the last time.

'For 40 years the *QE2* has striven to serve Southampton and serve her country with flair and fortitude, but now her sea days are done and she passes on to a new life in a new home. We wish her well.

'On behalf of *QE2*, I bid Southampton farewell and thank you for all the affection you have shown to her in all these years.'

The *QE2* sails down river past the QE2 Terminal. (Courtesy of Peter Ward)

The *QE2* backs up river to the Mayflower Park.
(Courtesy of Peter Ward)

BILBIOGRAPHY

Booklets and references
Arts and Heritage, Oral History.
150 years of Cunard 1840–1990, Official souvenir history of the Cunard line.
Ben Line, Fleet List and Short History, W.M. Thomson & Co.
British Airways Museum Collection.
Cunard, Queen Victoria, Limited Edition, Newsquest Southern, 2007.
King George V Dry Dock, British Transport Commission.
New Cargo & Passenger Building British Transport Commission, 1956.
Ocean Terminal, British Transport Commission.
Oriana Official Naming Ceremony Programme.
Southampton Container Terminals Ltd Booklet.
Southampton Docks Booklet, British Transport Commission, 1952.
Southampton Docks Booklet, Gateway to Britain, British Transport Commission.
Southampton Docks Booklet, Southern Railway.
Southampton Docks Centenary Booklet, 12 October 1938, Southern Railway.
Southampton Docks Handbook, 1929, Southern Railway.
Southampton Docks, Official Sailing List and Shipping Guide, June 1926. S.R.
Southampton Docks, Official Sailing List and Shipping Guide, June 1953. DIWE.
Southampton, Associated British Ports Booklets.
Southampton, Official Handbook & Street Plan, Southampton City Council, 1979.

Books
Archbold, Michael *Red funnel – A pictorial history* Red Funnel Group, 1997.
Arnott, Alistair and Rachel Wragg *Images of Southampton* Breedon Books, 2006.
Arnott, Alistair *Maritime Southampton* Breedon Books, 2002.
Brannon, Philip *The Picture of Southampton* 1850.
Bennett, A.E. and Barry J. Eagles *Coastal steam vessels of the British Isles* Waterfront (a division of Kingfisher productions), 2001.
Brannon, Phillip *Picture of Southampton* Published 1850.
Brooks, Clive *Life on the Liners* Brooks Books 1990.
Brown, Jim *Southampton's Changing Faces* Breedon Books, 2005.
Brown, Jim *The Illustrated History of Southampton's Suburbs* Breedon Books, 2004.
Cook, Robert *Southampton, Past & Present* Sutton Publishing Ltd for Marks and Spencer plc, 2005.
Cunard, Queen Mary 2, A Book of Comparisons The Open Agency, 2003.
Dawson, Philip Th*e Liner, Retrospective & Renaissance* Conway, 2007.
De Kerbrech, Richard P. and David Williams *Cunard White Star Liners of the 1930s* Conway, 1988.
Deeson, A.F.L. *An Illustrated History of Steamships* Spurbooks Ltd, 1976.
Ellery, David *RMS Queen Mary 101 Questions and Answers* Conway, 2006.
Emmons, Frederick *The Atlantic liners 1925 to 1970* David & Charles, Newton Abbot, 1972.
Hovey, John *A Tale of Two Ports*, Industrial Society 1990.
Howard Bailey, Chris *Down the Burma Road* Oral History Team, Southampton.
Howarth, David and Stephen Howarth *The Story of P&O* Weidenfeld and Nicholson, 1986.
Hutchings, David F. *QE2* Kingfisher Railway Production, 1988.
Hutchings, David F. *RMS Queen Mary* Kingfisher Railway Production, 1986.
Hyslop, Donald, Forsyth, Alistair and Sheila Jemima *Titanic Voices* Southampton Oral History Unit, 1994.
Lemon, Sir James *Reminiscenses of Public Life in Southampton 1866–1900* published 1900.
McCart, Neil *Atlantic liners of the Cunard Line* Patrick Stephens Ltd, 1990.
McCart, Neil *P&O's Canberra* Kingfisher Railway Productions, 1989.
McCutcheon, Campbell *Port of Southampton* Tempus, 2005.
Moody, Bert *150 years of Southampton Docks*, Kingfisher Railway Productions, 1988.
Rance, Adrian B. *Ship building in Victorian Southampton* Southampton University Industrial Archaeology Group, 1981.
Rance, Adrian B. *Southampton. An Illustrated History* Milestone Publications 1986.
Rance, Adrian B. *The Southampton Guide. A Historical Guide for visitors* Milestone Publications 1987.
Ransome-Wallis, P. *Merchant ship panorama* Ian Allen Ltd, 1980.
Robins, Nick *The Decline and Revival of the British Passenger Fleet* Colourpoint Books, 2001.
The Royal Jubilee Book 1910–1935 Associated Newspapers Ltd.
The Silver Jubilee Book, The story of 25 Eventful Years in Pictures, 1910–1935 Oldhams Press Ltd.
Williams, David L. *Docks and Ports: 1 Southampton* Ian Allen Ltd, 1984.

ND - #0358 - 270225 - C0 - 276/195/14 - PB - 9781780911137 - Gloss Lamination